Formalist Elements in the Novels of

JUAN GOYTISOLO

by Genaro J. Pérez

studia humanitatis

Publisher, printer and distributor
José Porrúa Turanzas, S. A.
North American Division
1383 Kersey Lane
Potomac, Maryland 20854
U.S.A.

cc

Dep. legal M. 1.065. - 1978
I.S.B.N. 84–7317–085–9

Impreso en Los Estados Unidos
Printed in the United States of America

Ediciones José Porrúa Turanzas, S. A.
Cea Bermúdez, 10 - Madrid-3

Talleres Gráficos Porrúa, S.A.

Formalist Elements in the Novels of Juan Goytisolo

For Terry

Acknowledgments

I would like to express my gratitude to Professor William J. Smither for his invaluable assistance in the writing of this book. I am also grateful to Dr. Gilberto Paolini for his helpful assistance. I owe a great debt to my wife Terry Naranjo Pérez for her patience and understanding. Special thanks to Debra Berthelot for the final preparation of the typescript. I also wish to thank the College of Liberal Arts Organized Research Fund of the University of New Orleans for generous assistance.

Some parts of this book have appeared in *Hispania, Hispanófila, Journal of Spanish Studies: Twentieth Century* and *Romance Notes*.

Regardez vous-même si vous voyez mieux avec ce verre-ci, avec celui-là, avec cet autre.

Proust

Table of Contents

Introduction

Juan Goytisolo was born in Barcelona, Spain on January 5, 1931, of Basque and Catalonian ancestry. Since the Spanish Civil War took place during his childhood, the conflict left marks on Goytisolo's life: his father, a chemical factory executive, was imprisoned by the Republicans and his mother was killed by a Nationalist bombardment in 1938. He lived most of the Civil War years in a small Catalonian village and spent the summer of 1939 in a country house, owned by his father, near Barcelona. The house, used as a school for orphan children, is the scene setting of one of his novels, *Duelo en el Paraíso*. He finished his *Bachillerato* at a Jesuit school in 1949 and studied law at the Universities of Barcelona and Madrid.

In 1951 Goytisolo founded the "Turia" literary group along with Ana María Matute, Lorenzo Gomis, Mario Lacruz and Juan Germán Schroeder. His first literary success came the following year when he won the "Joven Literatura" Prize for his short novel "El mundo de los espejos." It should be noted that Goytisolo's interest in literature is not an isolated instance in his family. His maternal great uncle was a poet, one of his two brothers, José Agustín, is a poet, and Luis, the other, is a novelist.

1

Goytisolo left the university in 1951 to devote his time to the writing of *Juegos de manos*, which he finished in 1952 and published in 1954. In 1957, feeling the pressure of the totalitarian Spanish government, Goytisolo left his country and went to Paris where he began working for the Gallimard Publishing House. The trilogy, *El mañana efímero*, composed of *El circo, Fiestas* and *La resaca*, was published between 1957 and 1958.

Problemas de la novela (1959), is a compilation of several articles Goytisolo wrote for the review *Destino* from 1956 to 1958. This collection primarily reflects his early theories about the novel, and Goytisolo had indicated he does not consider these views relevant to his mature works, those written after 1966. In *Problemas* he envisions the objectivist novel as the only valid means of writing fiction. He speaks of the need to humanize the novel (as opposed to Ortega y Gasset's concept of dehumanization) in order to portray society as it really is; the writer must mirror reality instead of manufacturing it. Consequently, literary creativity will be motivated by social conditions, and the theme will determine the technique utilized by the novelist.[1]

Goytisolo's travelogues, *Campos de Níjar* and *La Chanca*, were published in 1960 and 1962, respectively. *Para vivir aquí*, a group of short stories, appeared in 1960. A film script, *La isla*, was published as a novel in 1961 because the Spanish Government refused to allow its production in Spain. In 1962 four novelettes appeared under the title *Fin de fiesta*. *Señas de identidad*, published in 1966, is the first of Goytisolo's trilogy, comprised of his most recent three novels that reflect a new perspective in the writing of fiction in Spain and representing

---

[1] Most of this information appears in Kessel Schwartz, *Juan Goytisolo* (New York: Twayne Publishers, Inc.), *passim*, chapters I and II. It should be noted that Goytisolo (and Castellet as well, in *La hora del lector*) like many others, misinterpreted Ortega, who never advocated dehumanization of the novel; he merely identified a trend.

2

what this study calls his period of maturity. Some of the views that helped shape *Señas de identidad, Reivindicación del conde don Julián* (1970) and *Juan sin tierra* (1975) began to be expressed in a collection of critical essays, *El furgón de cola*, published in 1967. In these essays Goytisolo criticizes the Generation of 1898, the commercialization of Spain, and the mediocrity of most of the novels published after the Civil War. He also comments on the Spanish political conditions which force many novelists to deal with social matters by utilizing their most ingenious techniques to circumvent the censor, and he speculates on the means by which language might be used to destroy the old and create new.

Reivindicación del conde don Julián and *Juan sin tierra* are to date his best exponents of this theory. In a subsequent article in *Libre*,[2] Goytisolo elaborates on these views and expresses his admiration for the Russian Formalists, who, he indicates, have influenced his writings.[3] Goytisolo also explains here his assessment of the reasons for the appearance of the "novela social" in Spain and the abundance of mediocre novels published after the Civil War. To some extent, the views are a continuation of those already expressed in *El furgón de cola*, but some tenets of the Russian Formalists are presented here for the first time as possible means of invigorating the Spanish novel. In the Formalist vein he writes that "aunque desde el siglo XIX, para la gran mayoría de novelistas y críticos, lo más importante de una novela es su conexión con la realidad exterior que pretende representar, su trabazón con el *corpus*

---

[2] Juan Goytisolo, "La novela española contemporánea," *Libre*, Núm. 2 (diciembre, enero, febrero, 1971–1972), 33–40, *passim*. Hereafter pages cited will be given in parentheses at the end of the text.

[3] In an interview conducted by Claude Couffon, "Don Julian ou la destruction des mythes," *Le Monde*, 11 septembre 1970, p. VI, Goytisolo says: "Il y a, en effet, une coïncidence visible entre mes intentions artistiques et les problèmes posés actuellement par la 'nouvelle critique.' Comme la plupart de ses représentants, j'ai subi, au cours des dernières années, la double influence de la lecture de Benveniste et de la découverte des formalistes russes. . . ."

general de las obras publicadas anteriormente a ella es siempre más intensa que la que le une a la 'realidad' " (p. 37). He maintains that there will be an unavoidable influence of one literary work over another. This concept is what the Formalists call literary borrowing:

> Toda obra literaria aparece en un universo ya poblado de obras, cuya existencia prolonga o modifica, y mantiene con ellas una complejísima red de relaciones de jerarquía y dependencia. Un texto cobra sentido no aislado, sino en correspondencia con otros textos, con todo un sistema de valores y significaciones previos. Como nos han enseñado los formalistas rusos, no son las obras las que evolucionan, sino la literatura: el texto particular no es más que un ejemplo que nos permite describir las propiedades de la literalidad. (p. 37)

Goytisolo also views criticism of a language as a means to criticize the social realities of a particular nation. He feels that in the Western World, where the old taboos such as crime, drugs, and homosexuality are no longer shocking, language is the only subversive element left to the writer: "El lenguaje, y sólo el lenguaje puede ser subversivo" (p. 39). Goytisolo indicates that such has been his intention with *Señas de identidad* and *Reivindicación del conde don Julián*: "No he abandonado en ellas en modo alguno el compromiso que buscaba en mis obras juveniles, simplemente, lo he trasladado a otro nivel. Nuestro anquilosado lenguaje castellanista exige . . . el uso de la dinamita o el purgante" (p. 39).

Goytisolo's latest work, *Juan sin Tierra*, completes what in this study is called *The Mendiola Trilogy*, in which Álvaro Mendiola is the protagonist. Goytisolo himself indicated that this book may be "el *finis terrae* de mi propia escritura."[4] The work is a tour de force in which many motifs of previous

---

[4] In *Juan Goytisolo*, ed. by Julián Ríos (Madrid: Editorial Fundamentos, 1975), p. 128.

novels are brought together and Formalist theories are applied throughout.

Even though Martínez Cachero[5] subdivides Goytisolo's writings prior to 1966 into three groups, this writer believes that there are truly two distinct ones. Martínez Cachero places *Juegos de manos* and Duelo en el Paraíso in the first group; the trilogy *El mañana efímero* in the second; and *La isla,* the travelogues, and other writings in the third. This study divides Goytisolo's work into an early, conventional period, consisting of the novels listed in the first two groupings of Martínez Cachero, and a mature period comprising *The Mendiola Trilogy.* Between these two periods there is hiatus, a period of transition in which Goytisolo writes *La isla and the two travelogues, Campos de Níjar* and *La Chanca,* in addition to other works not examined here. This study concentrates on Goytisolo's novels and the two travelogues. The short stories, the critical works, and the political writings lie beyond the scope and purpose of this investigation. The analysis of the works chosen is undertaken from a Formalist viewpoint.

Before examination of Goytisolo's novels, it is pertinent to give a historical sketch and a brief summary of the theories of Russian Formalism, with particular emphasis on those aspects that have influenced him. The Formalists do not necessarily agree on all the points examined here; hence this study emphasizes those authors whose definitions and views are closer to what Goytisolo appears to be doing. Moreover, when it appears that the Formalists do not provide the means to examine or define Goytisolo's writings, some improvisions, as well as other critical sources and methods, are utilized.

The aspect of Russian Formalism to which Goytisolo refers is the resurgance of a school of literary scholarship

---

[5] José María Martínez Cachero, "El novelista Juan Goytisolo," *Papeles de Son Armadáns*, No. 95 (febrero 1964), 125–60.

5

which originated in 1915–16 and was suppressed in Russia around 1930. The two initial Formalist platforms were the Moscow Linguistic Circle established in 1915 and *Opoyaz* (Society of Poetical Language) established in Petrograd in 1915. According to Victor Erlich[6] there are many points of contact between the Russian Formalists and the later Anglo-American school called "New Criticism"; the concept of shifting the emphasis of study from the poet to poetry is perhaps one of the most important characteristics common to both schools.

When dealing with those aspects of Formalism most relevant to Goytisolo's work, it can be stated that the essential premise of the Formalists was that "a work of art was an esthetic unit obedient to its own laws."[7] Such a concept is a radical departure from established scholarship of the time which generally followed one of three paths:[8] the historical school, which limited itself to studying literary backgrounds and often ignored literature itself; the moral-social, which considered literature as an instrument for the ethical and social improvement of mankind; and the philological, which stressed linguistic and historical studies in folklore and comparative literature.

Superficially viewed, the Formalists give the impression that they reject any theoretical or methodological program, but, in fact, their primary contention is that the purpose of literary study is essentially the knowledge of literary writings as independent entities. Boris Eikenbaum, in his essay "The Theory of the 'Formal Method,' " indicates that the Formalists "are not concerned with definitions, for which the late-comers

---

[6] Victor Erlich, *Russian Formalism, History-Doctrine* (The Hague: Mouton and Co., 1955), p. 242. Hereafter cited in parentheses at the end of the text.

[7] *Russian Formalism*, ed. by Stephen Bann and John E. Bowlt (New York: Harper and Row, 1973), p. 4.

[8] *Russian Formalist Criticism—Four Essays*, translated and with an introduction by Lee T. Lemon and Marion J. Reis (Lincoln: University of Nebraska Press, 1965), p. X. Hereafter cited in parentheses at the end of the text.

thirst; nor do we build general theories, which also delight eclectics. We posit specific principles and adhere to them insofar as the material justifies them. If the material demands their refinement or change, we change or refine them" (Lemon, pp. 102–03). Eikhenbaum stresses that "the question for the Formalists is not how to study literature, but what the subject matter of literary study actually is" (Lemon, p. 102).

The Formalists also departed from the traditional dichotomy of form versus content. For them form was no longer a vessel into which content was poured; rather, a work of art was the sum of the devices utilized in it. Wellek and Warren, in *Theory of Literature*, point out that the Formalists objected vigorously to that conventional dichotomy because it "cuts the work of art into two halves: a crude content and a superimposed, purely external form."[9] Thus, commentators should ask "how?" rather than "what?"

Todorov holds that it is "essential to realize that the 'form' of a work is not its only formal element: its content may equally be formal."[10] Once this idea is established, the concept of literary evolution or manner in which a work of art is related to its predecessors must be taken into consideration because, according to Eikenbaum, "Form, once understood as the fundamental basis of the work of art, is constantly self-adjusting in relation to all previous works in the past."[11] Victor Shklovsky comments regarding this relationship that "The work of art is viewed in relation to other artistic productions and is assisted by associations connecting it up to them."[12] Victor Erlich explains this association, indicating that the Formalists felt that "a new art is not antithesis of the preceding one, but its

---

[9] René Wellek and Austin Warren, *Theory of Literature* (New York: Harcourt, Brace and Co., 1949), p. 140.

[10] Bann and Bowlt, p. 10.

[11] As cited by Todorov, in Bann and Bowlt, p. 10. This idea is called literary borrowing.

[12] *Ibid.*, p. 11.

reorganization, a regrouping of the old elements" (Erlich, p. 226).

For the Formalists then, according to Todorov, anything included in a work of art is *formal*. The only elements which can be considered as nonformal are the material of which it is composed, the self-same elements prior to their integration into a particular artistic form. Since there is no natural or qualitative differentiation between subject and material and formal elements, the distinction can be made only by examining the use made of these elements or their function. This fact leads Todorov to state that "Analysis of form, in other words, of the totality of the work of art, leads to the identification of its functions, i.e., the relation between its various components."[13] Thus, Formalists are not merely concerned with form as traditionally envisioned, but with the totality of the work of art. In order to prevent confusion with the terms form and content, the Formalists "tended increasingly to substitute for the static dichotomy 'form versus content' a dynamic pair of notions, 'materials' and 'devices' " (Erlich, p. 161). The materials comprise the raw stuff which acquired esthetic efficacy through the utilization of the device.

Certain devices identified by the Formalists are especially relevant to Goytisolo's novels. In their study of fiction, they distinguished between two aspects of narrative: Story (*fable*) and plot (*sujet*).[14] Story is the narrative as presented in chronological order; plot, the manner in which the story is presented. Whereas the story runs at the same speed, in the same order, the plot may reverse its course, breaking with time and space; plot depends totally on the will of its creator. Thus, "story" might designate a rather well-known tale which (via a different "plot") the author presents in a new and original way. An excellent example, cited by Erlich (p. 209), is a For-

---

[13] *Ibid.*
[14] Robert Scholes, "Formalism and Structuralism," *Novel*, VI, No. 2 (Winter 1973), 138.

malist reference to *Anna Karenina*. Its fable allegedly can be summarized in one brief sentence, but in no way approaches the richness and complexity of the work.

Since the terms *story* and *plot* have undergone many definitions and interpretations, there does not seem to be agreement as to what these two terms mean exactly. This study utilizes a combination of those views, defining *story* as the pre-literary raw materials of the narrative, given or viewed in a chronological order. In this context, the story can usually be summarized, whereas plot, being the form given to the story, cannot. There are instances when the author might present the story about to be narrated in the form of an epigraph. *Plot*, on the other hand, can be viewed as the original manner in which the raw materials—the story—are given shape through the use of many devices that the Formalists have identified and named.

An important element of both story and plot are motifs. In a novel, the major theme or themes usually comprise smaller, irreducible units. Robert Scholes, in "Formalism and Structuralism," states that *story* can be defined "as the sum of the motifs in their casual-chronological order" and *plot* as "the sum of the motifs ordered as to engage the emotions and develop the theme."[15] For his part, Boris Tomashevsky ("Thematics," in Lemon, pp. 61–95), writes that a work of art is unified by a theme which runs through it: "The theme unites the separate elements of a work" (p. 63). Whereas Tomashevsky views story and plot as a manner in which the thematic units of a theme are arranged (p. 66), this writer considers Antonio García Berrio's views, in *Significado actual del formalismo ruso*, more in keeping with Goytisolo's works: "Temas y motivos se alojan, por así decirlo, en la entidad superior, denominada por los formalistas rusos 'fábula.' "[16]

---

[15] Scholes, p. 141.

[16] Antonio García Berrio, *Significado actual del formalismo ruso* (Barcelona: Editorial Planeta, 1973), p. 208.

The present writer envisions the possibility of a plot, as well as a story, composed of themes in addition to many motifs wherein themes form building blocks of story and plot rather than the opposite, as Tomashevsky seems to consider it. The theme, in fact, is developed through the use of several sets of motifs and/or undeveloped themes (subthemes) with their own motifs. Tomashevsky's meaning for motifs differs radically from that used in historical poetics. Whereas the latter system considers motifs as thematic units appearing in various works, Tomashevsky sees them as "the theme of an irreducible part of a work . . ." (p. 67). The kind of motifs that determine how the novel will begin, in relation to the story, are called *introductory motifs*. If the author begins the novel by acquainting the reader with all the elements of the story material, the procedure is called *immediate exposition*; if the reader is gradually informed of what is occurring, it is *delayed exposition*. There is a manner, seldom used, called *premonition*; Tomashevsky terms it "an account of what will happen told prior to the approaching events to prepare the reader . . ." (p. 75). The reader is thereby informed of what will happen through predictions, auguries, and assumptions. Another device, not mentioned by Tomashevsky, is character exposition: by detailing individual flaws the author gives the reader the opportunity to envision the future of characters involved in the narration. Still another form of exposition is that called *transposed*: to clarify something that has already happened, the author shifts time and/or place, either through his own comments or those of his characters.

According to Tomashevsky, the narrator plays an important role in the indirect development of the story materials "because plot shifts are a common function of the narrative style" (p. 75). These styles are three: omniscient, limited, and mixed. Omniscient narration is that in which the author informs the reader of everything taking place in the novel. Limited narration implies that the reader perceives only the perspective of one or several of the characters, but this vision is never all-knowing as that of the omniscient narrator. Mixed narration utilizes both the omniscient and the limited narrators. Other means, perhaps unfamiliar to Tomashevsky, involve stream-of-consciousness and free association.

Other important devices are *time* and *place*. Tomashevsky believes that "In analyzing the plot structure of individual works, attention should be given to the use of time and place in the narrative" (p. 77). He posits a definite difference between "story time" and "reading time," the former being the amount of time required for events in the narration to occur, while the latter is simply the length of time spent in reading the work. He further states (p. 78) that the story time can be given in three ways: 1) there may be a definite date, a specific chronological indication as to when the narration is taking place; 2) the duration of events may be indicated by the author directly or indirectly; 3) an impression of time elapsed is given so that the reader indirectly may determine its passage.

Concerning space, Tomashevsky identifies two types of motifs, the static and the dynamic. When the action of the novel takes place in a determined location such as a house, static motifs are used. In a situation where the persons in the narrative travel or move from one place to another, dynamic motifs are utilized. There are other applications for these two types of motifs: the dynamic ones usually cause a change in the situation and keep the story moving. The static, on the other hand, lend local color or serve to describe nature, the characters, etc.

Tomashevsky points out that some motifs cannot be omitted without destroying the coherence of the narrative while others may be discarded without disturbing the course of events. He calls the former *bound* and the latter *free* motifs. The free motifs, however, sometimes dominate and determine the construction of the plot (through digressions, details, etc.).[17] Leitmotifs (p. 74, note 10) Tomashevsky defines as motifs which are repeated more or less frequently, particularly if they are free. The writer nevertheless, will define any motif which reappears frequently throughout the work, even if it is not free, as a leitmotif.

Tomashevsky sees a character as the grouping and stringing of motifs. In this manner the literary figure becomes a "guiding thread which makes it possible to untangle a conglomeration of motifs" (p. 88). "A character," writes Tomashevsky, "is recognized by his *characteristics*" (p. 88), the group of motifs providing the reader with a psychological portrait, as it were, of the person. This characterization may be direct or indirect, depending upon whether the author gives a straightforward report or lets the reader form his own judgment through the examination of the characters' actions and conduct. A special device of either direct or indirect characterization called the *mask* is "the development of concrete motifs in harmony with the psychology of the character" (p. 88). External appearance of the character, the clothes he wears, the apartment or house in which he lives, and its furnishings become part of his mask. Additionally, two types of characters exist: static and dynamic. The static character does not change throughout the story, whereas the dynamic does, and this transformation may be relevant to the situation in the story.

Another device recognized by Formalist criticism is *motivation*, a rather complex concept. Lemon indicates that "generally, motivation is the reason governing the use of a particular device and may include anything from the author's desire to shock his readers, to the necessity of including specific props required by the action."[18] For Tomashevsky, "The net-

---

[17] There are instances, as will be observed later, when a motif may be bound and dynamic at the same time.

[18] Lemon, p. 30, n. 9.

work of devices justifying the introduction of individual motifs or of group of motifs is called *motivation*" (Lemon, p. 78). Tomashevsky mentions three motivational devices: *compositional motivation* simply refers to the usefulness and the economy of the motifs utilized. "Separate motifs may characterize either objects (stage properties) brought to the reader's attention or the activities of the characters (episodes)" (Lemon, p. 79). Tomashevsky cites Chekhov as saying that if the narrator mentions a nail driven into a wall at the beginning of a story, then at the conclusion the protagonist should hang himself on it. The second device, *realistic motivation*, demands an element of "illusion" in the work. The reader should have the impression, no matter what happens in the narrative, that what is taking place is real. Even when presenting the fantastic, the writer should create the illusion of reality through some double interpretation, a logical explanation, such as drugs, sleep, delirium, or other motifs. The third device is *artistic motivation*. The system of realistic motivation denies that of artistic motivation. Thus, any nonliterary material introduced must allow a new and individual interpretation.

Defamiliarization is a special example of artistic motivation because the old, the habitual, must be presented as if it were new and original. "One must speak of the ordinary as if it were unfamiliar," says Tomashevsky (Lemon, p. 85). Defamiliarization, for the Formalists, is a very important device. Shklovsky approaches Tomashevsky's positions noting that because of continuous exposure to the same things, man usually responds automatically to them. Art exists, Shklovsky feels, so "that one may recover the sensation of life. . . . The purpose of art is to impart the sensation of things as they are perceived and not as they are known" (Lemon, p. 12).

Other important devices identified by the Russian Formalists are *laying bare* and *retardation*. *Laying bare* is the manner in which the author allows the reader to see how he is going about the construction of the novel. Retardation is the manner in which motifs are arranged or interwoven in order to cause the narration to be delayed; time and space can be suspended or broken at the will of the narrator. One purpose of interpolating *delaying* motifs in the narration is to create suspense; Shklovsky indicates that the second part of *Don Quijote* is a good example of retardation, which he describes as a "loose mosaic of anecdotes" (Erlich, p. 213). Closely resembling retardation is the device called *staircase-like structure*. According to Erlich, through this device "What could have been a straight-forward statement is twisted by artful detours into a bizarre, multi-storied edifice" (p. 121). The device consists of the recurrence of the same episode in a novel through the use of parallels and juxtapositions. Shklovsky gives as an example Tolstoy's short novel *Khadzhi Murat*, the opening passage of which parallels and, in effect, predicts the fate of the hero by presenting the image of a crushed weed. Another device mentioned by the Formalists is *literary borrowing*, usually a transformation and not a mere transcription. Erlich comments that literary influences, according to the Formalists, "should be viewed in terms of an interrelationship between two autonomous artistic systems" (Erlich, p. 235). Once an act of borrowing is clearly discernible, the commentator's concern "ought to be not with the 'where from,' but with the 'what for'; not with the source of the 'motif,' but with the use to which it is put in the new 'system,' " (Erlich, p. 235).[19]

As can be gathered thus far, the Formal method does not advance ultimate criteria for the esthetic evaluation of a given work of art. It explains how the work is composed, but does not pass judgment. It should be remembered that the devices and motifs discussed by the Formalists have been in existence for several hundred years. What the Russian Formalists have done is to identify and describe them in a number of literary

---

[19] In the following chapters terms such as *story, plot, motivation*, etc. will be used in the technical sense indicated in this introduction.

works. Goytisolo's novels, unlike those of other novelists examined by the Formalists, provide an additional perspective. Since Goytisolo, beginning with *Señas de identidad*, has consciously used Formalist devices, an interesting evolution of form is present. Examination of those novels written before he became acquainted with the Formalists' tenets as well as those composed after he began to be influenced by them will be undertaken. Thus, a remarkable contrast will be discovered between the earlier period and the later: there will be a revelation of most of the devices utilized, consciously or otherwise that disclose the evolution of form in Goytisolo's novels. This approach will also help to understand better the Spanish author's last three novels, *Señas de identidad, Reivindicación del conde don Julián,* and *Juan sin tierra.* [20]

[20] The importance of other Spanish writers in the post-neorealist experimental renovation of the Spanish novel (Benet, Cela, Juan Leyva) should be remembered while reading this study. Additionally, Goytisolo's indebtedness to Martin Santos, particularly in *The Mendiola Trilogy,* must be recognized.

Chapter I

Juegos de Manos and *Duelo en el Paraíso*

Juan Goytisolo's first two novels, *Juegos de manos* and *Duelo en el Paraíso*, will be examined in this chapter. His first novel, although written in 1952, was not published until 1954; his second appeared in 1955. *Juegos de manos* is a good first novel but has many flaws, understandable in a literary debut. It received the third place in the Nadal national contest, and was, according to Kessel Schwartz, "far superior to either of the novels which placed ahead of it."[1] Its title might allude to a well-known Spanish proverb, "Juegos de manos, juegos de villanos," which underscores the belief that gentlemen do not engage in games which involve touching each other with their

---

[1] Kessel Schwartz, *Juan Goytisolo* (New York: Twayne Publishers, Inc., 1970), p. 42. Hereafter the page number will be given in parentheses at the end of the text cited.

hands and that might lead to a violent outcome.[2] Most commentators, however, believe the title refers to the sleight of hand in a crooked game of cards, through which one of the characters in the novel, David, is chosen to assassinate a minor political figure, Francisco Guarner. Kessel Schwartz translates the title as *Sleight of Hand*.

The story of the novel is basically a psychological portrayal of a group of dissatisfied young men who want to demonstrate, through violent means, their disapproval of the government and values of the society in which they were born. The plot may be considered as the manner in which the group plans to demonstrate their dissatisfaction and the unexpected outcome. Within the story and plot are several undeveloped themes, essentially psychological sketches of principal characters of the novel. This study briefly examines those characters deemed most important, summarizing their psychological make-up and their place in the novel. The characters in question are Agustín Mendoza, David, Luis, Uribe, and Ana.

The leader of the group Agustín Mendoza, a painter, is unable to accomplish anything of value. Because of his failure as a painter, he finds himself relegated to a state of mediocrity he abhors: "Mucho antes que tú me conocieras me consideraba un ser privilegiado. Cualquier alabanza, por desmedida que fuese, la estimaba producto de una reflexión justa."[3] In contrast with Mendoza, David, a close friend, shy and lonely, develops a great admiration for the former, and his life

---

[2] José María Sbarbi in *Gran diccionario de refranes de la lengua española* (Buenos Aires: Librería "El Ateneo," 1943), p. 523, says that the proverb "Reprende el retozar y jugar con las manos, como impropio de gentes bien nacidas. . . ." Additionally, the *Diccionario de la lengua española*, Real Academia Española (18th ed.; Madrid: Espasa-Calpe, 1956), p. 774, indicates that the proverb is a "referencia que censura la excesiva familiaridad en jugar y tocarse con las manos varias personas a otras."

[3] Juan Goytisolo, *Juegos de manos* (2nd ed.; Barcelona: Ediciones Destino, 1960), p. 144. Hereafter the page number will be given in parentheses at the end of the text cited.

changes radically after meeting him: "Y allí encontró a Mendoza, rodeado de pintores, poetas y anarquistas. Hacía de ello cuatro años y su amistad significó, para él, el cambio más importante de su vida. Desde su encuentro, David había dejado de ser el muchacho aplicado, orgullo de las familias" (p. 139). It is David who, as a result of a crooked game of cards, is selected to kill Francisco Guarner. Failing to carry out the assignment, David is killed by Agustín Mendoza.

Luis Páez, the perpetrator of the sleight of hand by which David is chosen, and his sister Gloria participated from an early age in violent games. Luis had been the leader of a gang of youths notorious for their stealing, vandalism, and sadism. Ironically, Páez' motives for forcing Uribe to cheat as he dealt the cards was fear of being selected as the assassin, a fact perceived when he almost fainted as he watched Agustín kill David (p. 244). Uribe, "Tánger," the buffoon of the group, is a coward, a dipsomaniac, a masochist, and a latent homosexual whose desire to escape from reality, from his own self which he despises, is patent every time he appears in the novel. An example of his desire to escape from himself is found in his continuous use of disguises: "Frente al espejo . . . Uribe se dedicaba a su locura favorita: su amor a los disfraces, al ansia de huir de sí mismo" (p. 152). It is Ana who suggests Guarner as the target for their crime since he is the symbol of the bourgeoisie; he stands for everything they abhor and want to destroy:

> . . . Guarner era una figura decorativa, un figurín, un payaso de trapo, pero a los ojos de los burgueses—el mundo cerrado de los padres del que todos se sentían desvinculados—encarnaba el antiguo estilo, los modales y la concepción sosegada de la vida, todo aquello que los jóvenes que olían la revuelta y la cercanía de la lucha, aspiraban a desterrar para siempre. (p. 91)

Thus, the novel is dedicated primarily to a psychological examination of a group of dissatisfied young men (obvious products of the Spanish Civil War) who rebel against their elders and their middle-class values. Most of these young people lack political convictions; being in essence a representation of the "angry young men," of the "rebels without a cause" of the fifties. Since they need some sort of identification, each one joins the gang seeking, as indicated by Randolph Cox, "a personal identity and a meaningful existence in harmony with others and himself."[4] To this could be added the desire, already mentioned, to repudiate the set of values of a society they dislike. For this reason they create a world where only their values are valid and, in the process, the beliefs of their subculture collide with those of the culture at large. Yet even in their world not everyone is able to abide by their rules and, as a consequence, failure results. Unfortunately Goytisolo fails to develop these characters and they must be classified as static.

The reader is introduced to the narration immediately, as it develops. There do not seem to be introductory motifs directly connected with the narration except for what appears to be foreshadowing of David's death: Agustín dreams several times that he kills David with a knife. There are flashbacks, related to the development of the characters rather than to the elaboration of the plot. Goytisolo employs a combination of narrating motifs, the prevalent one that of a modified omniscient narrator who takes the reader from one place to another, following the different characters. Goytisolo also uses third-person viewpoint, anecdotal dialogue, first-person point of view, modified stream-of-consciousness, and dialogue. The novel follows a lineal sequence, and the temporal plane is broken only when background information about particular persons is given.

Through the modified omniscient narrator Goytisolo

---

[4] Randolph Calvin Cox, "Aspects of Alienation in the Novels of Juan Goytisolo" (unpublished Ph.D. dissertation, University of Wisconsin, 1972), p. 73.

presents the characters' surroundings, their dialogue and their thoughts. At no time does the author address the reader, nor reveal himself as the narrator. He maintains sufficient objectivity that he never becomes the judge of his creations. In this respect, Goytisolo is very close to Baroja, who departed from the technique of the psychological novel of the nineteenth century wherein the God-like author forever judges and criticizes the villains, praising and rewarding the heroes. Goytisolo's limited participation (as an omniscient narrator) in the novel functions to establish an adequate background atmosphere, as the following example demonstrates: "Cuando salieron a la calle no había cesado de llover. Las gotas desprendidas del alero se desgranaban sobre el pequeño saledizo de pizarra y, junto al bordillo de la acera, las bocas de alcantarilla engullían el agua de la calzada" (p. 10).

Goytisolo rejected the psychological novel in *Problemas de la novela*, several years after he wrote *Juegos de manos*, probably trying to allow the reader an objective perspective of the psychological make-up of the characters through the combination of viewpoints. This "hands-off-the-characters" approach Goytisolo calls behaviorist, referring to the vogue in France around that time. This technique's purpose is to broaden exposition beyond the usual selected minorities who can realistically examine themselves in a novel:

> El empleo de método psicológico o de análisis implica, como hemos visto, la exigencia de unos personajes que, por su privilegiada situación cultural y económica, tengan capacidad, tiempo y medios materiales de observarse. A causa de ello, la casi totalidad de las novelas publicadas en España durante los últimos treinta años se ocupan sólo de una minoría selecta. . . .[5]

Consequently, novelists sought new ways to present other sectors of society: "En Francia se le ha bautizado bajo el nom-

---

[5] Juan Goytisolo, *Problemas de la novela* (Barcelona: Editorial Seix Barral, 1959), p. 11. Hereafter page numbers will be given within the text.

bre de 'behaviorismo' o método objectivo del comportamiento externo . . ." (p. 19). That is, the author should present only that which an external observer can perceive of a person or animal. Essentially, however, Goytisolo engages in psychological analysis of some of his characters without appearing to be taking direct part in the process as did many nineteenth- and twentieth-century authors. Not only is there greater verisimilitude in most instances, but more freedom for the reader to reach his own independent conclusions. Additionally, this technique frequently allowed the author to escape censorship since his ideas are "performed" rather than explicitly stated. Not until *La resaca*, however, does Goytisolo manage to master the behaviorist approach. That approach is best illustrated in *Juegos de manos* by the viewpoints he uses: third-person point of view and bits of internal monologue (appearing within quotes). It is seen in "Tánger" in the following excerpt:

"Oh. La magia. Entregarse de lleno a la alquimia. Fabricar cocktails."

Recordó que, cuando niño, en el jardín de su casa de campo, ayudado por un grupo de pilluelos de los que era cabeza indiscutible, reunía cuantos ingredientes tenía al alcance de la mano. (p. 121)

Another variant employs the first-person viewpoint, utilized at times to give an insight into David's background and psychological profile. The reader, through the third-person point of view, first encounters David as he is about to write in his diary. Before writing he reads past entries:

. . . Se sentó en la mesa del escritorio y abrió el cuaderno al azar.

"Mi niñez, que me había parecido algo muy simple, ahora que trato de abarcarla por entero, me parece de pronto enormemente complicada. El recuerdo que conservo de ella es turbio y fragmentario." (pp. 172–73)

Through anecdotal dialogue Goytisolo provides the past and present of some of his characters, as when an individual tells another about his life: " 'Mucho antes que tú me conocieras me consideraba un ser privilegiado. Cualquier alabanza, por desmedida que fuese, la estimaba producto de una reflexión justa' " (p. 144). The most objective instance of narrative found in *Juegos de manos* is perhaps a dialogue recalling Hemingway's style: dry, very colloquial, and to the point:

—¿Dan algo bueno?
—No sé. No me ha dicho nada.
—¿A qué hora le aguardas?
—A las seis.
—Está bien, iré.
—Te espero.
—De acuerdo. (p. 75)

The place of the action in *Juegos de manos* can be considered dynamic since there is continuous movement of all the characters from one place to another in the present as well as in the past. The chronological motif, on the other hand, is not definite, if present at all. References to time are vague: "the next morning," "several years ago." The reader, upon finishing the novel, does not know how much time has elapsed. There are, however, many flashbacks which break up time and space and serve to enhance the reader's knowledge of the psychological make-up of some of the characters.

There are three important bound motifs in the novel: antisocial behavior, a task, and escapism. The first is perhaps the most important, because without it the novel could not develop. Dislike of Spanish society spurs the young men to kill, to destroy, without actually grasping the magnitude, the meaning, of their actions and, in most cases, without having definite political views to express. A case in point is David, who holds no political views and is a member of the group only because of Agustín. When the assassination is discussed, he seems to be the only one who has any reservations (in addition to Páez, as the reader will discover much later). In the following scene David betrays his true state of mind:

. . . El que se oponga, debe decírmelo a la cara, sin necesidad de andarse escondiendo. Si me demuestra que no sirvo, yo seré el primero en aceptarlo.

22

> Hablaba en voz pausada, pero el temblor de sus manos trai-
> cionaba sus verdaderos sentimientos. (p. 138)

Thus, the execution of Guarner becomes a task David must perform to prove himself, not only his being entitled to be part of the gang, but, particularly, his affection for and devotion to Agustín. The group's desire to escape a society they consider decadent leads them to create a subculture with values of their own which eventually clash with those of the culture in which they live.

Three dynamic motifs influence, to a large extent, the outcome of the events: executioner-victim, betrayal, and cowardice. The executioner-victim motif is observed not only in the plans to assassinate Guarner, but also in the relationship between David and Agustín, ending in the execution of the former.[6] The reader should notice David's docility while Agustín goes through the motions of shooting him in the neck, an act of ritual overtones in which David accepts his sacrificial role and Agustín becomes the executioner. From the stand-point of the gang, David's failure to execute Guarner is a betrayal of rules and agreements established by the group. From their perspective, then, the motif of betrayal is best illustrated by David's failure to act. From the reader's view-point, however, Uribe and Páez' treachery in the game of cards is a better example. Uribe and Páez' conduct also displays the cowardice motif—in the former, because he was afraid of Páez and could not refuse his demand, and in the latter because he feared the possibility of his being selected by the cards as the assassin.

The most important free motifs in the novel are the constant digressions, details about characters, homosexuality, and a protean figure. Through digressions and details, Goy-tisolo develops the characters, their social status, psychologi-

---

[6] Ramón Buckley in *Problemas formales en la novela española contemporanea* (Barcelona: Ediciones Península, 1968), p. 158, sees David as an example of the victim archetype frequently appearing in Goytisolo's novels.

cal make-up, and thus the motives for their antisocial behavior, leading to the assassination plot and David's death. Each person in the novel has a different reason for wanting to murder Guarner. Ana has followed the politician's career and, to her, the murder has political overtones. Agustín considers it an opportunity to take a stand, to put into practice what the group has spoken about many times. David merely follows the ideas of Agustín, whom he admires; he is an innocent bystander unable to avoid becoming directly involved. His attraction to Agustín has homosexual overtones, and the latent homosexuality seems to be reciprocated by the painter. The mutual attraction is supported by symbolic, as well as premonitory, dreams in which Agustín kills David with a knife: "Una noche, tiempo atrás, durante una pesadilla había soñado que mataba a David, con una de las dagas de su colección, sin que el muchacho ofreciera resistencia" (p. 258), and "Es extraño," le dijo. " 'también yo he soñado eso muchas veces' " (p. 259). The use of the knife in their dreams is an obvious Freudian symbol.[7] The homosexuality motif also appears in "Tánger" who seems to dislike women and is attracted to young men:

—¿A dónde me lleva?
El muchacho estaba detrás, inmóvil. Uribe le fulminó con una mirada.
—Eso no te importa ni te interesa. Si has quedado con una de esas horribles pirujillas que corretean por ahí dentro, puedes decirle que vuelves dentro de un minuto. Pierde cuidado: yo no te haré nada. Mis necesidades no son de orden físico. (p. 158)

The Protean figure is illustrated by "Tánger" who uses disguises to escape his unwanted state in life.[8] With him, then,

---

[7] Emir Rodríguez Monegal, in "El arte de Narrar," *Marcha*, No. 10 (julio, 1959), 22, also suggests this relationship.

[8] J. F. Cirre in "Novela e ideología en Juan Goytisolo," *Insula*, No. 230 (enero 1966), 12, calls this type of character a *mixtificador*. Cirre, however, sees all the characters with escapist tendencies as *mixtificadores*. This study, in contrast, concentrates on those who continuously change their personality or appearance through the use of masks, disguises, or behavior. Buckley's use (*continued on page 25*)

there is a combination of motifs. But, unlike the others, his escape is through masks and alcohol.

Throughout the novel, Goytisolo appears to strive for verisimilitude, in which case, the system of motifs comprising *Juegos de manos* should stress realistic motivation. The outcome of the novel, however, seems unmotivated and somewhat improbable. Agustín's apparent psychological breakdown and his obvious wish for punishment, as he makes the dramatic statement in the barroom that he has killed the young man across the street, is not in keeping with the cold-blooded leader who, making sure he leaves no clues behind, plans Guarner's murder. Nevertheless, to paraphrase Juan Goytisolo, *Juegos de manos* is a good first novel.[9]

The young adults of *Juegos de manos* could be considered as a later stage in the lives of the children of *Duelo en el Paraíso* (1955). Goytisolo's second novel is set in a small Spanish town during the Civil War. The story is almost an allegorical representation of the biblical tale of Cain and Abel. The action takes place as the defeated Republican troops leave the town and the victorious army arrives. Of the many characters, most important are the orphan children who, taking advantage of the chaotic situation, take over the school in which they have been kept. These children are the offspring of the war's casualties, and this circumstance, as well as the unwholesome atmosphere surrounding them, causes their rebellion and their regression to a savage state. Paralleling the acts of war,[10] in a

---

(*continued from page 24*)(p. 163) of the term *figura proteica*, referring to escape through disguises, is more in keeping with the term as used in this study.

[9] Goytisolo made this statement to the writer in an informal conversation in New Orleans on March 22, 1975.

[10] When a soldier asks one of the children the meaning of the arabesques on his face, the boy replies: "El mismo que las estrellitas que llevan en la gorra sus capitanes" (Juan Goytisolo, *Duelo en el Paraíso* [4th ed.; Barcelona: Ediciones Destino, 1968], p. 9). Hereafter the page number will be given in parentheses at the end of the text.

more primitive way, they assassinate Abel, plunder, steal, and burn. The title is perhaps a direct allusion to the story. The word *duelo* has a triple denotation in Spanish; it is a wake, a duel, or sorrow, each a valid interpretation since there is a wake, Abel's; a "duel" is taking place throughout the novel; and the boy's death causes sorrow. Kessel Schwartz translates the title as *Sorrow at Paradise House*, while the 1958 English translation is *Children of Chaos*. The plot is developed through a multivisional approach and by the suspension of time and space. The theme is immediately discerned upon examining some of the symbolic allusions. Abel, the protagonist, who lives with his aunt on a small estate called "El Paraíso," is the victim of his young friends and brothers in misery. In essence, what takes place in the small town and surrounding area is a reflection of the war, a microcosm within the macrocosm of the Spanish Civil War. Consequently, the most important theme of the novel is the appalling result of man's unchained savage nature; he will destroy even his own kin. Ironically, adults in the novel appear horrified by the crime committed by the children even though surrounded by corpses from both armies.

Several subthemes (carrying their own free motifs) unfold the main theme, some sketchy and many unfinished. They constitute psychological studies of characters in direct relation to the dead boy, Abel, who can furnish a partial picture of his life. Taken as a whole, they provide a composite, sometimes overlapping, picture of events that led to Abel's assassination. While providing the reader with information about Abel, through flashbacks and other means discussed later, they digress continuously, offering a perspective of their personalities and/or those of others. This technique of retardation creates suspense in the revelation of what has taken place and the reasons for its occurrence. Gonzalo Sobejano believes that, without the constant flashbacks of the different characters, the main theme (a young boy assassinated by a gang of children) could be reduced to a short story:

> Diríase que toda esta avenida de recordaciones es como
> una red de afluentes que por diversas partes llegan a engrosar el
> caudal de un río. Sin esos afluentes la obra sería una novela corta
> o un cuento: con ellos se forma la corriente densa de una nov-
> ela.[11]

The subthemes include that of Estanislaa, Abel's demented
aunt, an overpowering woman wishing she could bring back
the past; the colorful "Gallego," a veteran of the Spanish-
American War and a friend of Abel; Elósegui, the law student,
who enlists on the losing side and finds Abel's corpse; and
Lucía and Ángela, the town spinsters, owners of the rifle with
which Abel is killed. These subthemes and others have several
associated free motifs, through which the reader acquires a
perspective of the characters' psychological make-up, their
particular views about the war and life in general, as well as
Goytisolo's feelings about them. Examination of subthemes is
limited to their association with Abel and to some pertinent
free motifs.

Goytisolo utilizes delayed and transposed exposition
and regressive ending[12] in the presentation of circumstances
explaining the cast of characters, the events, and the interrelationship between characters, as well as that between characters and events. Delayed exposition is observed in the *ex-
abrupto* introduction to Abel's death, followed by a gradual
exposition of events leading to his assassination. In order to
clarify what has taken place, to give a biographical sketch of
Abel and his psychological make-up, and to introduce other
characters in the novel, Goytisolo suspends time and space

---

[11] Gonzalo Sobejano, *Novela española de nuestro tiempo* (2nd ed.; Madrid: Editorial Prensa Española, 1970), p. 270.

[12] Premonition and foreshadowing are observed in a complex incident involving present, past, and future. Doña Estanislaa is telling Abel about her first son's death, his wake, and burial when, suddenly, Abel sees through the window a group of children carrying a coffin (p. 153). It appears to be a premonition of his death which, in the chronological sequence of the novel, has already taken place. Consequently, it is diffcult to ascertain whether it is really premonition or foreshadowing. Perhaps premonition is the more suit-able term.

and, as a consequence, a continuous shifting of time and space ensues in the elaboration of the plot—a good example of transposed exposition. Furthermore, the finale can be called regressive since not until the end are the reasons for the boy's execution given.

Goytisolo uses a mixed system of points of view in the narration, but the omniscient prevails. The combination of narrative motifs used will become clear in a brief chapter-by-chapter examination. The novel is divided into six chapters with subdivisions in each. The first begins with an omniscient narrator who gradually limits himself to the third-person point of view, that of Elósegui. The soldier's perspective is maintained thereafter, with relatively few exceptions, where the omniscient narrator assumes command. The following segment is a good example: "La súbita irrupción de Elósegui bajo el dintel de la puerta produjo un instante de confusión. El soldado que iba delante, temiéndose una emboscada, se pegó a la pared del edificio" (p. 26).

Part of the second chapter is presented via the point of view of "El Arcángel," one of the young boys of the tribe. The omniscient narrator then focuses on the group of children as they confront the boy, next shifting to a group of soldiers who go to El Paraíso to notify its inhabitants of the death of Abel. The reader thus becomes acquainted with the three women living in El Paraíso: Doña Estanislaa, the demented aunt; Águeda, her aging daughter; and Filomena, their servant. Filomena is ordered to the schoolhouse to identify Abel's body, and the *alférez* in charge proceeds to question her about him. The reader thereby learns more about the life of Abel.

The third chapter narrates the search the soldiers undertake for the school children, located in the process of burning a windmill with a man inside. One boy is captured; the man rescued, the person in charge of the schoolhouse, Quintana, explains events after the Republican soldiers left: how the boys, armed with different types of weapons, tied him, held a

28

trial, and sentenced him to death. The remainder of the chapter tells the story of Doña Estanislaa. Point of view is difficult to determine. Since this portion is separated from Quintana's account by asterisks, the reader can assume that the author is intervening directly, elaborating upon Quintana's remarks in the preceding paragraph. It is also probable that some italicized segments constitute internal monologue or stream-of-consciousness. The following three segments embody, respectively, Quintana's last remarks, a brief glance at Doña Estanislaa as she picks up a toy violin, and part of six italicized lines:

—Dos, ¿comprende usted? Y ahora el sobrino, por si no fuera bastante.

* * *

Doña Estanislaa tomó el violín de juguete que unas horas antes había sustraído del. . . .

* * *

Los dos eran jóvenes y hermosos: aún inocentes, se los hubiera creído culpables. . . . (p. 138)

Thereafter, narration resumes from a third-person viewpoint which appears to be Estanislaa's. Many flashbacks are segments of conversations of many years ago. There are also dreams and some hallucinatory incidents in which reality cannot be separated from fantasy. Therefore, viewpoint in this section is complex, involving Estanislaa and her past, and Abel and his future; it is observed when, as Estanislaa tells Abel about the burial of her son, the boy sees a group of children carrying a coffin—a premonition of his future death which, in effect, has already taken place:

Y de pronto, por arte de magia (o del hambre que llenaba su sueño de visiones aéreas y le rodeaba de seres alados y flexibles), todo el paisaje se había poblado de fantasmas. Un cortejo de chiquillos descendía las gradas del sendero que llevaba a la terraza, con un ataúd sobre los hombros. (p. 153)

The purpose of Estanislaa's narration is to acquaint the reader with her psychological make-up, her past, and her relation to Abel, the recipient of her reminiscences. It also offers an insight into Abel's home environment. Estanislaa's accounts are largely subjective and inaccurate, causing Goytisolo to introduce shortly thereafter the servant's perspective of the events. A good example of Estanislaa's inaccuracies is her report of the affair between Romano (whom she loved with obviously incestuous overtones) and Claude, a girl he brought from abroad to live in El Paraíso. From Estanislaa's perspective, the young girl is selfish, unworthy of Romano, the cause of his death: "Esta chiquilla, con sus lacas de uñas, sus recortes fotográficos de artistas de cine y los ratoncillos blancos que, según descubrí un día, ocultaba en los bolsillos del pantalón, estaba reduciendo mis proyectos a cenizas" (p. 167). The servant's narration, however, differs sharply. Filomena sees Estanislaa as a very possessive mother, trying to push aside the recipient of her son's love: "Por fin, el mes de mayo, el señorito vino con la señorita estuvo a punto de desmayarse de rabia. Estaba muerta de celos, porque sabía que el señorito la quería y deseaba casarse con ella" (p. 176).

The fourth chapter introduces "Gallego," the town beggar, an unusual character who lives in caves and carries on his back several bags containing a large number of useless items. He presents another perspective of Abel since the boy has been a good friend of his. Unlike the other schoolboys who threw rocks at him, Abel is kind and spends hours speaking with him. Gallego's perspective is important, emphasizing the radical change in Abel upon his meeting Pablo, an important member of the gang: "Un día, Abel se presentó en compañía de otro chiquillo y desde entonces, las cosas cambiaron. El niño no era el mismo de antes y parecía no tener ojos sino para su nuevo amigo" (p. 107).

The fifth chapter shifts to the point of view of the two spinsters, Ángela and Lucía, who provide another insight into El Paraíso and thus a better perspective upon the relationship between Abel and Pablo. With the news of Abel's death, they reminisce about Estanislaa's other children and her life in general: "La pobre ha sido muy desgraciada. Con tantos accidentes. . . . De todas formas—dijo Lucía mientras se secaba los ojos con el pañuelo—hay que reconocer que también ella se ha buscado sus desgracias. Su forma de educar a los chiquillos . . ." (p. 218). Pablo is a member of a gang of children who roam the forest around El Paraíso. One day Abel is taken prisoner because he was spying on the group. Thanks to Pablo, the boy is released unharmed and thereafter the two develop a close friendship.

The sixth and final chapter, narrated from an omniscient point of view, explains events surrounding the death of Abel; Emilio, one of the children of the tribe, captured by the soldiers, explains the reasoning behind the execution. The children, influenced by the chaotic retreat of the Republican troops, develop a paranoid fear of the approaching army. This fear of the unknown is heightened by the radio which urges its listeners to be vigilant:

> "Vigilad; formad vosotros mismos vuestra policía: aprended a delatar a los traidores; si vuestros compañeros son facciosos, castigadlos," y sus consignas, recibidas por algún niño oculto tras las cortinas del cuarto de Quintana, corrían de boca en boca. . . . (p. 275)

> —¿Por qué causa? —dijo Santos—. ¿Acaso os había hecho alguna pasada?
> Emilio movió negativamente la cabeza.
> —No, ninguna; pero el *Arquero* decía que él pertenecía a otro bando y que era preciso matarle para sentirnos liberados. (p. 283)

None of the six chapters of the novel maintains the same perspective throughout. As Kessel Schwartz has noted, Goytisolo "employs interior monologue, flashbacks, objective and cinematographic techniques to narrate the novel" (p. 53). Many instances could perhaps be considered examples of free association. The sudden knowledge of the death of Abel triggers a trance in some characters during which they recall, either aloud, for the benefit of the bystander, or to themselves, their past association with the boy, in addition to some personal experiences. There are occasions as well in which the omniscient narrator may further elaborate on the recollections of the characters. The brief sojourn of Abel in El Paraíso is thus narrated by several persons, each one giving a personal perspective, which may or may not overlap that of others, and by an omniscient narrator who fills in certain gaps. Thus, through a narrative collage, as it were, the reader learns of the unhappy life and tragic death of Abel.[13]

Time and space are suspended and broken continuously in *Duelo en el Paraíso*. Events depicted occur within twelve to fifteen hours and their location is El Paraíso and its surroundings. Notwithstanding, the author manages to present the past, present, and sometimes the future through premonitions as well as to embrace Europe and America in his narration. The novel begins at 10:00 A.M. at which time Elósegui hears the shot which kills Abel: "El camión partió a las ocho con el sargento y los andaluces. Elósegui lo oyó traquetear por el camino de El Paraíso y no se sintió tranquilo hasta que desapareció tras el recodo. Desde entonces habían transcurrido más de dos horas" (p. 10). The moment of the action is dated absolutely as February 6, 1939, in the following two excerpts. Elósegui, interrogated by the *alférez*, looks at a calendar on a wall: "Miraba la hoja del calendario que colgaba de la

---

[13] Sharon Spencer, in *Space, Time and Structure in the Modern Novel* (New York University Press, 1971), p. 156, considers this mixture of events in a novel as the *spatialization* of time:

"At its simplest, the spatialization of time in the novel is the process of splintering the events that, in a traditional novel, would appear in a narrative sequence and of rearranging them so that past, present, and future actions are presented in reversed, or combined, patterns; when this is done, the events of the novel have been 'spatialized.' " (p. 156)

An important effect of this "spatialization" is simultaneity: two or more actions taking place at the same time in different locations could be presented by the author without taking into consideration how far apart or how close they are to each other. Time is also splintered in the process since events many years apart are juxtaposed.

pared, a unos palmos escasos de la cabeza del alférez: seis de febrero" (p. 37). The year is deduced from a conversation taking place between Abel and "Gallego," the year prior to the boy's death, when he thinks the following about the old man: "Le molestaba la manía de los viejos de restar importancia a lo presente y recargar los colores de los tiempos pasados. También deseaba mostrarle que el año mil novecientos treinta y ocho era capaz de heroísmos . . . " (p. 205). The novel ends the same day. As night falls, Estanislaa speaks to a soldier during Abel's wake:

> Se había dejado caer otra vez sobre los cojines y aspiró ávidamente el perfume de magnolia. Fuera, el viento soplaba fuerte en torno a las paredes de la casa y traía a sus oídos el crujido familiar de los postigos. La luna inundaba de gris la terraza cubierta de hierbajos y los eucaliptos recortaban en el cielo sus harapientas cortezas. Lejos, muy lejos las campanas repicaban. A júbilo. A alegría.
> Doña Estanislaa se volvió para mirarle:
> —Mire usted: una vez, hace de ellos bastantes años. . . . (p. 294)

The progression of the day, from morning to night, is maintained through several allusions to the hour, for example: "Consultó el reloj: las once menos diez" (p. 20); "El reloj de sol marcaba la una y cuarto . . . " (p. 77); "¿Qué hora es?" "La una y media" (p. 187); "Está anocheciendo ya . . . " (p. 269). The purposes of such references vary depending upon the situation: exact time could indicate to the reader a return from a flashback to the present, set the stage for a voyage to the past, or show a linear progression which would otherwise be lost because of the suspension of time and space. The time of Abel's death appears at least twice in the novel because his sentence is written on several pieces of paper by "Arquero": "Un rectángulo de papel, escrito con lápiz, rezaba: 'La rejecucíon será a las diez' " (p. 15), and "Ocho rectángulos de papel pautado con el aviso: 'La ejecución será a las diez' " (p.5). Additionally, references are made to hours and dates of events prior to the moment of Abel's death.

Because of the constant shifting to other settings through flashbacks, in which the characters are frequently transposed to other places, the place of action may be considered dynamic; but since such movement occurs only in the minds of the characters while either in El Paraíso or its surroundings, the place of action could also be considered static. Consequently, it may be valid to view the place of action as both, dynamic and static.

Some of the bound motifs in the novel are war, death, an atmosphere of unreality and absurdity, two rifles, and social criticism. The war, encircling and pervading the area where the children are, contributes to the creation of a chimeric atmosphere where logic ceases to be relevant. Elósegui senses this unreality shortly after he discovers Abel's corpse: "Le asaltó la impresión de hallarse en medio de un bosque encantado y tuvo que frotarse los ojos" (p. 18);" . . . eran otras tantas fórmulas, conjuros y ademanes faunescos por los que un mundo de magia y de crueldad . . . acabada de imponerse al ordinario, cubriéndolo como un tapiz de ensueño" (p. 37). Death is omnipresent, not only as result of the proximity of the war, but as a calamity prematurely besieging most of the characters, young and old, in the novel.[14] For example, Estanislaa's husband and two sons die; Filomena loses five children. The presence of death, particularly in El Paraíso, is illustrated by Estanislaa's purchase of several dolls, one of which depicts death: " . . . era un esqueleto de marfil, que agitaba su cetro" (p. 163). Romano, leaving home after an argument with his mother, takes with him all the dolls. He dies

---

[14] A leitmotif reminding the reader of death as it relates to Abel and to Estanislaa's son, David, appears frequently in the form of a sentence, "Dios nunca muere," the title of a waltz to which some children dance during David's wake. Abel has a morbid attraction to the story of the wake, which Estanislaa narrates; he repeats it to Pablo and "Arcángel," and the latter gives Abel a piece of paper with the sentence written on it, perhaps as a warning, shortly before the boy's execution. This message Elósegui finds in the boy's hand (pp. 18, 152, 255, and 285).

in an automobile accident shortly thereafter, and Águeda tells Antonio she did not see the doll portraying death at the site of the accident: " 'Busqué con la vista la efigie de la muerte, pero no la descubrí por ningún sitio".(p. 174). Schwartz sees death as "almost the unseen protagonist of the novel" (p. 58). Abel's assassination is committed, ironically, with one of the rifles Pablo and he steal from Lucía and Ángela. The subsistence of the children in this deleterious environment leads them to regress to a primitive, barbaric state where death is commonplace; their behavior, a direct reflection of their elders whom they are trying to emulate, presents the novel's social criticism. The name Abel, as indicated previously, emphasizes Goytisolo's view that Civil War is a form of mass fratricide which solves nothing and destroys everything.

The most important dynamic motifs in *Duelo en el Paraíso* are escapism, executioner-victim, betrayal, loss of innocence, and a mother-figure which seems to symbolize Spain. Escapism is prevalent throughout the novel since most characters are trying to escape the situation in which they find themselves. Abel wants to escape from El Paraíso and from what he considers a meaningless and hopeless existence. To gain his freedom he wants to go to war. Pablo appears to manage his escape through economic means, and thus he steals and cheats. "Arquero" wants to create a city governed by children, completely independent of adults. Estanislaa escapes through madness from a reality she cannot bear. The desire to escape their situation directly affects the characters who, more often than not, act in an erratic manner. Abel, who wishes to escape to a more heroic world, frequently fantasizes that he is the hero of an adventure novel. He sees himself as a swashbuckler, wearing a mask[15] as he rescues maidens in distress, and de-

---

[15] The mask, another leitmotif, appears several times in the novel. Elósegui finds Abel's discarded silk mask shortly after discovering the boy's corpse (p. 18).

sires to go to war and to become someone else: "Deseaba dejar de ser él mismo, metamorfosearse en alguien" (p. 102). Estanislaa and her daughter Águeda try to detach themselves completely from the rest of the world: "Pese a la vecindad de los soldados de la batería y de los niños refugiados de la escuela, los habitantes de El Paraíso vivían al margen de la guerra: doña Estanislaa evocando tiempos mejores y Águeda soñando en algún príncipe de cuento" (p. 89). Such an attitude towards life creates an environment unwholesome for Abel, undoubtedly causing his negative view of the world.

The victim-executioner motive prepares for the death of Abel and is observed in the boy's association with Pablo and later in his relationship with the tribe led by "Arquero." Abel is a victim whose desire to escape not only his environment but, in some instances, life as well is manifested by a death wish that changes briefly when his desire to leave El Paraíso with Pablo offers a brief new perspective on life. Prior to his meeting Pablo, he continually dreams and thinks about death. Standing before a mirror, he says to himself: "Abel, mequetrefe, ha llegado el momento de hacer tus funerales" (p. 102). After he meets Pablo, his life acquires new meaning, as seen by his metamorphosis which Filomena describes:

> La culpa la tenía uno de los niños refugiados, un diablillo, hermoso como un ángel, que había sorbido el seso al pobre Abel; por su culpa, el niño se había transformado en otro distinto, en apariencia igual al anterior y cuyo físico usurpaba. Ella, Filomena, apenas daba crédito a lo que veía: Abel había destrozado, una tarde, los nidos de golondrinas con su tirador de goma; charlar con las mujeres le aburría y no prestaba atención a sus palabras. (p. 118)

Unfortunately, his new personality does not endure because Pablo betrays him. Thereafter he regresses to his former state, or possibly to a worse condition, an easy prey to "Arquero" and his tribe who become his executioners or, in the words of

Elósegui, "niños verdugos" (p. 18). The physical act of terminating his life is opposed to Pablo's psychological assassination, perhaps more painful to the boy, as inferred first from his belief that laws are suspended during times of tribulation: "Los verdaderos hombres pisoteaban las leyes establecidas por los débiles y llegaban hasta el asesinato en caso necesario. Vivían en una época de violencias y de guerras y el que no era verdugo corría el fácil riesgo de ser sacrificado" (p. 240). After Pablo's departure, Abel's general disposition leads him to ignore Quintana's warning about the violent mood of the children and his death:

> —¿Imaginaba ya lo que iba a ocurrirle? —preguntó Santos.
> El niño vaciló antes de responder. Hablaba con la cabeza baja e interrogaba a su padre con los ojos temerosos.
> —Creo que sí—contestó—. La mayor parte de nosotros lo sospechábamos desde hacía tiempo y él mismo dijo al Arcángel que el profesor le había avisado. (pp. 280–81)

The loss-of-innocence motif is a constant concern of Abel. Estanislaa is probably responsible for the boy's obsession with the process of becoming an adult, as suggested by the following exchange between them: "Oirás decir qué ha sido de los niños que mueren cuando nacen, pero yo te pregunto: ¿qué es de los niños que no mueren, el que fui yo, el que fue Filomena, el que fue Águeda? ¿Dónde está su cadáver, su tumba, el cementerio?" (p. 191). Similarly, all the children in the novel are affected by this malaise which possibly causes their barbaric regression. Several statements, from adults as well as from the children themselves, emphasize premature loss of innocence, as seen in these two examples, Quintana and Pablo's statements respectively:

> —Nadie tiene la culpa. A esos niños que no tienen padre ni madre es como si les hubiesen estafado la infancia. No han sido nunca verdaderamente niños. (p. 137)
> A veces, Pablo tenía ideas extrañas, que Abel escuchaba sin

aliento. Estaba convencido de que ningún muchacho alcanzaba su mayoría de edad si no tenía en su haber al menos una muerte. Cuatro años antes, durante las luchas laborales, la fuerza pública había cargado contra un grupo de obreros, y Pablo conoció por primera vez la emoción de ver sangre. (p. 231)

The last dynamic motif to be examined is that of the mother-figure manifested in Dora, the schoolteacher. While she is alive and at the school, she maintains a degree of peace and happiness among the children. Unfortunately, war once again deprives the children of a parent or loved one. Dora, impregnated by the soldier Elósegui, leaves the school to die shortly thereafter in a bombardment. Her death unleashes anarchy, total chaos, among the children who do not respect the old schoolmaster, Quintana. As is indicated by the omniscient narrator, "el ídolo había caído y su rotura los dejaba en libertad" (p. 254). They cannot handle their freedom, and disorder and confusion ensue, possibly in unconscious protest against those responsible for their suffering and deprivation. In any event, the children regress to a primitive state and begin to ape the war games of their elders.

Free motifs in *Duelo en el Paraíso* dominate and, more often than not, determine the plot through digressions, flashbacks, and many details. The following motifs are connected particularly to the elaboration of the subthemes, but some are related to the major theme as well: the children's use of paint on their faces, protean figures, a festive atmosphere, the need for love, latent homosexuality, incest, the spinsters, *la vida es sueño*, an overpowering mother-figure, and the past as it relates to the present.

The children's use of paint on their faces has several levels of interpretation, and its purpose as a free motif perhaps is to underline each of them: first, it stresses the children's cultural regression; second, it parallels the adults' behavior; and third, it reiterates the children's desire to escape—an important bound motif of the novel. Kessel Schwartz supports the first interpretation, comparing Goytisolo's novel with Golding's *Lord of the Flies*, wherein the boys regress and "they wear feathers, in savage Indian style, don masks, and paint their faces" (p. 51). But unlike the feathers, pointing out the cultural regression, and the masks which indicate a savage state as well as a desire to escape, the manner in which they paint their faces underscores not only the first two ideas above, but also is a grotesque parody of the war games of the adult world. The best example, mentioned previously, is the occasion when the soldier García asks one of the boys the purpose of the drawings on his face:

—¿Puedes decirme, al menos, que valor tienen esos dibujitos que llevas en la frente?
—El mismo que las estrellitas que llevan en la gorra sus capitanes. (p. 131)

Another free motif, examined in *Juegos de manos* and present in other novels to be studied, is that of protean figures, or *mixtificadores*.[16] The individual either uses masks or behaves in an unusual manner in order to escape his monotonous, unrewarding life and give it some sort of significance. Escape is not the sole purpose, since such behavior may also be a means to accomplish a particular goal, to give insight into the person's true nature, as is the case with Pablo. Shortly before he betrays Abel, the reader is confronted with Pablo's protean nature:

Luego, cuando menos lo esperaba, Pablo comenzó a hacer payasadas: sus ojos se inmovilizaron igual que dos botones, su lengua asomó yerta como la de un ahorcado. . . .
Nunca había podido explicarse el porqué de aquella explosión. Pablo se llevaba su dinero, su tesoro, su amistad, sus esperanzas . . . ¿había sentido necesidad de ser sincero? (p. 261)

---

[16] The idea of the *mixtificador*, or protean figure, has been discussed above; see n. 8.

In the case of Estanislaa, there is a constant *desdoblamiento*, through which she sees herself in the past with her dead son, David: "Y ella, Estanislaa, en virtud de un extraño desdoblamiento, se veía también 'en personaje'; dialogando con la doncella del piso" (p. 147). According to Filomena, she also learns to imitate her other son's handwriting and engages in correspondence with those friends who do not know Romano is dead:

> "Con paciencia de chino, aprendío a imitar a la perfección la letra del señorito y escribió a sus amigos firmando con su nombre. Les decía que era feliz, que junto a su madre había alcanzado la dicha y que ya no pensaba casarse con Claude. La mayor parte cayeron en la trampa y le enviaron sus respuestas." (p. 177)

With a direct allusion to Proteus, Estanislaa describes her perspective on love: "Yo, que tanto he amado a lo largo de mi vida, me considero mucho más rica que el resto de los seres, y si me interrogan acerca del amor, diré que, como Proteo, se disfraza de máscaras cambiantes" (p. 290).

An ironic, grotesque but festive atmosphere is another free motif in the novel. Elósegui, or the omniscient narrator, mentions this as he describes the general attitude of the children:

> Los niños vivían a su manera la atmósfera de fiesta que flotaba en el ambiente y se entregaban a lo sangriento de sus juegos en medio de los más duro del combate. La carretera dejaba a sus orillas un reguero de muerte: soldados ametrallados por los aviones, presos fusilados al borde del camino, desertores con una bala en la nuca. Los niños se movían entre ellos como peces en el agua. (p. 19)

The need for love is also a prevalent motif. Most characters crave some sign that they are loved. The town's spinsters, the children, Estanislaa, Dora—everyone's behavior is indirectly affected by this need that no one is able to satisfy. The yearning punctuates Abel's general behavior: ". . . estaba solo, horriblemente solo y requería el afecto y compañía de alguien" (p. 107). For this reason, Pablo's appearance and subsequent friendship are extremely important to him. His love for Pablo is observed in his daily need for the young boy: "El muchacho era el centro de su universo y todo se lo debía a él. Los días en que no acudía a verle, Abel creía desesperarse" (p. 228).

The motifs of incest and an overpowering mother-figure appear in Estanislaa's behavior towards her sons, her desire to control Romano's life, as an overpowering, devouring female who causes, to some extent, her son's death. Possibly from guilt or from frustration, she sees life as a dream—another free motif—and tells Abel how vague and subjective reality is: "La realidad es algo tan vago . . . no somos más que apariencias, sombras que caminamos" (p. 154), and "Todo es ilusión. . . . Mucho antes de que nacieras, otros seres iguales que tú quisieron olvidarse de que eran sueño y fracasaron" (pp. 190–91).

The past too is an important free motif when juxtaposed with the present, delineating the tragic circumstances. For some characters, the children for instance, the past is little different—the war has been with them most of their lives. In other instances, the past is yearned for, as is observed in Estanislaa and the spinsters, Lucía and Ángela. In the first of the two excerpts that follow, Ángela criticizes Lucía for regressing to the past, and in the second, Lucía finds fault with Ángela for the same reason:

—Nadie te discute eso—dijo su hermana—. Todo el mundo sabe que tenías hermosa voz, pero estamos hablando del presente, de ahora. (p. 215)
—Ángela—dijo Lucía—vive con la cara vuelta al pasdo: que si esto, que si aquello, que si te hubieras casado, que si fuésemos ricas. . . . Yo siempre he dicho que lo muerto. . . . (p. 216)

A few of the static motifs in *Duelo en el Paraíso* describe nature, local color, and the personalities of the characters. Nature is sometimes beautiful and at peace, and such descriptions are almost prose poems:

41

El día prometía ser templado y suave. El sol estaba a punto de alcanzar su cénit y acurrucaba las sombras a los pies de los árboles. Las gotas de rocío que moteaban el mantillo del bosque habían desaparecido con el relente. Una mariposa blanca voló hasta su hombrera y agitó perezosamente las alas. (p. 12)

At other times nature is transformed into a sordid and evil entity:

Al correr, le parecía que las ramas de los árboles se oponían a su marcha, como si todo el bosque hubiera cobrado vida: las raíces culebreaban por el sendero: unas ráfagas de viento malhumorado lanzaban contra su rostro las ramas de las encinas; las zarzas se aferraban a los faldones de su camisa, le arañaban. (p. 66)

Local color is provided by the spinsters and an occasional presentation of the townspeople. "Gallego" is perhaps the most colorful character:

En el torrente cercano a la carretera solía acampar un mendigo conocido en los pueblos de los alrededores por el apodo del Gallego, cuya silueta hacía inconfundible gran número de mochilas y escarcelas que llevaba siempre a la espalda . . . y su figura, a fuer de conocida, había acabado por incorporarse a aquel paisaje cual un elemento más, tranquilizador y cotidiano, como el coche correro del mediodía. . . . (p. 184)

Duelo en el Paraíso is important in Goytisolo's development as a novelist since it shows some formal experimentation. The narrative technique utilized, however, appears contrived at times, lacking motivation in the transition from one viewpoint to another, and is frequently too abrupt. In the process of presenting a composite picture of a tragic event, Goytisolo loses the reader. Nevertheless, commentators in general consider Duelo en el Paraíso one of Goytisolo's better early novels. It is undoubtedly superior to Juegos de manos in technique as well as theme, and in it Goytisolo departs from a traditional mold. The novels discussed in Chapter Two show further progression toward the experimental stage of his more recent novels, as well as one instance of regression to a more conventional method.

Chapter II

El Circo, Fiestas, and La Resaca

The trilogy *El mañana efímero* is composed of three novels: *El circo* (1957), *Fiestas* (1958), and *La resaca* (1958). According to some commentators, the only thematic vein uniting these three novels, warranting the term trilogy, is Antonio Machado's poem, "El mañana efímero."[1] *El circo* and *Fiestas* have as epigraphs several verses of this poem, and *La resaca* has lines at the end which perhaps could be considered an epilogue. Because of the relevance of Machado's poem, a general comment on it will be given before studying the novels.

---

[1] Eugenio de Nora in *La novela española contemporánea* (2nd ed.; Madrid: Editorial Gredos, 1970), III, 297, says that "Ninguna relación argumental (ni siquiera, en rigor, temática) une *Fiestas* o *El circo* (1957) ni a *La resaca* (1958). . . . La afinidad viene dada, únicamente, por el común propósito crítico respecto a la sociedad española actual." Nora fails to give his definition of trilogy. That of William Flint Thrall, Addison Hibbard, and C. Hugh Holman, *A Handbook to Literature* (New York: The Odyssey Press, 1970), pp. 494–95, follows: "*Trilogy*: A literary composition, more usually a novel or a play, written in three parts, each of which is in itself a complete unit. . . . The trilogy is usually written against a large background which may be historical, philosophical, or social in its interests." In this study these three novels are considered as a trilogy. Baroja's trilogies may serve as further justification for this position.

44

According to Alice McVan, "Machado rose to rare heights"[2] with "El mañana efímero," which has Spain as its theme. It was "written in a stern mood, one of disappointment in its own generation coupled with the belief that the new one could lead Spain to its triumph."[3] Norma Hutman, in *Machado: A Dialogue with Time*, mentions the political and social criticism implicit in the poem: "Machado often leaves his political comments to Mairena, although attacks on the nation find their way into several poems."[4] The three novels have several motifs in common, the pervading one that of political criticism. The use of Machado's poem is evidence enough that Goytisolo wanted to give some sort of unity to the three novels, for it serves as a succinct statement of purpose at the beginning of the first two and an expression of hope at the end of *La resaca*. Consequently, the study of these three novels does not follow the chronological order in which they were written, even though it may appear to be the case, but depends instead on the order of the verses taken from Machado's poem.[5] It is felt that this is the order of thematic development of the novels envisioned by the author.

El circo will be examined first since it uses verses seven through ten:

---

[2] Alice Jane McVan, *Antonio Machado* (New York: Hispanic Society of America, 1959), p. 48.

[3] *Ibid.*

[4] Norma Louise Hutman, *Machado: A Dialogue with Time* (Albuquerque: University of New Mexico Press, 1969), p. 117.

[5] A brief background on the vicissitudes of their publication is in order. *Fiestas* was written between June and December of 1955, as was indicated by Ignacio Iglesias in "Juan Goytisolo: *Fiestas* y *La resaca*," *Cuadernos del Congreso por la Libertad y la Cultura*, Núm. 36 (mayo-junio, 1959), 114. Because of its srong social and religious criticism, Goytisolo could not find a publisher in Spain. It was eventually published in Buenos Aires by Emecé in 1958, an edition plagued with errata. A better edition, the one used in this study, was published in Barcelona by Ediciones Destino in 1964, but for some unknown reason, omits the epigraph with Machado's verses. *El circo*, written in 1956, was published in Barcelona in 1957, earlier than *Fiestas*. *La resaca*, perhaps the novel where social criticism is most poignant, was published in Paris by Editorial Clúb Libro Español in 1958.

45

> El vano ayer engendrará un mañana
> vacío y ¡por ventura!, pasajero.
> Será un joven lechuzo y tarambana,
> un sayón con hechura de bolero.

Fiestas will be studied next since it quotes verses fifteen through twenty-one:

> Esa España inferior que ora y embiste,
> Cuando se digna a usar de la cabeza
> Aun tendrá luengo parto de varones
> Amantes de sagradas tradiciones
> Y de sagradas formas y maneras.

The third and last novel of this chapter, *La resaca*, uses the last eight verses of the poem:

> . . . Mas otra España nace,
> la España del cincel y de la maza
> con esa eterna juventud que se hace
> del pasado macizo de la raza.
> Una España implacable y redentora,
> España que alborea
> con un hacha en la mano vengadora.
> España de la rabia y de la idea.

The story of *El circo*, in the technical Formalist sense, is found in its epigraph which speaks of a "joven lechuzo y tarambana," who must be Utah, the main character. The novel presents a brief span (roughly thirty-six hours, perhaps the end), in the life of Utah, an irresponsible man unable to cope with reality, who incarnates the situation in which Goytisolo finds most Spaniards, and relates the machinations of two young men, Atila and Pablo, who plan to rob Don Julio, the wealthiest man in town. In addition, it focuses, chaotically, on many inhabitants of Las Caldas, the small town in which Utah lives.

The plot develops from the manner in which Goytisolo juxtaposes two themes and several subthemes, not necessarily related to the major themes or to each other. One theme is a sketchy psychological examination of Utah, first seen in Madrid seeking financial assistance from his father; he then proceeds to rent a car to return to Las Caldas even though penniless. Upon arriving, he goes to Don Julio's home and finds his corpse. The Utah-theme is juxtaposed to that of Atila and Pablo, who are preparing to burglarize the home of the wealthy man. While conducting the burglary they are discovered by Don Julio and Atila kills him. Continuous shifting from one scene to another serves in part to develop the two themes mentioned. Many characters and situations, a few related to the subthemes, appear indiscriminately and, as a consequence, give the novel the chaotic atmosphere of a three-ring circus: in the center is Utah, while Atila and Pablo and the subthemes occupy the side ones.

The presentation of circumstances and the interrelationship between characters in *El circo* are, to some extent, delayed exposition and foreshadowing.[6] The two major themes run separately to converge in Don Julio's office, ending shortly thereafter without a clear resolution. Several questions remain unanswered: Did Atila and Pablo commit the perfect murder? Did Utah die? Goytisolo develops these two thems slowly, frequently shifting the viewpoint to other characters, who, more often than not, do not seem to contribute to the narrative's unfolding. An example of foreshadowing in the Utah-theme is very ironic. Telegrams announce his presence in Las Caldas, while he is in fact slowly approaching from Madrid. In the first he wires his wife: "Peligroso asesino avanza hacia las Caldas. Abrazos. —Utah."[7] At the end of the novel he himself is hunted as an assassin.

---

[6] Boris Tomashevsky says that "A coherent account of significant parts of an event which foretells what will happen in an episode before it is narrated is called foreshadowing [*Vorgeschichte*]" (Lemon, p. 74).

[7] Juan Goytisolo, *El circo* (Barcelona: Ediciones Destino, 1957), p. 15. Hereafter pages cited will be given in parentheses at the end of the text.

Another example of foreshadowing, related to the sub-themes, is observed also at the beginning when the *pregonero* reads the program of festivities (p. 12). Some action of the subthemes and, to a lesser extent, that of the major themes develops within this framework. Flora, the neurotic spinster, during that morning's mass makes a date for the afternoon with Juan de Dios, the town idiot. Elpidio's father-in-law is insulted in the afternoon by his drinking companion during the dedication of the home for the aged (p. 148). Conversations to some extent either explain or foretell future events. While Cecilia is visiting Elpidio, for example, she overhears his father-in-law protesting their wanting him to go to the cere-monies to receive a medal. The explanation for such behavior is that "el Canario" has had a bad influence on the old man: "Lo que occurre es que, desde hace meses, se ha hecho amigo de ese borracho medio anarquista que llaman *Canario*, y le ha dado por beber" (p. 31). Cecilia is also told that Atila is a *truhán* not to be trusted bcause of his social background particularly, and because he is a gigolo:

> —¡Bah, desconfíe usted! Esa gente de las barracas son una pandilla de tunantes. . . . (p. 33)
> —El Atila y otro de su grupo se pasaron todo el verano con una alemana divorciada. . . . Ya se lo puede usted imaginar: por dinero. . . . (p. 34)

Thus, there is a great deal of digression in the novel which could be considered retardation, a device frequently used to create suspense. As was indicated in the introduction, Shklovsky views the second part of *Don Quijote* as a "loose mosaic of anecdotes." But retardation as used in *Don Quijote* must have a uniting "string"; otherwise the reader is con-fronted with a handful of incoherent situations. *El circo* fre-quently shifts from one character to another with only a vague connection between them. The town idiot, for instance, is encountered several times; yet he has nothing to contribute to the story, although his inclusion probably contributes to the plot by retarding its development.

An examination of the divisions of the novel illustrates the desultory shifting of points of view and some weak connections. *El circo* is divided into three parts, each with a large number of subdivisions, some less than a page long. The omniscient point of view predominates throughout; occasionally the third person is utilized, but not limited to any particular individual. Kessel Schwartz is of the opinion that "Goytisolo does not always use clear narrative bridges in *El circo* and often dissipates even his tenuous narrative connections."[8] Schwartz enumerates several narrative techniques utilized, such as dialogue and fade-out. Because of lack of control and loose narrative links, then, the shifting of points of view results in chaos. Focusing on the whole town and portraying so many individuals may warrant the chaos and, thus, the title of the novel. Kessel Schwartz notes this association when he states, "The novel follows the same technique of interacting lives we have seen in his earlier novels, and the title itself comes from the grotesque aspect of much of the action, which might more easily take place in a circus atmosphere." (p. 60). Yet, as shown in the examination of *Fiestas*, there can be a more controlled presentation of a large number of characters, associated with one another and contributing to the development of the plot of the novel, without leading the reader into blind alleys as in *El circo*.

In *El circo* there are many characters, some associated with subthemes, whose only connection with one another is through third persons who might be mutual acquaintances, or who have appeared in the same scene. For example, Juan de

---

[8] Kessel Schwartz, *Juan Goytisolo* (New York: Twayne Publishers, Inc., 1970), p. 64. Hereafter the page number will be given in parentheses at the end of the text cited.

Dios serves to link Flora with Pablo, who during the football game, watches his friend Tarrasa poke fun at the idiot who becomes Flora's lover (p. 161). There is no further connection between Pablo and Flora in the entire novel except that both live in Las Caldas. Their awareness of Juan de Dios links them in the narrative string. Pablo, the son of Elpidio, owner of the store "El Refugio," plans with Atila to rob Don Julio. Pablo's grandfather is Fidel Betanzos who, while receiving a medal of "Mérito a la Vejez," is insulted by his old friend, the town's alcoholic and anarchistic physician (p. 148). Juana, Atila's lover, is also Pablo's girlfriend, while Celia, a sentimental schoolteacher to whom Don Julio sends flowers, is in love with Atila and through Pablo sends Atila a message requesting a meeting (p. 161). Since Atila is busy with the robbery that evening, he gives Tarrasa the slip of paper and tells him to keep the date in his place. Utah, who owes Elpidio a large amount of money and will find Don Julio's corpse, is well liked by Celia, who believes in his originality.

Through such associations, Goytisolo appears to be trying to build a chain connecting all the characters and situations in the novel, the bonds between some being stronger and better delineated than those between others. Unfortunately, such links are not sufficient to motivate some of the digressions, the delays in the flow of the main narrative vein. However, in some instances the subthemes offer brief psychological insights into the personalities of Utah and Atila, as given through Celia who, in her loneliness, misinterprets the behavior of Atila and Utah. When she is told about Atila in Elpidio's store, she quickly dismisses the possibility of such behavior: " '—¡Qué absurdo!' dijo Celia, enrojeciendo hasta la raíz del cabello. 'En mi vida oí nada igual' " (p. 34). She considers Utah a misunderstood artist, a victim of the environment: "Y aunque ella intentase explicarle que quería a Utah porque no era un hombre como los otros y porque todo cuanto hacía y decía era original y no imitado" (p. 70). Nonetheless, many scenes could be omitted from the narrative, increasing thereby its coherence.

The story time of *El circo* is given at the outset. It is late afternoon and children are returning from school: ". . . los chiquillos que volvían de la escuela manifestaban su regocijo con aplausos" (p. 11). The reader knows it is after 5:00 P.M. because Elisa, Utah's wife, is thinking about the visit she had at five, some time earlier; "Luego, a las cinco, había recibido la visita de dos acreedores" (p. 14).Eliza has just returned from the window where she listened to the *pregonero* giving the schedule of the festivities of San Saturnino for the following day. It is the *pregonero* who dates absolutely the moment of action taking place in *El circo*:

A las diez: Misa solemne en la Iglesia. . . .

A las once y media: imposición en el Nuevo Hogar-Asilo de las Medallas del Mérito a la Vejez . . .

A las doce: Audición de sardanas. . . .

A las tres: Encuentro de fútbol entre el Club Deportivo de Las Caldas. . . .

A las cuatro y media: Inauguración de la nueva ermita de San Saturnino, Procesión y Rosario.

A las siete, en el Casino, audición de sardanas y baile.

A las once, igualmente en el Casino, Gran Baile de Gala. (p. 12)

Frequent direct references to these festivities serve to establish the time of day. Many other chronological motifs directly or indirectly establish the time of day or night, either by mentioning the time or by alluding to one of the scheduled events. A direct chronological motif frequently appearing is that of Luz Divina's party. There are several allusions to its being held at 6:00 P.M. Unfortunately, because she is Utah's daughter and because there is a more glamorous party taking place at the same hour, her friends do not attend: "Cuando el reloj del vestíbulo dió las seis, su madre había puesto punto final a los preparativos de la fiesta" (p. 177). "El reloj señalaba las siete menos diez: la casa estaba como al acecho . . . las bandejas seguían llenas de pasteles, el chocolate se enfriaba en los tazones y los invitados no llegaban" (p. 180). The scene of Utah's entrance in Don Julio's home is an indirect chronological motif. According to the plans of Atila, Pablo, and Heredia, the last was to retrieve the ladder at 9:30 P.M.: "Heredia debía esperar a que el reloj de la parroquia diese las nueve y media" (p. 233). At that moment, however, Utah enters the rich man's home and remains there around twenty minutes: "Utah seguía sin aparecer. Desde su llegada habían transcurrido más de veinte minutos. . . . La brusca aparicíon del pintor por la puerta no le dio tiempo de actuar. . . ." (p. 234). The novel ends when the *Baile de Gala* in the casino is interrupted by rumors that something is amiss: "Luego, inesperadamente, la atmósfera pareció agriarse. Alguien había irrumpido en el salón dando voces y los de las mesas vecinas se levantaron a escucharle. . . . A todas luces acababa de ocurrir algo importante" (p. 246). Thus, the novel begins on the eve of the holy day of the patron saint of Las Caldas, perhaps around 6:00 P.M., and ends on the following day when the festivities are concluding with a gala celebration at the casino.

The setting in *El circo* is both static and dynamic. At the beginning of the novel specific sites of Las Caldas are given by the *pregonero*, locations serving as background for the development of some scenes. Movement of people within the town, as well as a roaming viewpoint, indicates that the place of action is dynamic. Utah's traveling from Madrid to Las Caldas exemplifies such a motif. On the other hand, if the town is considered as a microcosm, a place where all the characters in the novel gather, and distances within are disregarded, then the place of action could be thought of as static.

There are several bound motifs in *El circo*, escapism being the most important because of its effects. The character most afflicted by this malaise is Utah, in whom Goytisolo again portrays a character who cannot adjust to society and must escape through fantasy; in *Juegos de manos* Tánger used alcohol and masks, and in *Duelo en el Paraíso* the children regress to a primitive world. According to José Luis Cano, Utah represents "la rebelión de la fantasía contra el achatamiento y mediocridad creciente de la sociedad."[9] This rebellion, however, is not creative, but self-destructive. A frustrated painter, Utah is not able to cope with life's daily needs. He cannot manage to support his wife and daughter, and his creditors constantly harrass him. Some means he uses to escape are alcohol, traveling, tall tales, and theatrical poses. Elisa, his wife, elaborates on the last when she thinks about her husband's personality: "La fabulación era su reflejo de defensa ante las situaciones de peligro. Cuando se sentía amenazado, se evadía. Algo más fuerte que él le obligaba a escudarse en una sucesión alocada de antifaces" (p. 15).

Utah's defense mechanism is his tragic flaw because his escapist reaction upon seeing Don Julio's corpse leads people to believe he is the assassin: "Don Julio yacía en medio de la alfombra, el rostro rígido como una mascarilla. . . . El viejo actor de todas sus comedias pareció despertar de pronto. Transformado en Reina Loca, sus ademanes se llenaron de sigilo. '¡Chsst! . . . El rey duerme' " (p. 232). Leaving the dead man's home, Utah tells little Pancho he is escaping because he has killed Don Julio Álvarez. Pancho replies that he has killed one hundred Apaches. They start to run away, and when Utah finally grasps the magnitude of the situation and tries to retract his statement, Panchito reminds him that it is too late; he has already committed himself:

> —No he sido yo—balbuceó Utah—. No lo he matado yo. . . .
> —No vale, no vale. . . . Haz sido tú. . . . Tú mizmo lo has dicho. (p. 243)

The desire to escape is also seen in Atila for whom money is the only means available to break loose from his environment;

---

[9] José Luis Cano, "Tres novelas," *Insula*, XIII, Num. 36 (marzo 1958), 6.

crime becomes the vehicle to achieve a new station in life. Unlike Utah, his form of escape is physical: "Estoy harto de callejear por ahí como un Juan Nadie, mientras cuatro peor nacidos que yo lucen cuellos de pajarita y se pasean en auto. . . . Harto. Harto" (p. 80).

Betrayal, another important motif already examined in *Juego de manos* and *Duelo en el Paraíso*, appears in *El circo* in the relationship between Heredia and Don Julio. The gypsy owed the old man his education: "Heredia le miraba con devoción. Cuando niño, don Julio le había costeado la escuela" (p. 111). Yet, Heredia helps Atila and Pablo in the robbery and is instrumental in Don Julio's death. These two bound motifs, escapism and betrayal, are dynamic as well; they keep the story moving and bring about the outcome of the novel. Without Atila's obsession to achieve economic independence, the crime would not have been committed. Had Utah been a different kind of person, he would not have accepted guilt for a murder he did not commit. Perhaps more important, if Heredia had not betrayed Don Julio, it is probable that the theft would not have been committed; had Heredia not attacked Don Julio when the old man held Atila and Pablo at gun point, his employer would not have died.

Escapism and betrayal also appear as free motifs. Escapism is observed in the behavior of Celia and Flora. Sentimental Celia yearns for a romantic adventure, while Flora, with her sexual neurosis, continuously protests that men molest her wherever she goes. This is wishful thinking on her part since her age and appearance preclude such encounters. Celia is betrayed in her quest for love by Atila, who sends a friend to assume his identity on their date. In this respect, Celia could also be considered a victim, an example of the executioner-victim motif, another free one appearing in *El circo*. The relationship between Atila and Pablo could also be construed as one of executioner-victim, although involving a willing victim, Pablo, a masochistic, subservient friend who accepts passively Atila's insults and is led to crime by the young *murciano*:

> Cuando a la hora de despedirse, Pablo le preguntó si iría por la noche a la bodega, Atila no se dignó siquiera contestarle. La autoridad que ejercía sobre su amigo tenía esto de bueno: hiciera lo que hiciese Pablo se sometía siempre, sin indagar las razones de sus actos. Atila le hablaba siempre de un modo brusco. "Tráeme esto. Haz aquello," le decía. Y Pablo cumplía lo ordenado, contento de poderle rendir algún servicio, aunque sabía muy bien que él no iba a agradecérselo o que, en caso de estarle agradecido, se esforzaría en ocultarlo. (pp. 88–89)

Moreover, the relationship between the two young men has homosexual overtones, another free motif.

Social criticism, classifiable as a free motif as well, is observed in the portrayal of the young *murciano*, Atila. The difficulties encountered by the *murcianos*, relegated to the lower class because of their lack of education and skills, is more patent, however, in *La resaca*.

Atila is an exponent of the criminal behavior resulting from utter poverty. The sexual hypocrisy of the upper classes is illustrated by Juana, Atila's girlfriend, and Flora. Atila, ironically, manages to have an affair with the daughter of one of the best families in town and chides her for her cant when she is among her own class:

> —Sí, pero cuando estás con tus amigos, no dejas que me acerque. Entonces eres la señorita Olano. La señorita Olano alternando con gentes de su clase. . . .
> —Lo malo es que no le gustan los finolis esos. . . . Para eso prefiere a Atila, un hijo de murcianos. . . . Entonces, cuando nadie la ve, la señorita deja a sus amigos y se va a buscar al murciano que, en cambio, le hace pasar un buen rato. (p. 78)

Flora's seduction of Juan de Dios can also be classified as a criticism of the sexual hypocrisy of the upper social stratum in Spain.

Another free motif in the novel is a vague allusion to the United States. Whereas some novels by Goytisolo display overt criticism of U.S. materialism, in *El circo* the allusion appears to be more of praise than censure. As Utah and Panchito are running to escape from the police, a large sign advertising Chesterfield cigarettes appears just as the headlights of an automobile make them visible to the police. These two items, the sign and the lights from the auto, somehow awaken Utah and he begins to break away from his fantasy world. The sign, which perhaps symbolizes American materialism as well as pragmatism, shatters his quijotesque escapism.

There are many static motifs in *El circo*. Those describing the local color of the small Spanish town are a good example: "La gente aprovechaba la fiesta para levantarse tarde. Grupos de hombres y mujeres charlaban en mitad de la calle en animada tertulia" (p. 128). A description of nature, also a static motif, is observed as Utah returns to Las Caldas:

> Delante de los faros del automóvil, la carretera parecía una larga cinta blanca. Deshojados por el otoño, con sus muñones al desnudo, los plátanos que bordeaban se defendían miedosamente de la luz . . . la luna se barruntaba entre las nubes como una mancha de luz, redonda, plateada y brillante. (p. 97)

The most prominent flaw is Utah's characterization, since there appears to be insufficient motivation for his behavior. The possibility that Goytisolo intended him to be a quixotic figure is suggested by a few tenuous parallels: Utah is described as having a "barbita de chivo" (p. 207). Panchito is a Sancho of sorts as they run away from the police; Utah constantly assumes different personalities and discovers enemies everywhere. Nevertheless, he seems incoherent throughout most of the novel, and control is lacking in the integration of the shifting viewpoints. Because of these two flaws, *El circo* is perhaps Juan Goytisolo's weakest novel. But his experimentation with the rambling point of view sheds light upon his future creative intentions. *Fiestas*, to be studied next, better illuminates the direction taken in his second period.

The story of *Fiestas* can be summarized (considering the epigraph quoting five verses of Machado's poem) as a denunciation of the ossified social structure of Spanish society. The Catholic Church is portrayed as the principal abettor of the *status quo* though superstition and, particularly, by favoring acquiescence to a totalitarian government. There is also a diatribe against submission to the system and people's inability to react. Ortega, the old professor, may represent Goytisolo's voice in this respect. Evidence to support the preceding contentions is adduced later.

The plot of *Fiestas* is developed from a major theme and many motifs which interweave raw materials of the story, presenting the condition of Spain without allowing the novel to degenerate into a political pamphlet. The title ironically underscores the relationship between the Church, represented by a *Congreso*, and the people of Spain. The plot exposes different ways in which people react to the *fiestas* of the *Congreso*. Some utilize them to obtain money (the stands selling refreshments and food; the beggars who multiply during the period of the festivities), and others as a means to exhibit their social status; but, in particular, public (and reader) are subjugated by a constant radio voice, coming through large speakers placed in every neighborhood. The people, like chickens,[10] follow the precepts broadcast by the ecclesiastic structure. As the epigraph underscores, most inhabitants of Spain are "Amantes de sagradas tradiciones y de sagradas formas y maneras." Additionally, for some, the term *fiestas* lacks its literal denotation since for them the period involved is very traumatic.

---

[10] One section ends with a scene where a group of matrons struggle with one another to kiss a bishop's ring: "Atropellándose unas otras, curvando sus cuellos, se esforzaban en depositar un beso en la sortija que el prelado amablemente les tendía" (p. 184). The allusion to their necks and the general description bring to mind a group of starving old hens scrambling to reach a handful of grain. The opening of the following section underscores this interpretation. Don Paco is feeding several hens and the parallel is unmistakable: "Media docena de gallinas blanquinegras corrieron al encuentro de don Paco. Atropellándose unas a otras, curvando sus cuellos multicolores, se esforzaban en alcanzar la comida" (p. 184).

There is one major theme in *Fiestas* and perhaps two secondary ones which, to some extent, could be considered reflections of the major one. These secondary themes, examined later, exemplify the staircase device. The major theme of the novel is Pipo's traumatic loss of childhood innocence and his being forced to take his place in a closed society whose primordial concern is to follow a set of superstitious beliefs. At first, Pipo searches for the means to escape his environment, his state in life, his own self,[11] but finally decides that his efforts are futile and conforms. Paradoxically, one way he tries to escape from reality is through friendship with an adult, Gorila. The latter is also seeking escape through association with Pipo and via alcohol and comic books and so, perhaps, is not mature enough to be considered an adult; still he provides Pipo with access to an adult world. Such an association may reaffirm Pipo's childhood, since the adult world underscores his adolescence. The boy senses that he is about to lose his innocence and therefore tries desperately to cling to it. This is perhaps one reason he no longer plays with his old neighborhood friends: his growth is reflected in that of the other children. Another lure attracting him to a world where he does not belong is that it provides an opportunity to let his imagination run wild, an attentive, unquestioning audience for tall tales about himself. Pira and Gorila are, to some extent, reflections of Pipo since both seek escape through their stories. Pira, however, has reached the point where she believes her fantasies.

The central theme or narrative current of *Fiestas* is Pipo. Several weeks in the life of the young boy are related directly

---

[11] In one scene Pipo looks at himself in the mirror and, perhaps with echoes of Unamuno's *otro* concept, wishes he were someone else: "Pipo volvió a abrir los ojos; el otro continuaba siempre allí. Su rostro reflejaba sucesivamente odio, tristeza, adulación, alegría; . . . Siempre era él. Por mucho que se esforzaba no conseguía evadirse. Inútil cambiar de nombre, rodearse de gente desconocida, mixtificar el pasado, enmarañar las pistas; su cuerpo continuaba siendo el mismo y nunca lograría abandonarlo" (pp. 126–27).

or indirectly to everything else taking place in the novel. The period of narration is bound by two well-delineated chronological motifs which mark a not-too-specific time span—the *Congreso* and a raffle. Other sets of motifs develop and explain Pipo's character and that of some others, as well as to describe the environment within which the novel takes place. The beginning of *Fiestas* appears uneventful. The reader, at the end of two chapters, still has no idea of what the novel is about. After finishing it, nevertheless, reconsideration of those two chapters reveals intimations of later events. Premonition is perhaps the best term for the introductory exposition. Toward the middle of the book there appears evidence of the use of transposed exposition.

A brief summary of the first two chapters illustrates how Goytisolo provides clues to future events. The novel begins by focusing on the street where Pipo lives. Its name, Mediodía, "Noon," is another ironic touch, since it is more like dawn, separating day from night; or, it alludes to the South, where the *murcianos* come from. A truck arrives and the omniscient narrator juxtaposes one side of the street, where beautiful houses evidence middle-class opulence, with the slum on the other side where the *murcianos* live: ". . . allí donde la calle Mediodía iniciaba su serie escalonada de terrazas sobre la panorámica de solares cubiertos de chozas diminutas."[12] Children playing in a trash heap run toward the truck, attracted by its bright colors and electric sign. One of the men from the truck asks a group of girls their birthplace and they reply: "Murcia." Goytisolo thus intimates the social problem the *murcianos* represent. This motif, developed later, also demonstrates people's inability to behave in a Christian manner. When Pira appears at the end of the first section of Chapter One, her behavior foretells her future: The stranger from

<hr />

[12] Juan Goytisolo, *Fiestas* (Barcelona: Ediciones Destino, 1964), p. 7. Hereafter pages cited will be given in parentheses at the end of the text.

the truck calls her and she, without hesitation, walks toward the man: "Al descubrir la señal que se le hacía, la niña marchó al encuentro del hombre con paso decidido: '¿Me llamaba Vd?' " (p. 13). Her appearance in strange clothes and her brief exchange with the man evidence her inability to grasp reality, a naiveté which will cost her her life.

The second section takes the reader from the street into the apartment house where Pipo and most of the characters of the novel reside. This action is accomplished by shifting the point of view of the first section to Arturo, who is watching Pira through his binoculars. Thus begins the process of acquaintance with the tenants of the building. The third section shifts to another resident, and more background information is provided, information helpful in understanding future events. The fourth section provides further exposition of Pira's character: Pira's fantasies, her wanting to go to Italy where she believes her father is waiting. The first chapter thus offers a rapid exposition of the possible social problem of the *murcianos* and a brief psychological sketch of the tenants, with a particular emphasis on Pira.

The second chapter, subdivided into four sections, follows, to some extent, the pattern of the first. Premonitions of later events can be detected only after careful consideration. The protagonist, Pipo, is introduced for the first time through a brief, but revealing, psychological exposition in the first section, continuing into the second where he is seen with a homosexual who thinks of seducing him. The third section shifts to the "Venadito," a boat in which Norte and Gorila live. Through Norte the reader learns of some flaws in Gorila's personality, for instance, his violent temper, which will help to understand future revelations. The fourth section continues with seemingly desultory exposition: Gorila's psychological make-up is further explored, as Pipo is taken by Gorila to a barroom and the man's behavior amplifies the psychological sketch: he drinks copiously, is very popular, loves to tell tall stories, exhibits his brute force, and is devoted to comic books.

After two seemingly uneventful chapters, the reader may believe he knows very little of what the novel is about or the author's plans. Yet he has assimilated many apparently incidental remarks that foreshadow what is about to happen and the author's intentions. Pira's comments when asked by Piluca the date on which the raffle is to take place are an example: "Entonces," dijo Pira, volviéndose a guardar el boleto, "entonces, empezamos a vivir de verdad y todo esto se convertirá en un mal sueño" (p. 33). The irony of the girl's statement is discovered *postea*. The nightmare, for many people, will take place precisely around that date. Pira herself will die, the *murcianos* will be evicted from the lot where they constructed their *chabolas* and a church will be built, and Gorila will be jailed because of Pipo's betrayal. The psychological sketches of Gorila and Pipo also provide a basis for later developments or, in the case of Gorila, explain what took place in the past. Gorila's erratic behavior, as seen in his reaction to Norte, in the third section of Chapter Two, reveals a potential murderer. Pipo's thefts signal the absence of moral values. His being an orphan is perhaps the source of many flaws in his character which predict his betrayal and eventual surrender to the establishment. An example of transposed exposition appears in the second section of the fifth chapter where Gorila tells Pipo about his past in Africa and his life in the Canary Islands. He informs Pipo of his servant-lover called Lu-Baba in Africa and recounts the affair his wife was having with his own brother, together with the killing of a policeman who interrupted his love-making. In the fourth subdivision of the same chapter, further transposed exposition takes the form of a dream: Gorila seems to re-enact the murder of the policeman. Clearly Gorila, not a professional criminal, is a very strong man unable to control his emotions. Once this point in the narration is reached, the reader can better understand the author's design regarding the relationship between Pipo and Gorila. Goytisolo has used in *Fiestas* a combination of several types of introductions or expositions: premonition, transposed exposition, and perhaps even delayed exposition, although the last is not as prolonged in the novel as it usually is in this form of introduction (as seen in *El circo*).

Fiestas exhibits a multiple system of narrative motifs.[13] This multivisional approach is accomplished through division into eight chapters, each subdivided into several segments. In these subdivisions the viewpoints vary: There is an omniscient narrator in some sections, a third-person point of view in others, and in a few the narrating viewpoint shifts within the section. It is also important that the third-person point of view is not limited to any one character, but shifts from one to another. The following diagram shows the pattern of viewpoint:

	Omniscient	*Mixed*	*Third Person*
Chap. I			
Sec. 1	pp. 7–13		
Sec. 2		Arturo & Omn., pp. 14–20	
Sec. 3	pp. 20–26		
Sec. 4	pp. 26–33		
Chap. II			
Sec. 1			Pipo, pp. 34–39
Sec. 2			Pipo, pp. 39–47
Sec. 3	pp. 47–55		
Sec. 4	pp. 55–62		
Chap. III			
Sec. 1		Piluca & Omn., pp. 63–70	
Sec. 2	pp. 70–78		
Sec. 3			Pipo, pp. 78–89
Sec. 4			Gorila, pp. 90–93
Sec. 5			Pipo, pp. 93–98
Sec. 6	pp. 98–105		*
Chap. IV			
Sec. 1			Jiménez, pp. 106–13
Sec. 2			Pira, pp. 113–15
Sec. 3			Francisco, pp. 115–22
Sec. 4			Pipo, pp. 122–26
Sec. 5			Pipo, pp. 126–32

[13] See Introduction, p. 10.

In the novels written years later, the author utilizes a more controlled and smooth approach. The constant shifting observed above may be construed as undisciplined rather than experimental.

---

[14] In this section there is a more complex situation than a mere third-person or mixed viewpoint. The presentation of Pipo's state of mind is given through a combination of several things. There is a modified stream-of-consciousness, in which Pipo's thoughts are bared, juxtaposed with the voice coming from the radio, and the conversation with the prostitute and the attendant of the *quiosco*. The reader is able to differentiate between them because of the type used. Ideas in Pipo's mind are presented in Roman type, the sounds from the radio in italics and the conversation in quotes:

"¿Quieres sentarte un rato, pequeño? ¿Quieres beber un poco de agua?" Al abrir los ojos se dio cuenta del lugar en que estaba: un quiosco improvisado de bebidas . . . grupo de curiosos escuchaban el relato de la radio: "*Docenas de miles de personas. . . .*" (p. 224)

In *Fiestas*, chronological motifs allow the reader to determine indirectly the passage of time and aid independent deduction of the duration of the novel.[15] Through a careful reading the reader can ascertain the duration of the events and examine the chronological motifs: the raffle, sponsored by the powdered chocolate "El Gato," and the *Congreso*. The first chronological allusion appears at the end of the first chapter: Pira tells Piluca that the raffle will be held in thirty-eight days. While the *murcianos* are being evicted, in Chapter Six, Pipo finds a piece of paper on which is written: "Gran rifa de Chocolates 'El Gato.' Ustedes recibirán algo inesperado en el mes de Junio" (p. 183). Pira dies after Pipo finds the leaflet. References to the *Congreso* do not specify the date when it takes place; however, its climax occurs several days after the raffle's results appear in the newspaper. At the end of Chapter Five, Norte and Gorila comment on the results (p. 164). Chapter Six seems to be a continuation of the same day. The possibility exists that Pira, upon hearing the results of the raffle which she hoped to win, decides to find other means to go to Rome and falls prey to a pervert. Chapter Seven takes place several days after Pira's death.

Chapter Eight gives no clues as to the time elapsed between it and the preceding one, but narrates the culmination of the *Congreso*. The first of many allusions to the *Congreso* informs the reader that it will take place during the summer: "Cuando pienso en la impresión que se llevarán los millares de peregrinos que, este verano, asistan al Congreso" (p. 23). Thereafter its overwhelming presence is gradually increased as the work progresses. The novel's pace in the first chapters is slow, but, as the culminating days of the Congress approach, the tempo of the narration increases so that in the seventh chapter it seems to monopolize everything. Such develop-

---

[15] Tomashevsky's views regarding this device were given in the Introduction, see p. 11.

ment is a kind of Ravel's "Bolero," slowly increasing its rhythm until it reaches a vertiginous climax in the seventh chapter. There is a difference, then, between the two chronological motifs of *Fiestas* since the timing provided by the *Congreso*-motif could belong within the realm of musical rhythm.

With regard to space, Goytisolo's novel seems to combine static and dynamic motifs, but the static motif predominates because most characters live in the same building and thus tend to congregate in one place. On the other hand, the dynamic motif could be more suitably applied to Pipo and Gorila since they constantly move from one location to another. Other static motifs, not related to space, will be discussed later. One of the best static motifs introduces the building as the meeting place of all the characters; the meeting takes place in the first chapter and shifts the action from the street to the building through Arturo's binoculars. The fact that Arturo is an invalid underscores the concept of spatial limitation. In contrast, Pipo gives movement to the narration, continually leaving the building for other places by himself or accompanying Gorila.

There are several bound motifs in *Fiestas*. The most important ones are related to Pipo and thence to the main narrative line and development of the novel. The bound motifs are so interrelated that, when studying them, a seesaw approach must be followed. These include the loss of innocence, betrayal, the *Congreso*, escapism, and the executioner-victim motif. Pipo's loss of innocence should be examined first because the novel deals primarily with it, the traumatic experience he undergoes as he becomes an adolescent. A great deal of irony inheres in such a metamorphosis. This motif is directly related to the *Congreso*, to Pipo's betrayal of Gorila, to his escapism, and to the executioner-victim motif as well. In addition to its relation to Pipo's psychological growth and trauma, the *Congreso*-motif is significant for its catalytic influence. The other bound motifs are not limited to Pipo's character study, but are found as well in the behavior of other persons.

Upon first encountering Pipo the reader may question his being a child. The boy is precocious for his twelve years in his drinking habits, his perennial stealing from his grandmother, and his desire to associate with adults. At times, however, he appears naive. A good example of what can be called innocence takes place where Benjamín, a homosexual, is about to seduce him and Pipo seems completely unaware of the man's designs:

> Con sumo cuidado sacó del bolsillo un pañuelo de seda. . . . Pipo . . . al ver el contenido, su rostro se coloreó de emoción. El pañuelo estaba lleno de gruesas bolas de vidrio. . . .
>
> "¿Te gustan?" decía Benjamín. . . . "¿Quieres que te las regale?" . . . .
>
> Su mano esbozaba todavía el ademán de ofrendarle las bolas, y Pipo no pudo resolverse a aceptarlas porque, ahora, Benjamín también suplicaba . . . sus ojos decían a las claras que Pipo tenía que darle algo a cambio. (pp. 41–43)

Benjamín begins to cry because he does not dare to carry out his plan. Pipo feels sorry for the man and the two cry together. It is obvious, nevertheless, that he does not know what Benjamín's desires are, as can be gathered by the man's advice to Pipo as they leave the park: "Crece. Hazte hombre. No hagas caso de los que quieren llevarte a sitios alejados" (p. 44). Benjamín's change of heart is perhaps the result of his seeing Pipo's innocence. Another example is Pipo's sexual attraction to Pira while they are in a cave located in the cellar of the building where they live. It possibly is more of an instinctive than a conscious attraction to the girl: "Pira le oprimía la mano con todas sus fuerzas y su contacto tibio le llenaba de turbación" (p. 83). The excursion to the cave ends in a childish quarrel and his desires are not consummated. The probability exists, nevertheless, that if Piluca had not been present, Pipo would not have stopped himself.

The scene with a prostitute constitutes the definitive loss of innocence, and Pipo seems to consider that instant a turning point in his life. Nonetheless, there is a profound moment of self-examination later, in the last section of Chapter Seven, which could be construed as a more definite occasion for self-discovery, in which the boy is finally fully aware of what has taken place. Yet, the incident with the prostitute triggers the entire traumatic episode and should be viewed as the starting point of Pipo's change (p. 223). Pipo and the prostitute, trying to escape from a police dragnet, are seated on the stairs of the fourth floor in a building. As he sits next to the woman, the boy concludes that technically he is an accomplice of Gorila and, consequently, liable for the policeman's murder. Hearing the footsteps of the police below, Pipo, trembling, embraces the prostitute. There does not seem to be any sexual attraction involved but because of the intensity of the moment and the contact of the woman's body, Pipo has an orgasm: "Y entonces, como una condensación de todo su miedo, la cosa se produjo: Pipo sintió que sus manos se desprendían de la mujer como si algo fuese a estallarle, algo que brotaba ya, al excitado compás de su pulso, hasta dejarle dulcemente agotado" (p. 223).

In the next section, he examines the "affair" with the prostitute and his betrayal of Gorila. The pervasive influence of the *Congreso* contributes to his magnifying these incidents under scrutiny. Within the boy paradoxical emotions occur; he seems not to understand the religious, moral, legal, and ethical issues involved. He should have envisioned his betrayal of Gorila as deserving the blessing of the social order instead of associating it, as he does, with the betrayal of Christ. On the other hand, his reaction to the incident with the prostitute, which he finds repugnant and sees as a sign of his decadence, is more in keeping with the type of morality expounded by the Congress and is at odds with the liberal spirit Ortega is probably trying to instill in him. Goytisolo describes Pipo's feelings in the following manner:

> *Dictó* sentencia contra él mismo: era culpable. Confidente de
> un secreto terrible había traicionado su promesa. Por su infidelidad,

el Gorila moriría tal vez. Lo sucedido en la escalera junto a la mujer constituía una señal irrefutable de su pérdida. . . . Era un traidor, un nuevo Judas: como él, había vendido a su amigo por unas miserables copas con González. (pp. 223–24)

As he leaves the prostitute and starts for home, Pipo is confronted with the festivities of the *Congreso*. From large speakers placed in every block, a voice can be heard exhorting the populace to abandon their evil ways and embrace the Catholic Church. His psychological state cannot withstand the festivities and the harangue from the radio, and paranoia suddenly sets in. He begins to believe that every word he hears is addressed to him: "La voz acusadora de los altavoces le parecía una advertencia divina; como si, en vez de hablar para todo el mundo, él fuese el blanco especialmente señalado" (p. 225). Besides feeling guilty, he considers himself alienated from the rest of society because of his actions: "Él, en cambio, estaba fuera del orden, aislado, como un paria" (p. 225). Without realizing it, he stands in line to confession and, upon discovering where he is, decides that, since there is no forgiveness for his sins, talking to a priest will not make any difference. Whereupon he goes to the docks to kill himself, but a night watchman orders him out of the premises before he can carry out his plans. Concluding that his inability to end his life is another of his many failures, he goes to a barroom and orders a coca-cola. Ordering the soft drink is perhaps the first manifestation of Pipo's metamorphosis. As has been observed, the boy usually drinks alcoholic beverages, which act is in itself a paradox.

When he leaves the tavern, the *Congreso* "volvió a digerirle" (p. 228). For some time the Congress has seemed a giant monster ingesting everything in its path; Goytisolo's use of "digerirle" in that context confirms such a hypothesis. The overwhelming presence of the Congress thus seems to guide just about everything taking place in the novel. Because of it Pipo is delayed in finding Gorila to inform him of his betrayal:

"Al llegar a la Vía Ancha quiso tomar el tranvía de los muelles, pero no logró abrirse camino entre la gente apiñada en las aceras" (p. 211). The *Congreso*, thus, directly interferes in the lives of Pipo and Gorila. If Pipo had taken the streetcar to the docks, Gorila would probably have escaped the police dragnet. The continuous sermonizing over loudspeakers induces Pipo to see himself as a degenerate, guilty of unforgivable offenses. Because of the Congress, the *unijambista francés*, Pira's killer, goes to Barcelona, attracted by the crowd. The eviction of the *murcianos* is undertaken because the slum was a blemish to the city's appearance which had to be eradicated before the pilgrims arrived in Barcelona. Many other instances exemplify the influence of the *Congreso*-motif. The Congress, in addition to being a bound motif, is also dynamic because of its all-pervading, deleterious force.

A brief summary is now in order of Pipo's self-examination, which begins in the sixth section of Chapter Seven, and his metamorphosis, formalized in Chapter Eight. The festivities of the Congress overwhelm Pipo and kindle his awakening, and that night Pipo, trying to escape the noise and the crowd, sleeps in the park. The following morning, as the sun rises, he calmly watches the neighborhood, thankful for the peace and quiet. He thinks about his past behavior, concluding that he was ungrateful and uncompassionate towards his grandmother (p. 230). His association with Gorila is seen under a new light: it was a search for eternal childhood, a perennial innocence which cannot be realistically attained: " 'Hay algo más triste que envejecer; es continuar siendo niño.' Su amistad con el Gorila evidenciaba una nostalgia de la infancia, la busca de una inocencia imposible. Pero todo conspiraba contra esta inocencia y la hacía saltar hecha pedazos; el cuerpo crecía y se poblaba de deseos . . . " (p. 230). It is suggested that Pipo is now aware of his escapist tendencies, another bound motif. Through his loss of innocence Pipo discovers that his erratic behavior is perhaps an unconscious desire to postpone maturity and prolong his innocence. It should be remembered that the loss of innocence motif recurs in most of Goytisolo's novels.

After his self-examination, Pipo stoically accepts life in general and acquiesces to an existence under ossified religious belief and a reactionary political structure:

> La vida seguía su curso y resultaba imposible volver atrás. Uno era niño, se hacía joven, apuntaba a hombre y llegaba a viejo, sin saber cómo, sin protestar; porque la vida era así y era precisco resignarse. Vivir era ya elegir, y había que decir sí a todo, sin remedio. (pp. 230–31)

Thus, Pipo becomes a "yes man." The coup-de-grace is his final statement in that chapter indicating that he accepts whatever the newspapers tell him, becoming in effect another Don Paco, another Spaniard accepting the regime:

> Sin poderlo evitar se acordó de las protestas indignadas de Ortega e hizo suya la razonable respuesta de don Paco: "Si los sacan es porque los alojan en otro sitio." Y los alojaban, sin duda.
> Por algo lo decían los diarios. (p. 231)

This is another betrayal, because Pipo renounces Ortega's teachings. In the last chapter he dresses in Sunday clothes and leaves his home to join the festivities. When Ortega sees Pipo "vestido con el traje de los domingos y adornado con la escarapela del Congreso," he says "Tú también, Pipo" (p. 233), the familiar paraphrase of Shakespeare's Caesar discovering that Brutus was one of his attackers.

Pipo's development is complex, at times paradoxical. Orphaned at an early age, perhaps as a result of the Civil War, he is forced to assume responsibilities he would not have undertaken otherwise. However, not wanting to be an adult prematurely, he escapes from that world whenever he can with the help of Gorila, who brings him prolonged youth. The overwhelming presence of the *Congreso*, the death of Pira which unconsciously leads him to his betrayal of Gorila, and his "affair" with the prostitute provide a traumatic awakening to what he, mistakenly, assumes are his responsibilities. Therefore, his transformation is, ironically, another escape, a "cop-out," insofar as by accepting the establishment he finds another way to avoid his obligations as an adult and a human being. Goytisolo appears to say that Pipo's transformation, his awakening, is essentially an evil, the malaise contaminating every Spaniard.

Such an ill affecting the Spanish people is partially the responsibility of the Church, which appears in *Fiestas* in the form of the *Congreso*. The Congress, as it relates to the people, is an excellent example of another bound motif, one which recurs throughout many of Goytisolo's works: that of the executioner-victim. The *Congreso* is one of many ways in which the Church manipulates the sentiments of the people, and to some extent can be considered as the executioner of Pipo, because it forces him to submit to the *status quo*. Moreover, its relationship, direct and indirect, to several characters seems to have the earmarks of the motif. Pipo is without doubt the executioner of Gorila, but had he not been delayed by the festivities, Gorila might have escaped. The *unijambista francés*, executioner of Pira, goes to Barcelona attracted by the crowds of the Congress. Another case in point is the expulsion of the *murcianos* so that a Church can be built where their *chabolas* are located. A final instance of the motif, perhaps not related to the Congress, is González's behavior toward Pipo. He inebriated the boy to obtain information about Gorila, an instance wherein the betrayal motif is also present since Pipo considers González his friend.

From a large number of free motifs, only those deemed most important will be mentioned. Because of the constant shifting of viewpoint they recur frequently. In addition to social criticism expounded through the use of the *Congreso*-motif, there are several free ones concerning other aspects of Spanish society that Goytisolo feels should be denounced. The plight of the *murcianos* (the theme of *La resaca*), appears frequently throughout *Fiestas*. It is one of Arturo's main concerns, but for other reasons; he feels the slum dwellers are a plague that will devalue property and bring ruin (p. 117). Ironically, Arturo's hate for the *murcianos*, apparently shared by his mother, directly contradicts the family's religious beliefs, and Goytisolo plays with this paradox during the eviction. In the following excerpt, as Arturo, overjoyed, watches them being expelled by the police, the radio speaks of brotherly love, and his mother, Cecilia, wishes to thank the Virgin for their removal:

> Si de él [Arturo] dependiese hubiera hecho una hoguera con todos sus enseres.
>
> . . . *con lo que, hijos míos, al acercarse este gran acontecimiento, resuenan en la ciudad los himnos de amor y de ternura. . . .* (p. 176)
>
> De no haber sido por su dolencia, su respuesta hubiese sido un: "Gracias a Dios. Voy a rezar un Avemaría." (p. 177)

Goytisolo also seems to be saying that Spanish people look upon religion as a panacea for all social ills, as seen in the building of a church on the ground from which the *murcianos* were evicted.

Ortega, the old professor, voices another of Goytisolo's concerns: Spaniard have lost their ability to react and are no longer capable of rebellion. Ortega makes this idea clear to Don Paco during a heated exchange: "No, no me entiende usted. Lo que pretendía hacerle comprender era que ni usted ni yo, ni nadie, reaccionamos. Hemos perdido la capacidad de rebelión" (p. 187). Comic books, another free motif, underscore escapism, a bound motif. Gorila's avid reading of them points to his struggle to retain a perennial youth or innocence, another bound motif. Other free motifs which serve to describe Gorila's personality and stress his obsession to escape include his drinking and fantasizing.

The motif of homosexuality appears throughout Goytisolo's novels. In *Fiestas* it is overt as well as latent. Benjamín, the best overt example, could not bring himself to seduce Pipo whether because of the boy's innocence or other unexplained reasons. Another example appears in the first section of Chapter Four: Ortega gives Jiménez, the son of an old friend, the phone number of a young man he feels has something in common with his friend's son. Unfortunately, however, Jiménez encounters a homosexual instead. The scene is narrated from the third-person point of view so that the reader can grasp only Jiménez's perspective of the incident. Perhaps the homosexual encountered by Jiménez was Benjamín, as has been indicated by Kessel Schwartz.[16] Latent homosexuality appears in the relationship between Pipo and Gorila, and several scenes make it obvious. Pipo is not to be with Gorila when the fireworks appear in the sky. When he mentions to Gorila his wish to be with him at that moment, the man indicates that as long as they think of each other the distance between them does not matter. Another instance occurs after Pipo's "affair" with the prostitute. Reassessing his past behavior, he concludes that "Por su infidelidad, el Gorila moriría tal vez" (p. 223). The word *infidelidad* suggests that Pipo considers the orgasm a sign of infidelity to Gorila.

Some bound motifs, already mentioned, are also dynamic. The *Congreso*, Pira's death, González's betrayal, to mention only three, are central to the story and guide its development. The Congress's influence over Pipo and others in the novel has already been described. Pira's death is a possible motivating force behind Pipo's betrayal of Gorila. The boy establishes a parallel between the murder of Pira and the crime committed by Gorila, of which he considers himself an accomplice: "El asesino la atacó por la espalda," concluyó. Exactamente de la misma manera en que Gorila y yo *liquidamos* al guardia en Canarias" (p. 201). Thereafter, Pipo, unconsciously perhaps, allows González to intoxicate him in order to let his

[16] Schwartz, p. 67.

and Gorila's secret be discovered. Thus, a chain of events, generated by the preceding and other dynamic motifs, culminates in Pipo's acceptance of the establishment.

Static motifs include Arturo and his binoculars, descriptions of nature, local color, the personalities of the characters, etc. Arturo, a *voyeur* of sorts, is introduced to the reader in the second section of the first chapter, a section suggesting Robbe-Grillet's *Le Voyeur* because the objectivity of exposition is akin to that of the French writer. Whenever Arturo appears, he is seated in his wheelchair in front of a window, surveying the neighborhood with his binoculars, a perspective which could not be obtained through Pipo, Pira, Gorila, or any other character in the novel. Descriptions of nature in *Fiestas* are few and brief: ". . . el sol emergía entre los arbustos y el aire era transparente y limpio" (p. 229). Local color too is provided throughout the novel since it focuses on the Spanish character.

In *Fiestas* Goytisolo uses a principle Tomashevsky calls compositional motivation. [17] All of the episodes, all the activities of the characters, all the motifs, directly or indirectly, are geared to the developing of the novel. The chain of events unleashed by the Congress has already been mentioned, and nearly everything is motivated by social criticism. The work opens with the poverty of the *murcianos* and the raffle which might give some of them the opportunity to escape their environment. The deck, however, seems to be stacked against them since the winner belongs to the upper class. The reaction of the people to such injustices, as illustrated by Norte and Gorila, is one of apathy or stoic resignation. As Ortega indicates, Spaniards are no longer capable of reacting. Arturo and his binoculars best symbolize most people's perspective on the social ills of their country; they peer at them from afar and without compassion. The motifs thus are the outgrowth of,

---

[17] Relevant information has been provided in the Introduction, p. 13.

and serve to underline, Spanish social structure, emphasizing particularly the deleterious influence of the Catholic Church.

Of the novels written in his pre-Formalist period, *Fiestas* is Goytisolo's best. He departs from the type of novel written in Spain after the Civil War, his own as well, and will continue to diverge after 1966. Eugenio de Nora likewise sees in this novel (though for different reasons) a shift of direction in Juan Goytisolo: " . . . *Fiestas* queda como un paréntesis, como testimonio de un primer cambio de rumbo, aún vacilante, pero significativo."[18] In *La resaca*, Goytisolo departs somewhat from an objective narration following his views in *Problemas de la novela*, where he states that a well-written novel is one in which the author is not visible. But it is not until *Señas de identidad*, published in 1966, that the new route begun in *Fiestas*, is fully taken.

La resaca (1958), third novel of the trilogy *El mañana efímero*, ends with the last verses of Machado's poem:

> . . . Mas otra España nace,
> La España del cincel y de la maza
> con esa eterna juventud que se hace
> del pasado macizo de la raza.
> Una España implacable y redentora,
> España que alborea
> con un hacha en la mano vengadora,
> España de la rabia y de la idea.[19]

These verses seem to offer hope for Spain; the novel paradoxically does not indicate such a possibility. The epilogue could be an afterthought of the author, or perhaps Goytisolo's call to arms, where hope and desire for a better Spain are expressed. Additionally, the title, as pointed out by Kessel Schwartz (p.

---

[18] Eugenio de Nora, p. 298.
[19] Juan Goytisolo, *La resaca* (Paris: Libería Española, 1961), epilogue. Hereafter pages cited will be given in parentheses at the end of the text.

80), "implies that the undertow or surf tosses up an odd and often evil-smelling brew which comprises the Spain of the post–Civil War period." But the key to the meaning of the title perhaps resides in the epigraph—an excerpt from the *Diario de Barcelona:* "Pueden mezclarse en la resaca el truhán, el pordiosero de oficio y el maleante." Thus, in essence, the novel is a vivid examination of a social malaise present in Spain which the *Diario de Barcelona* designates as *la resaca.*

A few commentators have pointed out this documentary aspect of the novel, as well as Goytisolo's departure from the Objectivist method expounded upon in *Problemas de la novela.* Schwartz says that Goytisolo wanted to present facts through his characters and, consequently, "tried to abandon fantasy and poetry for a photographic reality of frustrated victims of society who try to forget in drink their despair and defeat" (p. 78). Eugenio de Nora alludes to the cinematic narrative techniques of the novel when he says that Goytisolo uses a "técnica, cinemático-literaria" (p. 299), and considers humorous the baptizing of one of the boys in the gang as "neorrealista." Evidence that the Objectivist method, propounded in *Problemas de la novela,* is not followed closely signals departure from earlier theoretical beliefs. Schwartz calls attention to Goytisolo's abandoning these views by saying that the Spanish author "combines his observation as a painter with an imagination a true objectivist would not use" (p. 79). Perhaps even more important than that aesthetic aspect is Goytisolo's overt social concern, which could not be voiced in a truly objective novel. Schwartz considers that factor a flaw in Goytisolo's presentation of an objective viewpoint: "His social consciousness also refutes his objectivism" (p. 79). Such a departure from views expressed in *Problemas de la novela* is an indication of Goytisolo's new direction; it indicates that he is no longer limiting himself to a constricted set of compositional norms. Breaking away from these views will permit him to embark upon a more rewarding and ample compositional approach.

The story of the novel, indicated in the epigraph and

implied by the title, is a study of the life of the lower class in Spain. From the first pages it is obviously a quasi-social study, almost naturalistic, of the *murcianos* in a Barcelona suburb. In *Fiestas*, the author gives a mere glimpse of the ignominy to which these people were relegated; in *La resaca*, he uses a magnifying glass to show their condition. Because of its social criticism the novel was banned in Spain. The story, in brief, is the presentation of several families, with special attention to several characters, in a *murciano* neighborhood. In order to develop the story of these people, Goytisolo uses a collage approach for his plot, somewhat similar to the one utilized in previous novels: there is a constant shifting of viewpoint from one character to another, from family to family, from scene to scene. Such changes contribute to the suspension of time and to several instances of regression—the latter appearing whenever the same situation takes place more than once. Repeated reports of the same action differ at times, as different characters appraise the situation from personal perspectives. Thus, the lives of the *murcianos* form a collage (montage?), portraying varied types of families ranging from the ambitious Saturio—an opportunist who aspires to leave the neighborhood after obtaining with the help of a priest a *piso* of his own—to Antonio, Coral the child prostitute, and the gang of young thieves (*guirlocheros*).

The theme centers on the life of a young *murciano*, Antonio, as he subsists from day to day in an economically as well as morally deprived environment. Several subthemes contribute either to development of the main theme and/or to display the conditions of the slum and the psychological state of its inhabitants. Two important ones directly connected with Antonio's senescence are the *guirlocheros* and Costa's wife. Subthemes belonging to the latter category are the lives of Giner, Saturio, Evaristo, and Coral. The manner in which the theme and the subthemes are interwoven will be shown in the section dealing with the narrating motifs.

At this time, a brief summary of the subthemes mentioned above is in order. The *guirlocheros,* a gang of youths led by Metralla, are involved in diverse manners of stealing, for sport as well as a means of livelihood. They reside in a beach bunker built during the Civil War, around which tide and waves have formed a mound:

> Construído durante la guerra, en previsión de un posible desembarco, las crecidas del río y el embate del mar habían formado a su alrededor un montículo, cerrado como un cráter. Un gigantesco anuncio de Lucky, emplazado en la cresta, le ponía a cubierto de todas las miradas. (p. 59)

Association between Antonio and the gang begins when Antonio comes upon the group as they are in the process of giving Jarque, an ex-member, a thrashing. Police appear, the group escapes, but in the rush Metralla forgets his hat. Antonio follows the group to return it to Metralla, gaining the sympathy of the leader and becoming a member of the gang. He undergoes a period of apprenticeship in the field and shortly thereafter becomes Metralla's assistant, subject to Metralla's whims, with suggestion of a possible homosexual relationship between the two boys.

The other subtheme which contributes directly to the main theme is Costa's wife, a lonely woman, frustrated by her husband's sexual indifference, who wants a child to replace the one she has lost and perhaps even a lover to placate her sexual needs. She eventually manages to have Antonio provide her with both. At the end of the novel she appears as an overpowering monster from whose net Antonio cannot escape.

Among the other subthemes, not necessarily related to Antonio's development, is Giner's life. He is the social activist of the *barrio,* continuously trying to find the means to awaken his fellow workers. He exhibits Emilio, a product of the neighborhood who goes to France where he lives much better economically, as a tangible example that his dreams are within reach. Unfortunately, however, his wife constantly reproaches him for the undesirable experiences that the family undergoes as a result of his political views. Because of her naagging and the indifference of his sons, he utilizes alcohol to escape. An elaboration of what took place in the past is provided through flashbacks in which Giner re-experiences the four years he spent in jail.

Saturio exemplifies the ambitious *murciano* who hates the *barrio*; he wants to escape at any cost and in order to do so capitalizes on his friendship with a priest. At the beginning, three priests appear in the neighborhood looking for Saturio's house, which will be used as a registering center for those children who want to take their first communion. As the novel progresses, the reader learns how Saturio and his wife Fuensanta consider themselves above the social status of the despised members of their neighborhood. Saturio's opportunism and his lack of true religious belief are best illustrated by his dramatic change of behavior after the tragic death of his daughter. He turns away from the church and becomes a dypsomaniac, spending most of his time at the neighborhood barroom.

Evaristo, an old man, a much-decorated veteran of five wars, lives in a precarious economic situation and may be evicted. Many, including Evaristo, mistakenly believe that, given the old man's reputation and his service to the nation, his being thrown into the street is highly unlikely. In the third section of Chapter Six, however, Evaristo is evicted. Such an act by the Spanish authorities is too harsh for the old man to bear, and he kills himself after returning all his medals to the army officer in charge of the Military District in which he served.

Coral, the child prostitute, contributes to the development of the character of Antonio, providing his first sexual experience. She also illustrated the decadence of the lower classes, possibly as a direct outcome of the environment in which she lives, since she becomes a prostitute after her father violates her. Through the subtheme of Coral's life, Goytisolo strongly criticizes those in authority who, instead of solving problems of the poor, compound them by taking advantage of their weaknesses and needs. A police corporal, for example, uses Coral's services, free of charge, whenever he pleases.

Even though the theme and most of the subthemes mentioned above, as well as many characters and situations not mentioned, are not related directly, their connection to the development of the plot is more definite than is the case in *El circo*. Goytisolo presents via these characters a composite picture of a *murciano* neighborhood and its deplorable social conditions. Such an approach brings to mind Dos Passos' *Manhattan Transfer*, in which the wasteland of the twentieth century is presented through the exposition of many individual lives. The following statement by Jon D. Brantley about Dos Passos' novel, is to some extent applicable to *La resaca*: "Unlike most thesis novels, however, the 'proof' is not developed in a narrative but is established through a series of some two hundred episodes, many of which have no direct relation to the other episodes except as they are related to the theme."[20] Goytisolo himself suggests this approach when he establishes an analogy between the amalgamation of many different items which make up Maño's tavern and the *murciano* neighborhood: "La taberna del Maño estaba como achicada a la luz del sol. Como el barrio del que era ilustraciíon y reflejo, parecía un rompecabezas compuesto de infinidad de piezas. Baldosas y mosaicos de diferentes formas y colores, ladrillos y adoquines arrancados de distintas aceras" (p. 8).

There seem to be no introductory motifs in *La resaca*. The reader is acquainted with what is taking place as it happens, without needing to be familiar with past occurrences since

---

[20] Jon D. Brantley, *The Fiction of John Dos Passos* (The Hague: Mouton & Co., 1968), p. 46. Brantley is not using the word *theme* in the same manner that this study is. Thus, the word *theme* should be substituted for story in his statement.

only what is happening during the narration matters. The novel thereby exudes an air of immediacy, of verisimilitude, which is perhaps Goytisolo's intention in using the documentary approach. Nevertheless, foreshadowing at times seems to occur. The possibility of Evaristo's eviction is discussed by Giner, Costa, and Evaristo himself early in the novel (p. 36). Additionally, as the three are talking, Costa's wife enters the house without greeting them. Her behavior embarrasses the group, and during the silence that ensues Giner stares at a picture of the couple's dead son (p. 28). As the reader discovers later, Evaristo will be evicted and Costa's wife will find a substitute for her lost son, who looks very much like Antonio. In the narration Goytisolo utilizes again the migratory point of view, a multivisional approach, dividing the novel into seven numbered sections which, for practical purposes, will be called chapters. Each is further subdivided into subsections ranging in number from eight (Chapter IV) to one (Chapter VII). This study will briefly examine each subsection, with the aid of diagrams, to exhibit its mixed viewpoint and thus illustrate the development of the plot, theme and the subthemes, and at times the simultaneity of action.

The first chapter of *La resaca* is subdivided into six sections, most of which combine a third-person viewpoint with a partially omniscient narrator. The first section begins the narration with an ironic touch, the source of which appears to be the omniscient narrator. There is a close-up of a sign, written on a wall, which says: "Ni un hogar sin lumbre, ni un español sin pan" (p. 1). The irony of these words permeates the entire book and the sign reappears frequently. From omniscience, the focus slowly shifts to Antonio, a follow-shot perhaps, as he walks around the neighborhood. These changes of viewpoint might remind the reader of cinematographic devices such as close-up, follow-shot, and panorama—devices that Goytisolo will use frequently in this work. Antonio's perspective and that of the omniscient narrator are interchanged in the first section providing a great deal of information about the *barrio*.

In the second section the device is used once again. The action begins with a third-person narrator, Cinco Duros, and then shifts to the omniscient viewpoint; this interchange continues throughout the section. The third returns to Antonio and the omniscient viewpoints, and the image-maker's wife appears before the reader for the first time. She follows the boy wherever he goes, much to his dislike. Upon discovering her, Antonio proceeds to get away. The woman's perspective of this scene will appear much later in the novel.

The fourth section concentrates on Giner as he walks out of Maño's tavern. Thereupon the reader enters Giner's thoughts, flash-backs recalling his friendship with Emilio, now in France, and their activities during the years of the Spanish Republic. The section ends as he drinks with Evaristo and Costa, the image-maker. Section five focuses on Ramón, son of Cinco Duros, who, with his brother Paco, watches his father drinking in Maño's tavern. Their admiration, as they peer through the window and see him gulp a bottle at one sitting, knows no bounds. The sixth section begins with the omniscient narrator summarizing what took place in Saturio's home that afternoon (registration for first communion), and thereafter the narrator provides an insight into the family's negative feelings about the neighborhood:

	Omniscient	*Mixed*	*Third Person*
Chap. I			
Sec. 1		Omn. & Antonio	
Sec. 2		Omn. & Cinco Duros	
Sec. 3		Omn. & Antonio	
Sec. 4		Omn. & Giner	
Sec. 5		Omn. & Ramón	
Sec. 6	Describes Saturio's home		

The second chapter is divided into six sections, the first describing the *refugio* where the young hoodlums live with general information about their picaresque adventures through their conversation with Antonio. Section two shifts to Giner, and the reader learns of his plans for improving the standard of living of the Spanish labor force via an interior monologue which Goytisolo presents as if voiced at the outset: "Sentado frente a una botella, en un rincón, Giner monologaba en voz baja. El vino hacía verlo todo sencillo. Poco a poco, su cabeza se poblaba de visiones que se sucedían sin orden ni concierto" (p. 72). The third section returns to Antonio, narrating his apprenticeship conducted by the *guirlocheros* and the relationship developing between him and Metralla. The viewpoint shifts continuously from Antonio to an omniscient narrator, as seen in the almost poetic description of the *chabolas*: "Construídas a la buena de Dios, con material apañado en diferentes lugares, sus fachadas tenían curiosos remiendos de alquitrando y lata que, milagrosamente, se mantenían en equilibrio" (p. 84). Section four describes, from an omniscient point of view, the children of the *barrio* entering the building *Fuente de Juventudes* to learn the catechism which will prepare them for their first communion. In the fifth section, the omniscient viewpoint continues, detailing the conversation of the *guirlocheros*. Upon occasions Antonio's thoughts are bared to the reader. In a similar manner, section six begins with an omniscient narrator who subsequently concentrates on Maño's thoughts:

	Omniscient	*Mixed*	*Third Person*
Chap. II			
Sec. 1	Describes *refugio*		
Sec. 2		Omn. & Giner	
Sec. 3		Omn. & Antonio	
Sec. 4	Omniscient		
Sec. 5		Omn. & Antonio	
Sec. 6		Omn. & Maño	

The third chapter has seven sections, the first told from the viewpoint of the image-maker's wife, whose name is never

83

given. The reader learns in this section details of her marital life and her obsession with Antonio. Section two combines the omniscient viewpoint with that of Coral, giving thus an understanding of the young girl. In the third section the omniscient narrator gives details of how Antonio carried out the plans of the *guirlocheros* to swindle wealthy Catholics. Section four returns to the *barrio* on Ascension Day, focusing on the people as they leave church speaking of trivialities. Thereafter the narrator follows Hombre-Gato to Maño's tavern to obtain cash from his father Cien Gramos. In the fifth section Antonio's viewpoint and that of the omniscient narrator shift back and forth, taking the reader to the *refugio* with members of the gang. Section six opens with the omniscient narrator describing the neighborhood, giving more background information, and concentrates thereafter on a procession taking place at that moment. The patrons in Maño's tavern look on and the barroom owner comments on Saturio's good fortune. Henceforth the viewpoint concentrates on Giner and his domestic problems. The seventh section focuses on Antonio as he learns that Costa's wife wants to adopt him:

	Omniscient	Mixed	Third Person
Chap. III			
Sec. 1			Costa's wife
Sec. 2		Omn. & Coral	
Sec. 3	Omniscient		
Sec. 4		Omn. & Hombre-Gato	
Sec. 5		Omn. & Antonio	
Sec. 6		Omn. & Giner	
Sec. 7			Antonio

The fourth chapter is formed of eight parts, the first narrated from an omniscient viewpoint and relating Cien Gramos' disappearance, Hombre-Gato's first communion (really his third), and the festivities of Saint John's Eve (or midsummer night). The second section continues with an omniscient narrator, but focuses on Saturio's house where there is a party celebrating San Juan's Eve. Section three continues with the same time-span, now concentrating on Antonio bar-hopping with Metralla. The fourth section, a continuation of the third, follows Antonio who, having lost Metralla, finds Coral. She takes the boy to an abandoned railroad car and seduces him. Section five returns to Saturio's party during which his daughter dies tragically. The sixth section, with the omniscient narrator, gives an account of Saturio's daughter's wake and burial. In section seven the omniscient viewpoint narrates a political gathering at Maño's tavern, which continues into section eight:

	Omniscient	Mixed	Third Person
Chap. IV			
Sec. 1	Omniscient		
Sec. 2	Omniscient		
Sec. 3			Antonio
Sec. 4			Antonio
Sec. 5	Omniscient		
Sec. 6	Omniscient		
Sec. 7		Omn. & Giner	
Sec. 8		Omn. & Giner	

The fifth chapter has three parts, with the first narrated from the viewpoint of Costa's wife. The omniscient narrator, however, briefly summarizes what she does to bring Antonio to her home and how the boy reacts. The section also provides insight into her unconscious, giving detailed information on the dreams she has been having. Section two combines Antonio's point of view with that of the omniscient narrator. The boy plans to steal a large amount of money from Costa's wife in order to escape to America with Metralla. The third section also has mixed viewpoints: Antonio's theft and Metralla's betrayal are described, as well as the triumph of the image-maker's wife. Even though most of the narration seems to be limited to Antonio's perspective, there are instances when the voice of Goytisolo, or that of the omniscient narrator, is distinctly heard:

	Omniscient	Mixed	Third Person
Chap. V			
Sec. 1		Omn. & Costa's wife	
Sec. 2		Omn. & Antonio	
Sec. 3		Omn. & Antonio	

Chapter six also contains three parts. In the first, the omniscient narrator tells how a heat wave seems to contribute to a greater number of violent incidents in the neighborhood. As usual, the people attribute the atmospheric disturbance to a conspiracy of the United States. In this section the reader is informed that Coral has been taken by the police and that Hombre-Gato has tried, unsuccessfully, to see her. In section two, the omniscient narrator brings other sub-themes to their conclusion: Emilio, frustrated, returns to France, while Giner, depressed, goes to Maño's bar where he encounters Fuensanta who recounts Saturio's transformation after the death of his daughter. Trying to escape, Saturio wanders around the neighborhood until he finds himself in front of Evaristo's home where a group of people are congregated. The third section shifts from Giner's viewpoint to Evaristo's as he is being evicted. The section begins with the omniscient narrator summarizing what has happened and then proceeding to describe Evaristo's feeling which leads him to suicide:

	Omniscient	Mixed	Third Person
Chapt. VI			
Sec. 1	Omniscient		
Sec. 2		Omn. & Giner	
Sec. 3		Omn. & Evaristo	

Chapter seven's single section combines Carlito's viewpoint with that of the omniscient narrator. The neighborhood is preparing itself to receive the visit of a governmental delegate, and Carlito, Saturio's son, is chosen to give a speech. This section focuses on the boy's endeavors to learn the speech under Father Bueno's direction and his exposure to the evils of the *barrio*. Because of the recent traumatic changes at his home, however, Carlito fails to give his speech and instead mumbles a few words about his family's domestic woes and begins to cry:

	Omniscient	Mixed	Third Person
Chap. VII Sec. 1		Omn. & Carlito	

The importance of the examination of these shifting viewpoints will be seen when those novels written under Formalist influence are examined. In this novel, however, one purpose of such shifting is retardation. Additionally, the viewpoints appear to change in order to present an objective narration in which the author's hand is invisible. Ironically, the author's presence seems more conspicuous because of the continuous shifting.

The story time of the novel is provided by many allusions. In the first section of Chapter One, a priest informs the people gathered around him that Easter will take place within a few weeks: "Dentro de pocas semanas," dijo, "Nuestra Santa Madre Iglesia celebra con gran solemnidad la festividad de Pascua Florida" (p. 5). Since Easter, a movable holy day, is usually celebrated between the twenty-seventh of March and the twenty-fifth of April, the novel can be established as beginning in the month of March. The omniscient narrator says the novel starts on a Sunday (p. 1): it ends also on a Sunday, and a definite date is given: "El domingo, once de agosto" (p. 269). Thus, the action of the novel occurs over several months. Further references to the holy days, specific events, and dates illustrate Goytisolo's use of the chronological motif: "El día de la Ascensión" (p. 134), "la víspera de San Juan" (p. 170), "A mediados de julio" (p. 253), "El día de Santiago" (p. 257). All these contribute to an awareness of the movement of time within which events develop, and thus provide an air of verisimilitude.

Upon examining the place of action, the static motif is probably more suitable to describe it if the *barrio* is considered as the meeting place where all the characters in the novel congregate. This assumption, of course, would require overlooking the mobility of Antonio, Hombre-Gato, and other characters. Otherwise, a combination of both concepts, dynamic and static would be the suitable description.

There are several bound motifs in *La resaca*, but social criticism is most important, being directly connected to the main theme as well as to all the subthemes. Other motifs are bound here, already noticed in earlier novels: betrayal, escapism, loss of innocence, and executioner-victim. Social criticism is particularly noticeable in the portrayal of Antonio as a victim of his environment. His behavior is the direct result of an upbringing in sub-standard living conditions. Goytisolo's denunciation of Spain is perceived in his portrayal of the *guirlocheros* who are products of their circumstances. The brief and sketchy psychological study of Coral illustrates effects of an impoverished environment upon people. The treatment of Evaristo by the Spanish authorities underlines the government's inhuman treatment of citizens and its inability to reward those who serve it well. Giner's concern with the improvement of the Spanish labor force is also Goytisolo's. Through Emilio, the author shows the gap that exists between Spain and the other European nations as concerns the standard of living of laborers.

Betrayal, as it relates to Antonio, is another important bound motif. The betrayal of Metralla cannot be omitted without destroying the coherence of the novel. Because of Metralla's treachery, Antonio cannot escape from the barrio and Spain, and finds himself at the mercy of Costa's wife. His loss of innocence is not solely the result of his affair with Coral; it is also in the realization that he was the prey of the image-maker's wife. He broods over his predicament as he lies nude next to the woman, several hours after Metralla leaves for America:

> Luego se despertó, en su habitación, llorando y delirando. . . . La mujer estaba tendida junto a él, como un amante. . . . Su cara flotaba sobre la de él, como una máscara, y, al mirar los ojos, brillantes y desorbitados por la alegría, Antonio comprendió, con una mezcla de tristeza y alivio, que su niñez había muerto y que, en adelante, jamás podría escaparse. (pp. 249–50)

The above scene also illustrates the executioner-victim motif since the woman may have known Antonio and Metralla's plans, and probably had even surmised Metralla's designs, yet did not intervene, allowing destiny to follow its course in order to keep Antonio to herself. In the above paragraph, her face floating over the boy could be associated with a monster, a spider rejoicing over its prey. The executioner-victim motif is also evident in the relationship between Antonio and Metralla. Throughout, in order to please the *guirlochero* leader, the boy is induced to perform a number of acts, which he masochistically carries out.

The motifs of escapism, betrayal, and executioner-victim in addition to being bound are dynamic because they change situations, contributing to the development of events. The desire to escape his environment leads Metralla to betray Antonio and thus make the boy his victim. On the other hand, Antonio's "victim" tendencies (as noticed in his association with Metralla), his admiration for the *guirlochero,* and his wanting to get away from his home influence him to perform many deeds he most probably would not have considered under other circumstances. His fate is thus provoked by his behavior. Belonging to a gang is also a form of escape. Schwartz writes that Antonio belongs to the gang in order to "achieve a sense of meaning in life, to escape his feeling of being a poor child from a district of shacks" (p. 81). Another dynamic motif is found in the behavior of Costa's wife, a combination of sexual deprivation and maternal love. The image-maker's wife does everything she can to possess Antonio, causing certain events that transpire in the novel.

Of the several static motifs in *La resaca*, perhaps the most important one, also bound, is that of social criticism. It appears in many guises, the most obvious being the wall sign that states: "Ni un hogar sin lumbre, ni un español sin pan." The most significant moments in which it appears are at the beginning of the novel, as was indicated earlier, and when Evaristo commits suicide. The local color evident in the description of the picaresque adventures of the *guirlocheros* can be considered a static motif too. Instances in which the omniscient narrator gives a bird's eye view of the barrio are also examples.

There are many free motifs in the novel. The most important are social criticism (which appears also as bound motif), homosexuality, loss of innocence, religious opportunism, deprecatory allusions to the United States, religious festivities (which in some cases have a negative force), and the language of the people. The motif of social criticism is omnipresent: most characters and situations are directly or indirectly related to Goytisolo's indictment of Spanish society. When some of the *murciano* children are being prepared for their first communion, for example, the classroom in which the catechism lessons are given have photographs of Franco and José Antonio, with the following inscription beneath: "El hombre no sólo vive de pan. Nuestro régimen no es materialista" (p. 94). Such a slogan, unfortunately, is of no value, Goytisolo seems to say, to a group of people who are starving. The title of the novel,[21] too, stresses the social situation, as we have noted earlier in quoting Schwartz's interpretation that the title refers to the foul social conditions of post-Civil War Spain.

Portrayal of the representatives of the Church is in itself a

---

[21] It is important to remember that the novel was originally titled *Los murcianos*, as Kessel Schwartz indicates in *Juan Goytisolo* (p. 78).

form of social criticism. Their only remedy for the illiterate and starving *murcianos* is copies of the catechism. Their hypocrisy is underscored when they transform the appearance of the neighborhood only because a governmental delegate is going to visit. Father Bueno's speech, which Carlito was to give, expounds the establishment's reactionary position. The injustice of the system is reflected upon by Antonio when he realizes that he could steal in one day what his father earned, by hard labor, in a week: "Sin trabajar ganaba en un solo día lo que su padre obtenía en una semana, partiéndose el espinazo" (p. 129).

The homosexual motif is noticed in the association between Antonio and Metralla.[22] The two boys sleep in the same bed and Antonio obviously seeks Metralla's approval for everything he does. Furthermore, upon occasions Antonio becomes a masochistic servant of sorts seeking to please Metralla's whims: "Lo que Metralla quería—y continuamente quería algo—se traducía más bien en forma de gestos y ademanes. Por acuerdo tácito, Antonio se había convertido en una especie de ayudante, enteramente consagrado a su servicio" (p. 81). In Costa the reader also finds the homosexual motif; sexual life between him and his wife is nonexistent. He develops a fetish for food and his sexuality appears limited to allowing pigeons to pick up grains of millet from his lips: "Un día, ella le había espiado desde lejos. Su marido se ponía granos de mijo en los labios. Envuelto en un remolino de aves, se abandonaba, con los ojos cerrados, a sus arrullos, mimos y zureos" (p. 116). However, there is no overt evidence of Costa's homosexuality. He may merely be impotent, a question taken up later. A latent homosexual relationship is also apparent in the friendship of Cien Gramos and Cinco Duros whose lives consist of a three-step cycle: fighting with each other

---

[22] Emir Rodríguez Monegal, "El arte de narrar," *Marcha* (10 julio 1959), 22, has also noticed this.

91

(somewhat like a domestic squabble between man and wife), reconciliation, and celebration with alcohol until they lose consciousness.

The loss-of-innocence motif occurs almost as often as that of social criticism. Nearly every child in the *barrio* undergoes a traumatic experience at an early age, losing his innocence. Coral is ravished by her drunken father; Hombre-Gato, Carlito and other *murciano* children are prematurely confronted by a cruel, unfriendly world. The religious opportunism of the people is patent at the beginning of the novel and throughout. Since the Church dignitaries fail to provide urgent, material needs, they try to obtain from the priests as much as possible by feigning religious devotion. The first section of Chapter One where most residents of the *barrio*, in unison, stop their activities (gambling, listening to loud music from the radio) and rush to greet a group of priests. There is no religious fervor involved in the action; they merely want to secure clothing and perhaps food, both of which usually accompany the visit of priests. Once the group leaves, the cards reappear and radios are heard once again. Another example is Saturio's volunteering his house for registering children who plan to take their first communion. He is trying to gain Father Bueno's sympathy in order to secure an apartment and move away from the neighborhood, and his lukewarm religious beliefs disappear altogether after the death of his daughter. Another example is the low esteem in which communion is held by both children and adults. In the fourth section of Chapter Two as the boys are queuing to take their catechism lessons, their dialogue reveals that many have taken first communion several times because of the clothes and other items they will receive. Hombre-Gato, for instance, had taken it three times.

Several deprecatory remarks against the United States can be classified as a free motif. The people of the *barrio* look upon the United States as a source of many of their chronic woes. Whenever there are atmospheric irregularities, a heat wave for example, the people say it was manufactured by the U.S.: " 'Para mí, la culpa la tienen los americanos,' opinió Saturio" (p. 134). Religious festivities, as in *El circo* and *Fiestas*, have a negative and unhappy effect on some people. In *La resaca*, Saturio's daughter dies tragically on San Juan's Eve while he is giving a party. The same night Antonio loses his virginity, and his dream of going to America (which he "lives" during coitus), does not materialize. Another free motif is that of an over-powering, castrating female (possibly representing Spain as it relates to Antonio), observed in the characterization of Costa's wife. Her attitude towards her husband is one of disdain and hate. In section one of the third chapter, for instance, she watches her husband contemptuously as he gorges himself: "Sentado frente a ella, Costa seguía dando buena cuenta del desayuno. Si su aritmética no fallaba, aquella era su séptima tostada" (p. 115). After watching how he let pigeons pick grains of millet from his mouth, she is revolted to the extreme that she slashes the canary's throat: "De vuelta a casa, ella abrió la jaula y le cortó el cuello con las tijeras" (p. 116). The act is an evident symbolic form of castration of the husband who has not touched her in a long time, if at all. There is no definite statement about Costa's sexual behavior, only veiled allusions, such as "¿El capón?" (p. 234), suggesting impotence. But there is the following statement, "Se lo tuvo que explicar el médico. Yo había ido a verle creyendo ser estéril" (p. 117), which seems to indicate that Costa did not have an orgasm during sexual relations with his wife. The mystery of their dead son is partly explained when she tells a friend of the information she has given Antonio about Costa: "Se lo he explicado todo. . . . La forma como tuve mi hijo, y lo demás. . . . Quiero que día de mañana lo desprecie también" (p. 234). The hypocritical relationship between Costa and his wife is a criticism of the institution of marriage in Spain where many couples are pressured by society and the Church into remaining together even though they detest each other.

Costa's wife also exercises an overpowering, almost castrating force upon Antonio. A morbid bond between the two evolved from the boy's stealing: "El robo, conocido y admitido por los dos, creaba, en cierto modo, una especie de lazo" (p. 235). Antonio steals from her and she is aware of it, but does nothing to stop him. On the contrary, she makes it easier for Antonio to find the money he wants, a fact which indicates that she is using the theft as a bait to draw him into her net. Throughout, when *murcianos* speak, Goytisolo uses words underscoring their regional or social origins. At the end of the novel there is a glossary which aids the reader in determining the meaning of those unfamiliar words. Here, once again, is an aspect which will be observed in his later works: the use of language to convey a particular idea without necessarily relying on the connotative aspect of it. In *La resaca* this motif is not as complex as in *Reivindicación del conde don Julián* but emphasizes the cultural differences of the *murcianos* in particular and the lower classes in general.

The Formalist device of retardation is best illustrated by the shifting points of view. Its purpose, in addition to delaying the action of the main theme, is to develop the subthemes. But the most obvious utilization of the device, in which the development of neither the theme nor the subtheme is helped much, is the series of comic interludes presented by Cinco Duros and Cien Gramos. They do aid in building up tension as the theme and the subthemes unravel. In one case, their entrance reminds the reader of the knocking at the gate in *Macbeth*: in the eighth section of Chapter Four, while Giner and Emilio hold a political gathering in the backroom of Maño's tavern, there is loud pounding on the door and a voice orders the people within to open in the name of the law. Tension in the room, high prior to the knocking, becomes critical. When

Maño opens the door, however, he discovers that it is only Cinco Duros and Cien Gramos.

Composition of *La resaca* can be described as the result of realistic motivation. Goytisolo told Francisco Olmos García that the novel came from a direct contact with a world he was not aware existed. Consequently, he went out and did research for the novel:

> Cuando niño, mi vida se había desenvuelto como a los acordes de una música melodiosa y alegre: Yo no conocía otra gente y otro mundo que los que me brindaba mi medio social. Deseoso de conocer otras cosas, un buen día descubrí la vida de los foburgos de Barcelona, donde todos decían hallarse allí huyendo de *algo*.[23]

The above explains the documentary approach, and, thus, every action in the novel has a realistically motivated reaction. Antonio joins the *guirlocheros* to escape his environment and to have an identity of his own. Costa's wife is attracted to Antonio because the boy resembles the son she lost. Even Giner notices the resemblance (p. 151), which underscores the validity of her love for the boy. That her maternal love becomes a sexual one can also be explained by pointing out her marital unhappiness. Antonio, on the other hand, decides to reside with the woman, even though he dislikes her, because Metralla asks him to do it. Antonio steals from her both at Metralla's request and because he plans to save the money to go to America. Giner's behavior is consistent with that of a political activist, as in Saturio's with that of an opportunist. Coral's state is the result of poverty and depravity. Taken separately, each of the above is a story in itself with only traces of political and social protest; together, however, they are another matter. The novel's many threads are woven into a political manifesto.

In the three novels examined in this chapter there is a unifying bond: social criticism, although *El circo* does not man-

---

[23] Francisco Olmos García, "La novela y los novelistas españoles de hoy. Una encuesta," *Cuadernos Americanos*, 129 (julio-agosto, 1963), 231.

age to carry it out as well as the others. Many ideas are expressed and many philosophical views are propounded, but it is evident throughout that Goytisolo feels that the novel is an instrument for the ethical and social improvement of mankind. Not until *Señas de identidad* and *Don Julián* will his political views be relegated to a less pervasive level and his novels cease to be political pamphlets.

Chapter III

La Isla, Campos de Níjar, and La Chanca

This chapter examines three works which cannot be considered novels per se, *La isla* (1961), *Campos de Níjar* (1960) and *La chanca* (1962). *La isla* was originally written as a film script to be produced in Spain. After the Spanish government forbade its shooting, Goytisolo published the script as a novel. According to him, this is the reason it centers on one character, Claudia, and the others are mere caricatures.[1] *Campos de Níjar* and *La chanca* are travelogues of an unusual type since the narrator uses the genre to criticize the Spanish government for allowing the social ills he witnesses. As a consequence, he is highly selective in what he shows; the works should be considered written documentaries of the social conditions of the people and areas of Spain displayed. An important reason for studying the travelogues is their relationship to later novels; some motifs of these two works appear in *Señas de identidad*, *Don Julián*, and *Juan sin tierra*, and the novel genre is related to history and the travelogue form.[2]

---

[1] Juan Goytisolo made this point to the writer during an informal conversation in New Orleans on March 22, 1975.

[2] According to Eichenbaum, "The novel has its source in history and travelogue," (Victor Erlich, *Russian Formalism*, p. 215).

97

The story of *La isla* reminds one of Federico Fellini's *La Dolce Vita*. It portrays the decadence of the Spanish bourgeoisie and that of the wealthy Americans they are trying to emulate. As the title implies, the group focused upon is isolated from the rest of Torremolinos. The plot is not too different from the story, being limited to one point of view without deviations from the story line. Hence, "the action" [story]; "and how the reader learns of the action"[3] [plot], are the same. It is pertinent to note what Tomashevsky says about causal connections in a work: when these are weak, chronological connections are stronger. Therefore, when "the story line becomes weaker, we move from the novel to the chronicle, to a simple statement of the sequence of events" (Lemon, p. 66). *La isla's* title in French translation is *Chronique d'une île*. The strong chronological connections in the novel arise from its theme—eleven days in the life of Claudia, the narrator, and her experience in Torremolinos. The reader is also provided with a few glimpses into her past and grim future.

The introductory motifs are either absent or not very definite. The work begins without explanations and ends eleven days later. The reader learns what is taking place day by day, without much depth in any of the situations encountered. Because the prevailing narrative motif is first-person point of view, supplemented by dialogue and letters, there is no elaboration. The time motif is also influenced by the first-person point of view. It is absolutely established at the end of the book by Claudia, as she departs, that eleven days have elapsed. In addition, references to waking up in the morning, having lunch or supper, and going to sleep, provide an almost hour-by-hour account.

---

[3] *Russian Formalist Criticism—Four Essays*, translated and with an introduction by Lee T. Lemon and Marion J. Reis (Lincoln: University of Nebraska Press, 1965), p. 67. Hereafter pages cited will be in parentheses at the end of the text.

The motif of place is perhaps both dynamic and static, dynamic because there is a continuous movement from tavern to tavern and one party to another. But, at the same time, most occurrences take place in Torremolinos, a resort town where all the characters gather, a fact which would support contention that the static motif is appropriate to describe the setting.

There are four bound motifs in the chronicle: escapism, boredom, physical and spiritual erosion, and social criticism. All characters in the novel, particularly Claudia, are trying to escape their lives through sex, alcohol, and food—a closer examination would possibly indicate that all the capital sins are assiduously practiced. Their reason for wanting to escape their existence is boredom with their meaningless condition; they somehow have reached a point in life where they no longer hold any values and only debauchery provides comfort. Such behavior leads to physical and spiritual erosion, not only in the characters, but also in Torremolinos and ultimately Spain. Claudia points this out at the end of the novel: "El tiempo corría de prisa y la erosión continuaba."[4] Kessel Schwartz notices this aspect when he says: "Claudia leaves, realizing that time is passing her and Spain by, and that the spiritual and physical erosion will continue."[5] Thus, social criticism is the most important of the bound motifs because it is, in essence, the whole purpose of the chronicle.

There are a few free motifs, a prevalent one being continous criticism of the United States, which is very ironic since most Spaniards appearing the chronicle are aping the decadent values of those U.S. citizens in Torremolinos—who in no way necessarily reflect the culture of the United States. The materialism of the people involved is also a free motif; they

---

[4] Juan Goytisolo, *La isla* (Barcelona: Editorial Seix Barral, 1961), p. 171. Hereafter pages cited will be given in parentheses at the end of the text.

[5] Kessel Schwartz, *Juan Goytisolo* (New York: Twayne Publishers, Inc., 1970), p. 86. Hereafter the page number will be given in parentheses at the end of the text cited.

are shown as they live from day to day. This is perhaps the reason for the hour-by-hour type of narration. Another free motif is adultery: most characters appearing in *La isla* commit adultery at one time or another. The idea of celebration, of *fiesta*, is also a free motif—the people go from one party to another so that their lives are a continuous celebration.

It is difficult to establish the presence of dynamic motifs in the chronicle. If there are moving forces in the narration, occurrences that make things happen, they are not very evident. Perhaps their indistinct presence is part of the mood of the life of leisure in which the characters move. Two facts, however, might be conceived of as dynamic since they, to some extent, influence Claudia's behavior. One is Enrique's impotence and the other is Rafael's career. Claudia is no longer in love with her husband, Rafael, but because he is a newspaper writer and a governmental official, she has remained with him—yet another example of Goytisolo's criticism of the institution of marriage in Spain which keeps together people who do not love each other. Claudia is in love with Enrique, whose impotence probably influences his not wanting to leave his wife. Thus, these two deterrents may be responsible for Claudia's immutable life. There is, in effect, a paradox here since if these motifs are dynamic, it is because they prevent her life from changing. Nevertheless, they are responsible for something happening or not happening in the narration.

The local color of Torremolinos, the beaches, a few nature scenes are some of the static motifs of the novel:

> El 403 dejó atrás los anuncios de colores de la plaza, la doble hilera de casas blancas adornadas con macetas, las colinas boscosas de El Pinar, las luces de la estación de servicio. La carretera subía y bajaba y en una de las revueltas divisé el mar, encharcado de luna. (p. 120)

There are flaws in the logical construction, in the motivational aspect of the chronicle. The narrator does not explain how the reader has managed to become acquainted with eleven days in her life. Is she writing her memoirs? What motivates her writing them? Is she criticizing the society in which she lives, yet does not seem to reject? These and other questions are unanswered, the probable result of transforming a film script into a novel.

Campos de Níjar and *La chanca* are neither novels nor conventional travelogues. Kessel Schwartz writes that they "are not novels in the classic sense, neither are they travel books only" because they convert reality into a "novelistic and lyrical experience" (p. 121). Gonzalo Sobejano is of the opinion that these books "representan el extremo límite de la narrativa social, puesto que tratan de ser reportajes económico-sociales sobre regiones españolas menesterosas y olvidadas."[6] The best study on *Campos de Níjar*, underlining its social content, is perhaps Gil Casado's *La novela social española*; Gil Casado considers Goytisolo's work as one "de intención plenamente testimonial."[7] What Goytisolo does is to present a totally "involved-observer" in the travelogue, one dramatically opposed to the travel narrator, who objectively provides a painting of the landscape and the people he encounters—a good example of which is Cela's travel books. Goytisolo believes the narrator should be involved by calling attention to those socio-economic flaws he discovers in his travels. Gil Casado enumerates five points which are present in every testimonial travelogue:

1) recorrido de la región; 2) propósito testimonial e intención crítica social; 3) veracidad y realidad precisa. . .; 4) pinto-resquismo expuesto a través de "tipos," de la indumentaria de la gente, del

---

[6] Gonzalo Sobejano, *Novela española de nuestro tiempo* (2nd ed.; Madrid: Editorial Prensa Española, 1970), p. 278.

[7] Pablo Gil Casado, *La novela social española* (Barcelona: Editorial Seix Barral, 1968), p. 228. Hereafter pages cited will be given in parentheses at the end of the text.

aspecto de los pueblos y del paisaje; 5) estilo basado en un realismo objetivo, en la instantánea descriptiva. La prosa intenta recoger la fonética popular y el vocabulario local. (p. 228)

Goytisolo, according to Gil Casado, satisfies the preceding five requirements in *Campos de Níjar*. When Francisco Olmos asked Goytisolo about the purpose of the travelogue, he said that it was a new genre, needed urgently: "Este género de literatura que no tiene precedentes, es muy urgente."[8] He also stressed that the travelogue should be motivated by the desire to know the reason for certain social conditions; his own desire to discover what caused some Spaniards to leave certain regions of Spain prompted his travels and his writing of *Campos de Níjar*: "El acuciante deseo de conocer ese *algo* de que habían huido los habitantes de los barrios obreros de Barcelona hizo nacer en mí la necesidad del viaje. . . . Lo que descubrí en esos primeros viajes lo he contado en *Campos de Níjar*" (p. 232). Goytisolo also points out the necessity of being well informed on social and historical aspects of the region visited: "Con *La chanca*, mi segundo libro de viajes, he querido demostrar que el escritor-viajero que no conozca de antemano la vida económica, social e histórica de los lugares que visita no puede ver nada" (p. 232). He then proceeds to call to task Cela and other writers of this genre for not following his approach: "Para mí, en oposición a Cela y sus predecesores, la literatura de viajes requiere una previa labor de investigación y debe ser una literatura-documento" (p. 232).

In *Campos de Níjar* and *La chanca* there is one distinct dynamic motif and a large number of free ones. The prominence of the latter is the obvious result of the free aspect of the genre which does not need to follow any particular pattern in

---

[8] Francisco Olmos García, "La novela y los novelistas españoles de hoy. Una encuesta," *Cuadernos Americanos*, 129 (julio-agosto, 1963), 232. Hereafter pages cited will be given in parentheses at the end of the text.

order to develop characters or situations. Since Goytisolo does not limit himself to static description of the landscape and its people, but dynamically asserts his views on what he sees and hears, the prominent dynamic motif in the narration is the attitude of the traveler-narrator: he determines the course of the testimonial presentation. Because of such an approach, this travelogue verges on the thesis novel. Another dynamic motif, apparently uncontrolled by the narrator, appears in *Campos de Níjar*. He oversleeps, missing the bus (p. 58) so that he has the opportunity to walk several miles and speak to many interesting inhabitants of the region. Even though most of the free motifs examined appear in both works, there are a few which are limited to either one or the other. This study will first examine those present in both *Campos de Níjar* and *La chanca* and then those which appear in only one travelogue.

The most prominent free motifs recurring in both works are economic, social, and political criticism of Spain, a constant reference to the Arabic culture prevailing in the area visited, the language spoken by the people in the region, the behavior of foreigners in Spain, and the narrator's feelings about situations encountered. As indicated by Goytisolo in the paragraph cited, economic, social, and political criticism is the primordial purpose of the two travelogues. Throughout both, the reader finds examples of poverty, social injustice, and the failure of the present political system to undertake the proper measures to remedy the situation. Trachoma and silicosis, for instance, are very common ailments which the majority of the inhabitants of the area contract. In one instance a miner, wanting to improve his living conditions, goes to France. French physicians discover silicosis and he is asked to return to his country; the company for which he worked in Spain refuses to indemnify him because he quit. Thus, he finds himself ill, without any means of sustenance (p. 37).

Allusions to Arabic culture comprise historical references and mention of similarity of the landscape to that of

103

Africa. An example of the former is found when Goytisolo indicates that Almería reached a period of splendor under the dominion of the Arabs and its decadence began once Fernando and Isabel conquered the area:

> Almería conoció un breve período de esplendor durante los albores de la dominación musulmana. "Cuando Almería era Almería—dice un proverbio que los viejos repiten melancólicamente—, Granada era su alquería." Desde su conquista por los Reyes Católicos la región ha sufrido una interrumpida y patética decadencia.[9]

The continuous interpretation of the landscape so as to emphasize its similarity with Africa is observed in the following scene:

> Las casas de El Barranquete son rectangulares, con ventanucos cuadrados y cúpulas. De lejos recuerdan las caperuzas de los *trull*: de la campiña de Ostuni, y Martina-Franca en el sur de Italia, pero aquí los casquetes son únicos. . . .
> —Parece África, ¿Verdá? —dice leyéndome el pensamiento. (p. 20)

A great amount of dialogue between the narrator and the people he encounters provides opportunity to appreciate the regional differences of spoken Spanish. Gil Casado mentions this aspect of *Campos de Níjar*, which intends to reflect the language of these people; however, he feels that it is mostly literary creation:

> En los diálogos con los naturales se tiende a reflejar la lengua del hombre del campo, pretendiéndose a darle un aire de autenticidad mediante el uso de ciertos vocablos y giros locales. . . . En realidad se trata de un lenguaje convencional, simplificado, que, excepto por algunas palabras regionales, es creación literaria. (p. 237)

The following examples from both works illustrate this lin-

---

[9] Juan Goytisolo, *Campos de Níjar* (Barcelona: Editorial Seix Barral, 1960), p. 120. Hereafter pages cited will be given in parentheses at the end of the text.

guistic motif, and in them Gil Casado's contention seems
doubtful:

> —¿Cine, en tu pueblo?
> —Han venío unos de Murcia con el portátil.
> —¿Y qué película echan?
> —Una, no lo sé. . . . Pá mí son iguales toas. (*Campos*, p.
> 33)
> —¿El Sable? ¿Qué le ha ocurrío?
> —Ná. Que le dió un tembló y no para ni un segundo. Asín,
> asín como el primo de Antonio cuando enfermó de silicosis. [10]

The foreigner encountered by the traveler is either
pedantic and condescending or disregards totally the local
mores and, consequently, causes culture shock and problems
for the populace. An example of the former is found in *Campos
de Níjar* when the narrator is walking along an untraveled road:

> —*Pardon*, señor. *Est-ce que vous savez* dónde agua—dice
> cuando llego junto a él.
> —Je ne sais pas, c'est la première fois que je prends cette
> route.
> El hombre amusga la vista con cierta sorpresa.
> . . . .
> Por la ventanilla del coche asoma una cabeza de mujer,
> colérica, con la nariz despellejada.
> —Je te l'avais dit quarante fois. Toute cette région là c'est le
> désert. Maintenant essaie de trouver de l'eau. Cela t'apprendra à
> m'emmener dans des pays pauvres. (pp. 62–63)

In *La chanca*, an old woman tells the traveler about what appears to be her realization of the reasons some French tourists
have for taking her family's picture and her desire to react in a
dignified manner:

> —¿Se acuerda usté de aquellos franceses que subieron a
> vernos y retrataron a mis nietecitos?
> . . . .

[10] Juan Goytisolo, *La chanca* (Paris: Librería Española, 1962), p. 109. Hereafter pages cited will be given in parentheses at the end of the text.

–A veces una hace las cosas sin comprender. . . . Creo que si vinieran ahora les escupiría. (p. 137)

In *Campos de Níjar* a Swedish couple's sexual freedom creates a stir among the inhabitants of a small town by the beach:

La sueca se lió con el Gabriel y la mujer los enganchó a los dos en la playa y armó la de Dios es Cristo.

Argimiro sonríe ladinamente y enseña sus dientes grandes y picados.

—Tal como se lo digo. Y el sueco, sin enterarse. . . . (p. 90)

Another free motif mentioned continuously is the need for water and trees in the region. Signs everywhere indicate this, and the narrator speaks to the local people about it. *La chanca* ends with the narrator saying before he goes to sleep: "Faltan árboles, ¿comprendes? Faltan árboles. . . ." (p. 140). The narrator's emotions about what he encounters in his travels are openly displayed: he may offer a verbal outburst about a particular injustice he feels should be corrected; there are moments when he describes his frustrations at not being able to remedy a given situation, and a few instances of sentimentality in which the traveler weeps over what he sees. The following scene is from *Campos de Níjar* as the traveler wanders around a small town, drinking and crying: "Unos niños rondaban alrededor mío a respetuosa distancia y, al levantarme, oí decir a uno: . . . 'Parece que se le ha muerto a alguno. Mi madre le ha visto llorando' " (p. 138). In *La chanca*, after heavy drinking, the narrator says:

—Vitorino—dije—¿Me oyes?
—Sí—repuso.
—Almería ha perdido el sol. Ha perdido el aire. (p. 140)

Campos de Níjar has two free motifs which do not seem to be present in *La chanca*, references to time and to the music of the region. An example of the former is seen when the narrator muses: "Revivía los incidentes de mis tres días de viaje y la idea de lo que había visto todavía—o me había pasado inadvertido tal vez—me abrumaba" (p. 133). "Treinta y seis horas después, lavado y afeitado . . ." (p. 139). The narrator discusses music with one of the men of the region, after hearing the men singing:

> —Tiene muy buena voz.
> —Debería habé oío usté la de un chaval que trabajaba con nosotros. . . . Era un campeón. Fandangos, serranas, tientos, tó lo que quiera usté. . . . (p. 36)

La chanca, on the other hand, makes continuous reference to the historical sins which, to some extent, led the area to its present underprivileged condition. An appendix of roughly forty pages is dedicated to historical data about the area. Another free motif, not present in *Campos de Níjar*, is a scene in *El Club de los Bacilones*. Goytisolo criticizes the way in which some men of the area escape their frustrations and their social condition by using *grifa* (cannabis):[11] "En la mesa vecina los jugadores se pasan un cigarillo de grifa de mano en mano, recogidos y dignos, igual que comulgantes" (p. 126).

The purpose of this chapter has been to examine other forms of narrative in the writings of Goytisolo in order to give the reader a better perspective of the transformation beginning with *Señas de identidad*. What appear to be excerpts from these travelogues reappear in the three novels to be studied in the following chapters, while the sexual behavior portrayed in *La isla* is parodied. The short stories of Goytisolo are not studied because they are not relevant to the scope and purpose of this study.[12] *Pueblo en marcha*, on the other hand, is too much a political pamphlet to be examined from a literary standpoint. In essence, then, *La isla, Campos de Níjar*, and *La chanca* could be considered as transitional, perhaps a hiatus, between the early works and the mature ones.

---

[11] It is interesting to note that the use of historical data, the Arabic culture, and cannabis will be found in *Don Julián* and *Juan sin tierra*.

[12] *Fin de fiesta* appears to have one theme with four variations. Such a countrapuntal device could yield a great many combinations and juxtapositions from a Formalist standpoint.

Chapter IV

Señas De Identidad

With *The Mendiola Trilogy* Goytisolo begins a new period in his literary career, marked particularly by a conscious utilization of the Formalists' theories. The three novels composing it, *Señas de identidad* (1966), *Reivindicación del conde don Julián* (1970), and *Juan sin tierra* (1975), show a progressive complexity and sophistication not seen in contemporary Spanish literature. In addition to the very obvious typographical layout, these novels use Formalist devices such as laying bare, literary borrowing, retardation, and defamiliarization, but most important is the noticeable awareness Goytisolo has for the relationship between form and content. There are radical differences among these novels as well: *Señas de identidad*, flawed from a Formalist viewpoint, has certain conventional aspects; *Don Julián*, on the other hand, a radical departure from conventional works, can be called a novel; *Juan sin tierra*, however, must be considered a new genre for which there are no precedents. The following three chapters will show how they differ from Goytisolo's conventional period and from one another.

The title, *Señas de identidad*,[1] alludes to the psychological state of the protagonist who searches for some "signs of identity." The story is thus an intense psychoanalysis of the main character from his birth to his present. Yet the work is in no way a psychological novel *à la* nineteenth century, particularly because seldom does an omniscient narrator assume control of the events.

There are instances, however, in which the author's intentions are revealed and the novel becomes a testimonial of sorts, as can be gathered from the following statement made by the protagonist: "Evoca (transcribe) esta escena por que no muera contigo" (p. 389). Furthermore, the novel contains three epigraphs relevant not only to Álvaro's characterization, but to Spanish civilization as well:

Ayer se fue: Mañana no ha llegado;
FRANCISCO DE QUEVEDO

Vamos claros, dije yo para mí; ¿dónde está el cementerio? ¿Fuera o dentro? . . . El cementerio está dentro de Madrid. Madrid es el cementerio.
MARIANO JOSÉ DE LARRA

Mejor la destrucción, el fuego.
LUIS CERNUDA

The story concerns Álvaro Mendiola, a Spanish emigré living in France, who, shortly after suffering a heart attack at the age

---

[1] This study uses the second edition (1969), revised by the author. Juan Goytisolo, *Señas de identidad*, (2nd ed.; México: Editorial Joaquín Mortiz, S.A., 1969). Hereafter all references will be given in parentheses in the text. In the following excerpt from a letter to Christian Meerts published in *Technique et Visions dans "Señas de identidad" de Jun Goytisolo*, Analecta Romanica Heft 31 (Frankfurt Am Main: Vittorio Klostermann, 1972), p. 81, Goytisolo stresses his view that the 1969 version of the novel is the definitive one: ". . . aunque halle Vd. referencias en ellos que sirvan de apoyo a su análisis, este 'apoyo' me parece inútil, puesto que no forman parte del libro en su versión definitiva."

of thirty-two, begins a sentimental journey back to the past. This retrospective voyage to two time-frames, the distant past of his ancestors and the very near past, a few days prior to the moment in which the narration begins, serves a twofold purpose: one is self-discovery, a search for his *raison d'etre*, as well as his "true" identity, and is also a panoramic examination and reflection upon the many ills afflicting Spain during the first half of the twentieth century. The novel, in brief, is primordially an *examen de conciencia* which transcends the individual engaging in the act allowing the reader a peek into every secret thought, at the same time it exposes critically his cultural background, his Spanish collective unconscious.[2]

The plot of *Señas de identidad* is a significant departure from the modest degree of experimentation found in *Duelo en el Paraíso* and *Fiestas*. Here it consists of combining the main theme, the life of the protagonist, with a few subthemes and a score of free motifs, which give a great deal of background material about Álvaro. Basically, the subthemes and free motifs complement and expand the main theme, directly or indirectly. The many events which make up the life of the protagonist are presented through different layers of time and space. These emerge from Álvaro's reaction after he examines certain documents and photographs. The usual result is a voyage into the past, giving the reader a fascinating perspective of remote events involving long-dead ancestors, things Álvaro never knew, as well as his own childhood. Additionally, there seems to be a somewhat veiled self-analysis from which the reader may gain more information if he makes a careful examination of the protagonist's extremely subjective allusions and statements. The reader not only finds a perspective of the past and the present, but may also speculate about Álvaro's future. Álvaro's life is interwoven with anecdotes

---

[2] This aspect will be more patent in *Reivindicación del conde Julián*.

about his friend Antonio. The political activism of other Spaniards and the manner in which the police react and try to destroy any form of subversion are also presented. In addition to these subthemes, many free motifs contribute to a panoramic perspective of the environment within which the novel develops, and frequently construct a tableau beyond the purview of the protagonist himself.

Álvaro's friend, Antonio, a hardened revolutionary, lives for the moment when Spain will have a Marxist form of government. He has been in jail many times for his subversive activities and at one point is confined to a small town, Hornillo. He must report once a week to the local police office to sign and cannot leave the general area: "Los sábados Antonio se presentaba a firmar en la casa cuartel y platicaba unos minutos con el teniente" (p. 186). His general behavior contrasts sharply with Álvaro's, which could lead the reader to believe he is Mendiola's alter ego. Whereas Álvaro's political perspective has changed dramatically with the years, Antonio continues active in his struggle to free Spain from Franco's regime. Since his characterization is indirectly related to Álvaro's and underscores the general struggle of Spaniards unsympathetic to totalitarian government, it cannot be classified as a fully developed theme.

A similar judgment must be passed upon the subtheme of political activism in which Álvaro and Antonio collaborate with the large number of Spanish exiles who appear in the novel. While focusing on this subtheme, Goytisolo criticizes not only the Spanish government and all its injustices, but also the exiles with their petty quarrels which lead them to chronic divisionism:

> La convocatoria llevaba el aval de una veintena de personalidades de nombre remotamente familiar que representaban, a su vez, agrupaciones tales que Izquierda Republicana, Partido Republicano Federal, Unión Republicana, Esquerra Catalana, Partido Republicano Gallego e incluso una Alianza Democrática Valenciana Sección Exterior. (pp. 264–265)

111

The last subtheme to be examined seems designed to provide the cold and dehumanized perspective of a police state. The text of police reports is interpolated with the account of the confinement of Antonio in Hornillo, illustrating the day-by-day, hour-by-hour police vigilance of deviants, one of whom is Antonio, and their eventual incarceration:

> Domingo, día 3—A las 8'45 salen Gorila y Gitano de casa de éste y se trasladan en autobús al final de la calle Mallorca, en las inmediaciones de la Sagrada Familia. En la portería del 530 contactan con un individuo bautizado Ramallets. Van los tres al bar Compostela y toman un café. (p. 168)

It is interesting to note the humor involved in some of the code names used by the police. For instance, Gorila is perhaps an allusion to *Fiestas*. In another police report, one of the subversives is called Cocteau. The direct connection between the police vigilance subtheme, the main theme and the Antonio subtheme can be observed in this report:

> Jueves, día 11—Identificado Ondulado como Antonio Ramírez Trueba, natural de Águilas, Murcia, domiciliado en la Pensión Zamora, Calabria 116. Doctor en derecho y alumno de la escuela diplomática. Señalado en la universidad por sus simpatías marxistas en su expediente figura como acompañante de Álvaro Mendiola autor del film antiespañol sobre la emigración obrera intervenido por la guardia civil de Yeste, Albacete, el 23–8–58. (p. 228)

Since most of the events have already occurred and the reader is exposed to them piecemeal, *Señas de identidad* is an excellent example of delayed exposition. The climax is Álvaro's heart attack and his realization that his death is probably near. Most events in his past, the environment in which he grew up, his ancestors, his psychological state are revealed through hints and incidental remarks, a characteristic of delayed exposition. Many instances, however, facilitate clarification of incidents whose ramifications the reader must understand. Such undertakings call for time shifts in the narration of the story material, a good example of transposed exposition.

The narration follows a seesaw approach, shifting between subjectivity and objectivity. Schwartz comments on this, saying that Goytisolo "employs every imaginable technique. . .first, second, and third-person singular; first, second and third-person plural; interior monologue; flashbacks; stream-of-consciousness; and rapidly shifting images and scenes."[3] Other techniques not mentioned by this critic include: dialogue, typographical changes, the cold bureaucratic exposition of the police reports, and also a somewhat complex narrative style which could be considered as oral transcription. Had there been the means to do it, it is plausible that those portions of the novel would have been presented on magnetic tapes for the reader to hear rather than read, a technique of oral transcription rendered much better in *Juan sin tierra*. From among the wealth of narrative motifs, this study will present examples only of those viewpoints deemed particularly significant.

The novel opens with a chorus which voices disapproval of Álvaro's behavior:

> Instalado en París cómodamente instalado en París con más años de permanencia en Francia que en España con más costumbres francesas que españolas incluso en el ya clásico amancebamiento con la hija de una notoria personalidad del exilio residente habitual en la Ville Lumière y visitante episódico de su patria a fin de dar un testimonio parisiense de la vida española. . . . (p. 9)

This viewpoint is that of a collectivity representing the Spanish establishment and its perspective on the exiles.

From the chorus the novel shifts to a second-person

---

[3] Kessel Schwartz, *Juan Goytisolo* (New York: Twayne Publishers, Inc., 1970), pp. 102–03. Hereafter the page number will be given in parentheses at th end of the text cited.

singular viewpoint that explains what has taken place on the preceding pages:

> Así hablaban de ti, al divulgarse el incidente del documental, en cafés y tertulias, reuniones y veladas, los hombres y mujeres satisfechos que un decreto irrisorio del destino te había otorgado, al nacer, como paisanos, barrosos amigos de infancia, inocuos compañeros de estudio, parientas de mirada frígida y torva, familiares virtuosos y tristes, encastillados todos en sus inexpugnables privilegios de clase.... (p. 11)

From this point of view Álvaro begins a series of "Proustian" flashbacks triggered by an old album of photographs, some religious books and documents belonging to his ancestors. In the excerpt to follow, the reminiscing takes place while he is looking at some old photos:

> ... y buscar entre los estantes de la maciza biblioteca el álbum de retratos que tal vez te permitiera recobrar la perdida clave de tu niñez y tu juventud. De nuevo podías volver al jardín y acomodarte con aquél en la mesa de mármol, aspirando el aroma antiguo y mohoso de sus págins; observar con aplacado sosiego el paisaje insomme, el cielo y mar maleables, el sol enrojecido y moribundo: .... (p. 16)

The first-person plural point of view is employed to rationalize the conformism that followed the Civil War:

> ... Nosotros no tenemos la culpa en realidad no sabíamos nada cierto que en el 39 adherimos masivamente a la Falange o al Requeté y vestimos a nuestras hijas de Luceros o Margaritas y a nuestro hijos de Flechas o de Pelayos pero lo hicimos por razones de puro patriotismo como reacción lógica contra los desórdenes funestos de antes desórdenes que ni tan siquiera hoy ningún hombre de buena fe puede negar sin equivocación.... (p. 32)

Some of the most objective portions of the novel are narrated in the third-person singular viewpoint:

> En las melancólicas semanas que precedieron al fallecimiento de su madre, Álvaro había seguido con inquietud la erosión lenta pero continua de las posiciones alemanas en el frente del Este. Tíos

y primos se habían instalado en el piso al acecho del desenlace y en el duermevela de las pesadillas y los insomnios las frases hoscas y premonitorias del tío Eulogio cobraban una tangible y angustiosa precisión. . . . (p. 36)

The second-person plural perspective is best illustrated by this segment in which the "narrators" establish a simile between an anthill and the Spanish people:

> Allanad con el pie las múltiples bocas de un hormiguero, pacientemente construido grano a grano sobre terreno ingrato y arenoso y pasad el día siguiente por el lugar· lo veréis de nuevo sutil y floreciente, como una plasmación del instir.to gregal de su comunidad laboriosa y terca, así la habitación natural de la fauna española, la ancestral y siempre calumniada barraca de caña y latón, ... (p. 64)

Dialogue is frequently used in its familiar function of providing insights objectively and serves to keep the author outside the narration, unable to intervene in what is taking place. In the following narrative motif two or three conversations appear to occur at the same time (spacing is Goytisolo's):

> —Esto me recuerda una anécdota que me ocurrió la víspera del levantamiento de Fígols, durante el segundo ministerio de Azaña. . . .
> —Yo pensaba escapar de alli camino de Alicante, cuando me entero por la radio de la caída de Madrid y la victoria de los fascistas. . . .
> —. . .A mí había enviado el Sindicato desde Barcelona para discutir con los representantes de los patronos. . . .
> —. . .La casa lindaba justamente con el comedor de Auxilio Social y, como yo no quería comprometer a mi amigo, me descolgué una noche por la ventana sin prevenirle. . . . (p. 281)

In a few instances stream-of-consciousness plays its normal role, giving perspective to the narrator's most intimate thoughts:

> Consecuencias físicas y morales del acto impuro. Clasificación de las jerarquías celestiales con las propiedades específicas de cada una de ellas. Tesino, Trebia, Trasimeno, Canas. Pichincha, Chim-

borazo y Cotopaxi. Binomio de Newton. Ovíparos, vivíparos, ovi-vivíparos. Barbara, celare, darii, ferio. Fórmula del bicarbonato sódico. Teorema de Pitágoras. (p. 58)

The cold bureaucratic exposition is observed in a police report which gives an account of the surveillance of some subversive elements:

> ... Son las 21'01. Del automóvil se apean una mujer y un hombre, el último con aspecto de extranjero, que son bautizados respectivamente Escuchi y Cocteau. Escuchi abraza y besa a Gorila. Cocteau le estrecha la mano, entra en el coche y saca una maleta. La cartera de color claro debe de quedar dentro pues no se la vuelve a ver más. Escuchi y Gorila paran un taxi y llevan la maleta al domicilio de Gitano.... (p. 210)

"Oral exposition" appears in italics, usually presented through the first-person singular viewpoint. In most instances it seems to be the voice of a Spanish émigré who tells Mendiola the woes he has suffered. The source of what appears to be a biographical sketch is perhaps a manuscript for Álvaro's documentary. He is either reading or remembering what some inhabitants of Almería and other deprived sections have told him about their social condition. The presentation is so done that the reader has the feeling he is listening to a tape rather than reading, (indentation is Goytisolo's):

> Y a los seis meses de haber llegado a Tarrasa me mujer tuvo una niña que nació antes de hora y nosotros buscamos un poco de ayuda porque no teníamos dinero para que la enterraran y todo el mundo se desentendía de nosotros así la tuvimos tres días metida en un cesto que es en mi vida lo que más pena me de pues no se ha visto cosa así en el mundo entero tener que llevarla en un cesto a la funeraria esto es justicia esto es dignidad tener que llevar esta niña coma si fuera un cesto. (p. 382)

At times either internal monologue or stream-of-consciousness is combined with dialogue. Álvaro recalls events, his trend of thought interrupted by italics which indicate that somebody is speaking. In the following segment he thinks about Dolores' abortion, and Luisito, her nephew, interrupts him, asking about the film they are watching.

estará acostada en la cama quién sabe si querrá abusar de ella *por qué se esconde* pour vous élargir vous comprenez *oh mira que hacen* los labios viscosos sobre su piel *son buenos o malos* la deprimente habitación de la clínica del Bel-Air los abetos el panorama suizo del lago *quién es el señor gordo* la bufanda anudada a la falleba la maldita semilla *se quiere escapar verdad* todo ha sido inútil estaba escrito que debía terminar en Suiza en alguna cloaca inmunda en el fondo del Léman. . . . (p. 353)

Because of the numerous narrating motifs the novel has an appearance of prose-collage. Unlike previous novels, however, the shifting of viewpoints is not rough and chaotic. There is now a smooth transition from one motif to another, and all the narrative pieces are so compatible that they seem to flow into one another.

Since the novel is a voyage through time, there are many direct and indirect references to dates and historical events, as well as a myriad of devices that provide a chronological compass for the excursion. The first instance in which a time-motif occurs is when the second-person singular narrator indirectly informs the reader that a person, Álvaro, is listening to Mozart's *Requiem* and is drinking Fefiñanes, a Galician wine (p. 13), establishes that it is ten minutes to seven and that there is a record player in the room. The wine and record player are important as sign posts of the present. After numerous flashbacks, the music and the bottle inform the reader that Álvaro has returned to the present, for example, on pages 13, 31, 41, 60, 125, and 148. The entire narration appears to take place on three and a half days during the month of August: " . . .Agosto del año de gracia del 63" (p. 414). Through flashbacks Álvaro goes to an era in which he was not yet born, as does Stern with

Tristram Shandy.[4] The following segment in which he speaks of his uncle Nestor is a good example:

> ... de revolucionario y dandy, héroe catalán y vagabundo (el tío abuelo Néstor había dilapidado una fortuna en el casino de Montecarlo, vivió amacebado con una tumultuosa poetisa irlandesa, separatista catalán militó en favor de la rebelión de los Sinne-Fein y se suicidó a los treinta y cinco años en un sanatorio suizo, colgándose de la ventana de su habitación con su propia bufanda). (p. 56)

Álvaro returns to his childhood during the Civil War (p. 19) and to many other moments of importance in his life. The heart attack obviously triggers this constant reminiscing, recalling the common belief that a dying man recalls all his life, in a flash, shortly before he expires. Certainly, fear of the nearness of death seems to have had that effect on Álvaro Mendiola.

The place of action in the novel is both static and dynamic. It is static because most events take place in the mind of the protagonist; he recalls, while sitting down or reclining, most of what occurs. Nevertheless, there is a considerable amount of movement, of traveling. Antonio, for instance, does move about. Thus, the novel's place of action may be viewed as static as well as dynamic. Two important bound motifs directly related to the development of the story frequently fuse into each other. The first is the protagonist's obsessive wish to compose a documentary to show the world the social conditions of contemporary Spain. The second portrays the psychological state of Álvaro Mendiola that causes him to embark on a profound self-analysis, frequently merging with a painful dissection of Spanish culture.

The first bound motif mentioned above is evident

---

[4] Goytisolo mentioned in an interview conducted by Claude Couffon, cited in the Introduction, his having read and translated into Spanish Victor Shklovsky's essay on *Tristram Shandy*:". . . les essais de Chlovsky, en particulier, me paraissent remarquables, et j'ai même traduit en espagnol celui qui est consacré à *Tristram Shandy*. . . " (p. VI).

throughout the novel. Álvaro is filming a sociological documentary exposing the reasons for the Spanish exodus to other European countries:

> La idea de un documental sociológico sobre las razones de su emigración, la exposición filmada de su doloroso periplo (la lenta y penosa huida de la miseria a partir de sus orígenes campesinos) se impuso de pronto en tu conciencia como una empresa no sólo apasionante sino (por la rebeldía que implicaba contra tu destino común de español heredero de la situación creada como resultado de la guerra civil) estrictamente necesaria. . . . (p. 378)

The documentary, however, is never finished because Spanish authorities confiscate the portion Álvaro has filmed and forbid him to continue shooting.[5] As a consequence, he decides to use prose as the means to present the situation. After his heart attack, Álvaro engages in self-examination and, in order to do a thorough job, finds he must analyze the environment in which he was reared. This leads to his bitter criticism of the Spanish establishment as well as the exiles residing in Paris. His overwhelming need to find some means to identify himself while undertaking a concrete and precise form of protest is best observed in this segment: " . . .aquí se ahorcó tu tío Néstor antes de que tú nacieras en su habitación del sanatorio de Bel-Air y su rebeldía contra la sociedad española de su tiempo murió con él como morirá sin duda la tuya si no le das forma concreta y precisa . . ." (pp. 345–46).

Four important dynamic motifs in the novel influence the development of the story and the outcome: the heart attack, a sort of abulia overcoming Álvaro, the confiscation of his documentary, and Dolores' abortion. Álvaro suffers the attack in March, 1963 (p. 365), causing his life and psychological make-up to undergo a metamorphosis. He looks upon it as rebirth of sorts:

---

[5] Much of this portion seems to combine his experience in *La isla* and the travelogues. There is no evidence, at the moment, as to whether Goytisolo had a heart attack.

> En aquel hospital anónimo de la anónima y dilatada ciudad, durante las largas noches en vela y su silencio puntuado con toses y con ayes, había vuelto a la vida horro de pasado como de futuro, extraño y ajeno a ti mismo, dúctil, maleable, sin patria, sin hogar, sin amigos, puro presente incierto, macido a tus treinta y dos años, Álvaro Mendiola a secas, sin señas de identidad. (p. 367)

His resurrection awakens him to the realization that he has no signs of identity. He thereupon proceeds to find a means to provide his life with some meaning, some purpose. In order to acquire it, a profound self-analysis and an examination of his cultural background are deemed necessary.

Acute introspection induces an abulic state that slowly detaches him from the present and submerges him into a continuous scrutiny of his past and of his ancestors. The confiscation of his documentary film and Dolores' abortion are also instrumental in preparing the outcome triggered by the heart attack. The abortion, which Álvaro could have stopped, is considered a form of rebellion against Spain; it is another means to break away from his culture, his religion, and even his life.[6] Mendiola draws an interesting parallel between himself and his great-uncle Nestor, whose suicide was in the same city where Dolores is having the abortion (the punctuation and form are Goytisolo's):

> como él quisiste romper con todo lo que recibiste de prestado con todo cuanto sin pedirlo tú te dieron ellos dios religión moral leyes fortuna . . . . (p. 349)

> Ginebra es una estación terminal nadie puede vivir impúnemente en ella tío Néstor no pudo elegir sitio mejor para acabar ni Dolores para destruir el germen de la odiada semilla . . . . (p. 351)

Such an act could also be construed as a death wish, a form of suicide.

---

[6] There is an interesting parallel between Álvaro Mendiola and Camus' Mersault. The latter goes to see a comedy the day on which his mother dies, and the former goes to see a film starring the Marx Brothers while Dolores is aborting their child (p. 352).

The confiscation of his film by the Spanish authorities is a great shock to Álvaro, perhaps conducive to the abulic state brought on by the heart attack. These four dynamic motifs keep the story moving; they are the reasons for Mendiola's state of mind and his general behavior. The reader has no way of knowing whether Mendiola has managed to transcribe what he has experienced and witnessed. Toward the end of the novel, however, where he states, "adelante pues" (p. 414), there seems to be the suggestion of a possible move to make a tangible presentation. *Reivindicación del conde don Julián* and *Juan sin tierra* will show Mendiola's metamorphosis.

The complexity of the plot of *Señas de identidad* is the direct result of the mass of free motifs appearing in the novel. Here Goytisolo begins to build more complex plots. Since free motifs dominate and determine the construction of the plot, their numbers are increased. One group of motifs triggers flashbacks *à la* Proust and causes digressions. These are directly responsible for some of the narrative techniques, but are also free because they bring about a thickening of the plot. These include the photographs, the Atlas, the voices Álvaro "hears," and the old documents he utilizes for his voyages back in time. The flashbacks are in essence digressions; yet to a great extent they contribute to the development of Álvaro's character, giving the reader a wealth of information which would otherwise be unknown. In the following example Álvaro looks at some old pictures among which is one of his uncle Eulogio, who was in Cuba when the Spanish Civil War began and whom Alvaro finds interesting:

> Por las páginas mustias del album el tío Eulogio aparecía a intervalos con su misterioso material científico, de visita en los umbrosos cafetales de Nicaragua o huesped insólito de los Mendiola residentes en Cuba. En su juventud se había entregado en cuerpo y alma al estudio y prospección de los astros. . . . (p. 34)

The Atlas brings forth more contemporary memories: "Pasabas despaciosamente las páginas del atlas y cada lámina en colores de la accidentada y mudable geografía política europea traía a tu memoria alguna imagen que, como acusación o descargo, se agregaba al expediente de tu historia común con Dolores y, de modo sutil, lo modificaba . . ." (p. 341).

Homosexuality, another free motif, is also prevalent in earlier novels. Álvaro apparently had several homosexual affairs. One, latent or actual, was with Jerónimo, a laborer on his uncle Cesar's ranch. He frequently slept in the barn with Jerónimo:

> Jerónimo te recibía con una sonrisa, encendía dos cigarrillos, te dejaba su manta, apagaba la luz. Hablar, lo que se dice hablar, poco os hablabais. ¿Qué había en común entre él y tú? Sólo el tuteo amigo y la sonrisa, la llaneza del gesto y el acuerdo animal, más allá de la palabras. ¿Confiaba en ti? Seguramente. Más de una vez extendiste el brazo durante su sueño y presentiste, agradecido, el bulto bienhechor del revólver en su cinto. (p. 47)

There is nothing definite here from which one might derive a clear conclusion about Álvaro's homosexuality, other than the possibly symbolic reference to the gun. In the following passage, however, Álvaro seems to be speaking of love, a possible basis for arguing that there are aspects of latent homosexuality, if not overt consummation:

> Fue a comienzos de octubre—lo recordabas bien: en víspera de reanudarse las clases y tornar la familia a Barcelona—la noche en que lo esperaste en vano y él no regresó. Volviste a tu habitación aterido, con una ansiedad y un tormento que no reconocerías sino mucho más tarde, enamorado ya de Dolores, en el estudio de la rue Vielle du Temple concebido, diríase, para el amor y la ventura, y privado tú, por tu culpa, del uno y de la otra, en uno de aquellos años mutilados y harapientos que luego bautizarían Años de Paz. (p. 48)

In the same paragraph there occurs an allusion to a brief homosexual encounter Álvaro was to experience many years later in Paris:

> . . . El árabe se demora a mirar con expresión ausente. Al llegar tú y seguir su ejemplo te examina unos segundos con sus ojos profundos y negros. Ha sacado la mano derecha del bolsillo de la

zamarra y, de modo mecánico, se acaricia el bigote con el índice y el pulgar.

El metro pasa zumbando encima de vosotros y su sacudida estremece brutalmente el suelo. Sustraído de pronto al tiempo y al espacio recuerdas que un día, en un hotelucho cercano, hiciste el amor (¿con quién?) aprisa y corriendo (era tarde, tenías una cita en la France Presse) y tu eyaculación había coincidio exactamente con el temblor provocado por el tránsito de los vagones. . . . (p. 340)

In the same vein of thought, Álvaro remembers Jerónimo and how he has been reincarnated several times:

(Como necesario horizonte para ti, el rostro de Jerónimo, de las sucesivas reencarnaciones de Jerónimo en algún rostro delicado e imperioso, soñador y violento había velado en filigrana los altibajos de tu pasión por Dolores con la fuerza magnética y brusca con que te fulminara la primera vez. Cuando os separasteis se fue sin darte su dirección ni pedirte la tuya. Tenía dos mujeres, seis hijos y nunca supiste cómo se llamaba.) (p. 340)

Furthermore, Álvaro comments to himself on Dolores' boyish appearance: "El pelo corto, peinado sobre la frente, le daba una apariencia ambigua (feliz) de muchacho" (pp. 324–25). The comment in parentheses is perhaps an allusion to the overt homosexuality—or bisexuality—of the protagonist. The homosexual motif appears in the traumatic experience of Álvaro's landlady, Madame de Heredia. Crying, she tells Álvaro, ". . . le salaud il a foutu le camp avec mon fils" (p. 335). It appears that the man she thinks is courting her is in love with her son.

Another free motif is that of the overpowering mother, illustrated by Ana, Sergio's mother. Álvaro meets Sergio when he is a student at the university, and the two young men become close friends. As Álvaro recalls their friendship, the reader perceives a possible incestuous attraction between mother and son. Sergio tells Ana about his sexual escapades, and his narration pleases her immensely: " 'Contadme,' decía. '¿Qué tal ha ido hoy?' Sergio refería las incidencias eróticas de la tarde y Ana reía silenciosa y exigía precisiones" (p. 90).

Eventually, however, when Sergio seems to have fallen in love with a girl of his own age, Ana's behavior changes, and jealousy overcomes her:

> Cesasteis de frecuentaros y, a escondidas de él, Ana te telefoneaba todos los días, interminablemente, confiándote sus temores respecto a una hipotética boda e informándote de paso que tu amigo jamás venía a dormir a casa: "¿Qué crees que debo hacer? . . . Ha descubierto que no puedo virvir sin él y se divierte jugando conmigo. Ayer se asomó sólo a pedirme dinero y no quiso siquiera que le besase. . . ." Aquella primavera os habíais visto alguna vez en secreto y Ana tenía los ojos irritados de llorar y parecía haber envejecido de golpe. . . . (p. 93)

She begins to use Álvaro as her confidant, wanting him to intercede on her behalf, which leads to dissolution of the friendship between the two young men. Ana's behavior reminds the reader of the image-maker's wife in *La resaca*, whose love for the boy was maternal as well as sexual.

The spider[7] motif appears in this novel, related to heterosexual intercourse. There seems to be an innate fear of either the female or of the sexual act—perhaps both. In the following scene Antonio brutally requests a prostitute to perform *fellatio* on him. As he lies back on the bed, the *mosquero* above becomes a spider:

> La cabeza de la mujer bajaba y subía entre sus piernas a un ritmo a la vez intenso y entorpecedor y Antonio se tumbó hacia atrás con las manos bajo la nuca y la vista fija en el mosquero de papel que—como una araña immensa que amenazara engullirlo todo—se balanceaba en el techo suave, muy suavemente. (p. 208)

It appears that Antonio, to some extent Álvaro's alter ego, has an innate fear which induces the sort of free association indicated above. Furthermore, Antonio's visit to the prostitute

---

[7] Erich Neumann, in *The Origin and History of Consciousness*, trans. R. F. C. Hull, Bollingen Series XLII (New York: Pantheon Books Inc., 1954), p. 87, says that the spider can be classified as a symbol of devouring chasm; it represents the female in general, who spreads nets for the unwary male.

occurs immediately after an excruciating evening at the home of the town physician, embodiment of the *status quo*. Thus, Antonio is releasing his anger by humiliating the prostitute.

Another free motif is the deficiency of a Catholic education. Álvaro Mendiola's behavior is the result of a religious upbringing in Spain where sex is looked upon, according to Goytisolo, as an unwholesome and sinful act. In the following scene the young Álvaro confesses his sins to a priest:

> —Padre, me acuso de haber faltado tres veces contra el sexto mandamiento.
> —¿De pensamiento o con acciones, hijo mío?
> —De las dos maneras.
> —¿Solo o acompañado?
> —Un amigo me enseñó una revista con mujeres y yo se la compré.
> —¿La miraste con él?
> —Sí.
> —¿Os tocasteis?
> —No, cuando se fue él pequé yo solo.
> —¿Sabías que cometías una falta grave?
> —Sí.
> —Entre todas los pecados es ése el que ofende más a Dios y a la Virgen Santísima. ¿Te arrepientes sinceramente?
> —Sí, padre. (p. 57)

The religious criticism implicit above needs no further elaboration. There is also an inclination towards masochism in the Church which dates back to the Christian martyrs, Goytisolo seems to be saying. As a young boy, Álvaro has a governess, Lourdes, whose only ambition in life is to become a martyr. She buys him books about the lives of children who die martyrs. On one occasion, during the first months of the Civil War, Lourdes tries to martyr Álvaro and herself by walking into a burning church.

> —¡Alto! ¿Adónde van?
> Un hombre malo, barbudo y mal vestido, se había plantado ante vosotros con los brazos en jarras.
> —A la única y verdadera Iglesia fundada por Nuestro Señor Jesucristo—dijo de un tirón la señorita Lourdes.

—¿No ven ustedes que está ardiendo?

—La gracia del Señor nos protegerá de las llamas.

Otros hombres armados y sucios se habían acercado a vosotros y os contemplaban—creías recordarlo—con una miscelánea de humor y curiosidad. (pp. 29–30)

Evidently her behavior leaves a sadomasochistic vein in Álvaro, an aspect of his character more evident in *Reivindicación del conde don Julián*.

Another free motif is the desire to return to the womb, perhaps caused in Alvaro by the many traumatic experiences of his upbringing. During those moments when depression overcomes him, he would like to crawl back into Dolores' womb:

Aproximarte a la cama de Dolores, oír su respiración, palpar su cuerpo, deslizar los labios sobre su vientre, bajar al sexo, demorarte en él, buscar un refugio, perderte en su hondura, reintegrar tu prehistoria materna y fetal.

Ojala, te decías, no hubieras salido nunca. (p. 158).

The loss of innocence motif appears frequently throughout Goytisolo's novels. In *Señas de identidad* Álvaro loses his virginity at the hands of a prostitute:

La habitación era pequeña, mal ventilada. El lecho sucio. El armario deprimente. Te desnudaste, temblando, sin atreverte a mirar su cuerpo avergonzado como estabas del tuyo propio, maravillado, al fin, al comprobar que el roce experto de sus dedos hacía de ti un hombre que, aunque con torpeza, se tendía sobre ella y, más torpemente aun, la penetraba (siempre guiado por su mano), encendidas las mejillas, rojos los pómulos, fundidos los dos hasta el placer crispado que te había devuelto a la vida tras aquellos segundos inacabables de olvido, de muerte. . . . (p. 78)

The executioner-victim motif also appears in this novel, associated with the Civil War in the following passage:

. . . Evocados unos y olvidados otros, fusilados del verano del 36 y de la primavera del 39 eran todos, juntamente, verdugos y víctimas, eslabones de la cadena represiva iniciada meses antes de la guerra a raíz de la matanza acaecida en Yeste en pleno gobierno del Frente Popular. (p. 110)

Álvaro probably considers himself a victim of his cultural circumstances and looks upon Spain as a "severa e inmortal Madrastra" (p. 375).

The betrayal-motif is encountered throughout the novel. There is a faint suggestion that Antonio betrays his comrades in exchange for his confinement in Hornillo. In a conversation between Dolores and Antonio, the latter informs her of gossip against him in Barcelona:

> En la terraza del balneario, mientras cenaban al borde del agua, Antonio le puso al tanto de los chismes que corrían sobre él en Barcelona: uno de los detenidos—condenado después a siete años a causa de sus propias revelaciones—pretendía que Antonio había denunciado también a los compañeros y—pese a la total carencia de pruebas—algunos amigos del grupo aconsejaban, contra toda lógica, una política de vacío. . . . (p. 197)

Even if Antonio is innocent, the motif of betrayal is present because of the reactions of Antonio's friends—they abandon him. Álvaro sometimes feels he has betrayed his friends and his country because he has not taken an active role in the liberation of Spain.

> . . . tu aventura propia y la de tu patria habían tomado rumbos divergentes: por un lado ibas tú, rotos los vínculos que te ligaran antaño a la tribu, borracho y atónito de tu nueva e increíble libertad; por otro aquélla con el grupo de tus amigos que persistían en el noble empeño de transformarla pagando con su cuerpo el precio que por indiferencia o cobardía habías rehusado pasar tú, . . . (p. 159)

The escape-motif is observed throughout the novel as well. Álvaro's behavior is, to some extent, a form of escape. His overwhelming desire to return to the womb is an obvious desire to retreat from reality. Closely knit to the escape-motif is that of splitting his personality, keeping himself detached to examine his cultural heritage as both participant and witness:

Pese a tus esfuerzos de sítesis los diversos elementos de la historia se descomponían como los colores de un rayo luminoso refractado en un prisma y, en virtud de un extraño desdoblamiento, asistías a su desfile ocioso simultáneamente como actor y como testigo, espectador, cómplice y protagonista a la vez del remoto y obsesionante drame. (p. 110)

The *fiesta*-motif also appears in *Señas de identidad* and, as in previous novels, the celebration is overcome by a negative aspect. The "Programa Oficial de Fiestas" of Yeste is reproduced in its entirety (p. 126). Thereafter Goytisolo juxtaposes a gory *novillada* withe the massacre of La Graya, the two events merging so that spectators of the *novillada* seem to be witnessing the assassination of a groups of peasants:

> . . . Olivadados en medio del campo yacen cuatro cadáveres. Una mujer llora arrodillada junto a uno de los cuerpos. El hombre herido en el brazo y la pierna agoniza aún, perdiendo sangre y escupiendo baba. El sol brilla implacablemente y hormigas y moscas se disputan el inesperado festín bajo la presencia agorera de los buitres que, en círculos tenaces y concéntricos, planean sin prisa sobre los olivares.
> Gorras, boinas, calzones de pana, blusas, mandiles, pañuelos amudados al cuello, chalecos sucios, alpargatas: mozos, adultos, viejos, chiquillos se amontonan en las trancas horizontales de las talanqueras al acecho del portal en donde está enchiquerado el novillo. . . . (p. 145)

The description of both events is very explicit and should be considered a step beyond *tremendismo*. The following scene in which two young men tear off the bull's tail is a vivid example: "Unos mozos se agarran al rabo del bicho y tiran con tanta fuerza de él que, medio desprendido ya por el corte de la cuadrilla, lo arrancan de cuajo. El novillo parece insensible al nuevo desastre y observa el espeso caldo humano con ojos sanguinolentos . . ." (p. 147).

Perhaps the most important motif of the novel is its experimental linguistic aspect.[8] Goytisolo himself writes that

---

[8] In *Reivindicación del conde don Julián* the linguistic experimentation is even more important.

"el lenguaje, y sólo el lenguaje puede ser subversivo" (*Libre,* p. 39). In one essay of *El furgón de cola,* he writes about Ferdinand de Saussure's dichotomy of *langue* and *parole.* The former is a social institution, whereas the latter is subjective and varies from one individual to another. Goytisolo deems this dichotomy of great importance to writers and says that "La oscilación del escritor entre el lenguaje ideal y el efectivo no es . . . un fenómeno secundario y circunstancial por el contrario . . . se sitúa en el centro mismo de la creación artística."[9] Carlos Fuentes in *La nueva novel hispanoamericana,* however, sees the language utilized by Goytisolo in *Señas de identidad* and *Reivindicación del conde don Julián* as a form of social criticism:

> La implacable intención crítica de Goytisolo es demostrar la falsedad y corrupción del tradicional lenguaje literario español y demostrar en qué medida las instituciones morales, económicas y políticas de España se fundan en la consagración de una retórica en la que los valores de la "pureza" y del "casticismo" justifican una cultura cerrada y un sistema de dependencias y relaciones de sumisión. . . . (p. 80)[10]

He also considers the juxtaposition of different forms of narrative an ironic and destructive endeavor leading to a totally new language; the novel is thus the vehicle for both destruction and creation.

The language motif of *Señas* is presented in numerous ways, some of which have already been mentioned; five examples will suffice to illustrate its major applications. They are the employment of anagrams, puns, literary borrowing, blasphemous prayers (which touch upon the religious criticism motif), and the use of foreign words and phrases. By the use of anagram in the following segment the narrator changes the headline in a newspaper to read in disparate ways (the following quotation marks are Goytisolo's):

---

[9] Juan Goytisolo, *El furgón de cola* (Paris: Ruedo Ibérico, 1967), p. 136.
[10] Carlos Fuentes, *La nueva novela hispanoamericana* (México: Joaquín Mortiz, 1969), p. 80.

. . . "Manolo Cuevas y Carlos Ribero cortaron orejas en San Sebastian de los Reyes." (p. 278)
. . . "Manola Orejas y Carlos cortaron riberos en San Sebastian de las Cuevas." (p. 278)
. . . "Sebastian Cuevas y Manolo Ribero cortaron reyes en San Carlos de las Orejas." (p. 279)
. . . "Sebastian Rivero y Reyes Orejas cortaron cuevas en San Manolo de los Carlos." (p. 279)

As for puns, the name of the town to which Antonio is confined is Hornillo. Again, while in the cemetery, during Ayuso's burial, Álvaro reads inscriptions in the tombs, one of which says: "EL ATENEO SINDICALISTA A SU CAMARADA AGUSTIN GIBAHELL" ((p. 106). A Catholic prayer becomes a blasphemous *esperpento* as Álvaro fuses religion with pagan ceremonies by invoking exotic deities. Perhaps in an allusion to his rebirth, he intones: "Alma de Ochún santifícame/cuerpo de Changó sálvame" (p. 410), a sharp contrast with the young Álvaro's recitation of the litany: "Alma de Cristo, santifícame . . . Cuerpo de Cristo. . . " (p. 29).

Literary borrowing is seen in his treatment of Machado's poem, "El mañana efímero," from which some lines are used within the text of his novel (the spacing is Goytisolo's; italics added):

Bruscamente un cuplé aflamencado sustituye la voz desfallecida del locutor
una vertiginosa síntesis de tópicos de *la España de charanga y pandereta* cerrado y sacristía
de gemidos de hembra sexilocua con rejas balcones claveles mantillas peinetas. . . . (p. 368)

Toward the end, typographical structure changes radically. There is very little punctuation; the lines are frequently short, sometimes leaving large margins at one side or the other; and in some instances lines are centered on the page. Frequently, foreign words and phrases give a collage appearance to the prose:

SALIDA
SORTIE

                    EXIT
                    AUSGANG
                    tout le monde est parti
                    come here my darling. . . . (p. 421)

Such typographical experimentation, which occasionally appears in earlier chapters, predominates in Chapter VIII. In his next novel, *Don Julián*, Goytisolo will utilize creative typography throughout. Frequent allusions to Arabic culture constitute another important free motif. Although observed in previous works, this motif predominates in the next two novels, the last one stressing the importance of this culture to Goytisolo.

Static motifs appear throughout in the descriptions of nature, local color, furnishings, and the behavior of secondary characters, many of them caricatures. The techniques of laying bare, defamiliarization, and retardation are continuously used throughout *Señas de identidad*. Laying bare is observed at the beginning of Chapter Four. The narration in such passages is presented by the second-person singular viewpoint:

> Tus esfuerzos de reconstitución y de síntesis tropezaban con un grave obstáculo. Merced a los documentos y pruebas atesorados en las carpetas podías desempolvar de tu memoria succesos e incidentes que tiempo atrás hubieras dado por perdidos y que rescatados del olvido por medio de aquellos permitían iluminar no sólo tu biografía sino también facetas oscuras y reveladoras de la vida en España. . . . (p. 159)

Defamiliarization may be seen in the juxtaposition of the massacre at *La Graya* and the bullfight. By presenting the two incidents side by side, the familiar becomes strange and thus more shocking. In the same vein, prayer is made strange by the introduction of pagan deities. The use of retardation is observed in the narrative technique and in the constant shifting of time and space. The usual purpose of the device is to build suspense by postponing the outcome of the narration. In *Señas de identidad* it seems geared to giving the narration a realistic flavor because it takes into account the protagonist's frame of mind; Álvaro does not seem capable of thinking in a straightforward, orderly manner: thus, the constant digressions.

Goytisolo's approach to the construction of *Señas de identidad* can be viewed as an example of artistic motivation. By using the techniques of defamiliarization and laying bare, he has broken the "illusion" of reality which would be present in a "realistic" novel. His intention appears to be that of presenting a work of art and, at the same time, a certain amount of social criticism. Nevertheless, unlike previous novels, that criticism is more objective and no longer the primary concern. *Señas de identidad,* the first of three novels from Goytisolo's mature period which this study calls *The Mendiola Trilogy,* is by no means his best work since it still has some compositional flaws.[11] The next two novels, *Don Julián* and *Juan sin tierra,* are Goytisolo's best to date.

---

[11] Goytisolo indicated to the writer in a conversation on March 23, 1975, that he is not satisfied with the novel as it is, and believes *Don Julián* is a better novel.

Chapter V

Reivindicación del Conde Don Julián

Reivindicación del conde don Julián (1970) follows more closely than previous novels many of the Formalists' theories. It is a continuation of what *Señas de identidad* began, Álvaro's search for a *raison d'etre,* and it appears that in *Don Julián* he has moved closer to his objective. The epigraphs provide a succinct preview of what is to happen. Two of them present a brief historical background of Don Julián, and the third evokes de Sade's means of achieving immortality: through evil. The protagonist is embarking on an immense evil deed seeking revenge, immortality, and an identity, a self of his own creation:

> Je voudrais trouver un crime dont l'effet perpétuel agît, même quand je n'agirais plus, en sorte qu'il n'y eût pas un seul instant de ma vie, où, même en dormant, je ne fusse cause d'un désordre quelconque, et que ce désordre put s'étendre au point qu'il entraînât une corruption générale ou un dérangement si formel qu'au delà même de ma vie l'effet s'en prolongeât encore.[1]

---

[1] Juan Goytisolo, *Reivindicación del conde don Julián* (México: Joaquín Mortiz, S.A., 1970), epigraph. Hereafter all references will be given in parentheses in the text. Goytisolo does not use periods in this work. To maintain uniformity of style in this study, final periods are inserted.

The story of the novel could be summarized by saying that *Don Julián* is a violent voyage into the mind, history, and myth; it is a treatise on linguistics, literature, philosophy, psychology, sociology, and religion as well as a political manifesto. The novel depicts the metempsychosis of the mythic-historical figure of Count Julián—considered by many as one of the most perverse characters in history of Spain. Throughout, the soul of the Count takes possession of an exiled Spaniard living in Tangiers (the Álvaro of *Señas* and *Juan sin tierra*). This action, considered by the protagoinist as a rebirth of sorts, takes place progressively. It depends on the psychological development—or degeneration—of the narrator, who is also the protagonist. Such progression in the narrator's character is the result both of his traumatic past and present circumstances. The narrator-protagonist is alienated for a number of reasons from his native country which he left in anger. The reasons for his exile are slowly revealed to the reader. The narrator, by birth a Spaniard yet through rejection deprived of an identity, seeks a personality of his own and a means of revenge against those who now control his country. He eventually achieves these two objectives by assuming the role of Don Julián. The story portrays the progressive development of a personality (which could be considered authentic from an existentialist point of view), penetrating the protagonist's mind from the instant just before he opens his eyes and gets out of bed in the morning until he lies down in the same bed to return to sleep the evening of the same day. During his waking hours, he vindicates himself by sublimating, through a symbolic, literary, and hallucinated invasion and destruction of his native country, all the bitterness, hate, love, and frustration he feels as a Spanish émigré, while at the same time attaining a new and authentic identity. However, this ritual must be repeated each day in order for the protagonist to maintain his identity. The novel thus displays a circular structure in which the narration returns to the point at which it began. Essentially it is a circle divided into four parts: the first chapter gives general background information about the protagonist; the second describes his traumatic childhood experiences, the latter part of the second, the third, and part of the fourth chapter represent the planning and the invasion of Spain; in the latter part of the fourth are the outcome of Caperucito's tale and the reaffirmation of the character's purpose, while he prepares to begin anew the following day.

The plot is extremely complicated in its composition. There is a combination of several themes, developed by their own set of motifs as well as countless free motifs. All these are interwoven with one another and connected by a set of symbolic bridges, leading directly and indirectly to the portrayal of the protagonist.

This chapter concentrates on eight themes deemed to be the most important; the Catholic Church, the police state, sexual mores, false tradition, literature, the economic prostitution of Spain, the Spanish language, and the invasion and destruction of Spain. The last theme, accomplished literarily and symbolically, is directly related to most of the other themes.

In *Don Julián* especially, the Catholic Church emerges as one of the most ossified and reactionary structures in Spanish society, one which must be ridiculed and destroyed. Holding extraordinary power within the state, it prevents the nation from assuming a realistic position in the modern world, directly and indirectly giving rise to many other flaws and myths in Spanish culture. In *Don Julián*, the attack on the Church is sadistic and direct in order to produce the horror the author knows these acts will inspire in believers. Goytisolo besieges mercilessly the cult of the Virgin, as in this description of Mary holding the infant Jesus:

> ...estás junto al camerino de la muñeca : maniquí de madera articulado, vestido con manto azul y oro y con el corazón atra-

vesado de alfileres como el acerico de una costurera : en sus brazos, el Nene, con pelo rubio natural peinado en tirabuzones conforme a la moda de Shirley Temple. (p. 232)

He continues the narration with the sack of a temple by the Moors during which Mary is dispossessed of all her jewels: "...pausadamente, comienzas a despojarle de sus joyas y adornos : tu vista se detiene en los aretes de diamantes que cuelgan de sus orejas..." (p. 232). Goytisolo seems to feel that it is not only barbaric but absurd for a mannequin to be royally dressed when so many, reduced to the lowest degree of poverty, could benefit from the Church's forgotten vows.

Goytisolo also shows that the Church has an indirect influence on the preservation of totalitarian rule in Spain. It supports the "Ubicuo" (Franco) and the evil he represents: atrophy of the arts and the mediocrity to which art has been reduced. There is no forward movement in this type of regime. Its lay supporters are another important target of criticism. They are that segment of Spanish society composed of what he calls *capras* and *carpetos* who constitute, in their majority, the conformist stratum of Spanish society. *Capra*, she-goat, is probably an allusion to the abundance of goats in certain regions of Spain, and Moscardón, a minor figure in the novel, identifies the odor of goat feces, in Unamunesque parody, as the fragrance of Gredos: "...se inclina a recoger una cagarruta y, llegándosela a las caudalosas narices, aspira el aroma con éxtasis...esencias metafísicas! ¡Gredos, Gredos!...la capra encarna nuestras más puras esencias" (p. 82). The term *carpeto* refers to the people and contains as well the geographical reference to the *Sistema Carpetovetónico Central*. Both the term and its significance derive from Cela's *El gallego y su cuadrilla y otros apuntes carpetovetónicos*. Zamora Vicente explains the expression: "Las personas ilustradas que lo usaban, carpetovetónico, en la conversación, aludían siempre a la sequedad...de la Castilla abrasada y polvorienta: se encerraba siempre, de una u otra forma, una idea de 'brutalidad'...."[2]

The *capras'* and *carpetos'* support of a totalitarian regime and their acceptance of the economic prostitution of Spain have led to mediocrity and pollution, economic mass production and standardization of the way in which people live and think: "estaciones de servicio y moteles... con bikini en las playas: different, yes . . . : lleno de sabor castizo..." (p. 26). The *capras'* and *carpetos'* attitude has also contaminated the arts. The author indicates that the promiscuous dissemination of literary awards to those who follow a conventional approach in their novels has led to mediocrity in the genre. In *Don Julián* those *premios* are given by the Fundación Al Capone, a pun on the notorious criminal's name and the Spanish word suggesting eunuch (*capón*). It also implies a dishonorable American source of funds for writers. Thus, with few exceptions, only the exiled artists have managed to produce anything commendable. In addition, Goytisolo feels that the totalitarian system of government is too precarious to allow deviations from established norms, a situation which compounds the problem of literary mediocrity. Promising artist are limited in their creative scope, are coerced into producing what appeals to public taste and abides by the censor's standards, a situation that has brought deteriorating Spanish culture to the verge of total ruin.

Both church and state have also had a direct effect on sexual mores; the perspective on sex in Spain has remained Victorian. This attitude creates another problem for the arts and life in general, preventing the introduction of new ideas. Consequently, this perhaps untouchable idol is the taboo subject that may incite the greatest controversy. The novel is

---

[2] Alfonso Zamora Vicente, *Camilo José Cela* (Madrid: Editorial Gredos, 1962), p. 144.

supersaturated with sexual "happenings" as well as a large number of Jungian and Freudian sex symbols, perhaps its most abundant motifs. The author's reasons for using sex as a vehicle of protest are, for the purposes of this study, threefold: to criticize the Catholic Church whose dominance in education has kept a Victorian perspective on sex; to flay Spanish society for its hypocrisy, since it shows equally Victorian licentiousness; and to defy the all-pervasive censorship exercised by the government since the author knows his novel will enter Spain.

Criticism of Catholic education is observed in the depiction of a child's unhealthy sexual development. When a priest addresses a group of adolescents that includes Alvarito, the protagonist's child-figure, they are taught to fear sex and women:

> . . . el desgraciado joven sucumbió a los encantos de la sirena . . . y por esa brecha escurrirá poco a poco toda la energía, todo el vigor del cuerpo . . .amados jóvenes, los placeres prohibidos se parecen a esa caja de oro que simula un contenido mirífico: pero, ¡ay de quien imprudentemente la abre! (pp. 102–03)

In other scenes Alvarito is caught practicing *voyeurism* and, as punishment, is forced to look at an old woman's genitals. He is also sodomized and flagellated several times by a Moor. Alvarito's doom, Goytisolo seems to indicate, is the result of the lack of proper education, which leads either to fear of the libido or to perversion of it.

In *El furgón de cola* Goytisolo says that the hypocrisy of Spanish society is perhaps a direct result of the totalitarian government's censorship and false laws. The Spanish people have so degenerated that falsehoods and hypocrisy exist everywhere:

> . . . la astucia e hipocresía entronizadas por un sistema político opresor contagian al fin a la totalidad del cuerpo social. En un país donde las leyes que rigen el mecanismo social son falsas, las relaciones personales de sus miembros tienden a ser falsas también.
> . . . . Oficialmente España se vende por un país de moral sana. En

realidad, las relaciones matrimoniales... son más inmorales y sucias que en la mayoría de los países de nuestra civilización y cultura.[3]

In the novel, as the invasion is about to begin, one of the things to be stimulated in the Peninsula is sex: "...inteligencia y sexo florecerán" (p. 127). Goytisolo's purpose in portraying so many sexual events is to shock the reader into some form of understanding of the problems facing Spain. He evidently feels that the presence of overt sexual matters in his novel is relevant to the social issues he raises, and, consequently, the shock-value of unadorned sex and sexual perversions has a redeeming social purpose.

The abundance of sexual motifs merits closer study. The theme of sexuality is underlined by the constant appearance of a variety of devices, one being the animal motif. The novel abounds with allusions to serpents, roosters, horses, spiders, and bulls, to name a few. Associated references include syphilis, a scar, and caves. The rhythmic effect achieved by the use of colons (an important stylistic device in this novel) may also be considered, on an intuitive level, as related to the theme of sexuality.[4]

---

[3] Juan Goytisolo, *El furgón de cola*, pp. 173–74.

[4] The most interesting way of permeating the novel with the sexual theme is through the abundant use of colons. (Carlos Fuentes used colons in parts of *La muerte de Artemio Cruz* and Martí also used them in some of his writings.) By limiting himself to the use of colons and commas in his novel, Goytisolo gives his prose a waiving motion, a galloping quality, a peristaltic rhythm: the sort of movement exercised during coitus. As the novel begins, this movement or pitch slowly rises, until a crescendo is attained (during the invasion of Spain), to drop gently back to its slow rhythm as the novel ends. A detailed study will be needed, however, to establish whether there is any truth to this hypothesis. It is also interesting to note what Goytisolo says about the erotic theme in Spanish literature in his prologue to *Obra inglesa de D. José María Blanco White* (2nd ed.; Barcelona: Editorial Seix Barral, S.A., 1974), p. 63: "A la presión ideológica que siguió al Concilio de Trento nos atreveríamos a sumar, con todas las necesarias reservas, un último factor mencionado por Blanco: la desaparicón de los musulmanes del horizonte español, que tan señaladamente influyó, por otra parte, en el extrañamiento del tema erótico."

The serpent is perhaps the predominant animal figure in this work. In addition to being a phallic symbol, it has other important connotations. According to tradition, Rodrigo's punishment for ravishing Cava was to be defeated by the Moors, to have his penis devoured by a serpent and to die as the serpent penetrated his body. Jung holds that for the old, the serpent represents fear of death; for the young, it represents repressed sexuality because it puts an end to childhood.[5] Noting that in "Deluge" by Rubens a serpent emasculates a man, he asserts: "This motive explains the meaning of the 'Deluge'; the maternal sea is also the devouring mother."[6] The serpent, then, seems to represent in the novel a fear of sex present in Spanish culture throughout history, a fear that has led to censorship and the attempt to repress the libido, one situation that Goytisolo is trying to change.

The rooster, perhaps the most obvious phallic symbol, serves to emphasize the theme of sexual fears present in the protagonist as well as in the culture he is trying to destroy. Several violent scenes deal with the mutilation of roosters. In one, a rooster is seen wobbling along a street in Tangiers with his head partially cut from the rest of his body, while a large, black dog follows, licking the trail of blood left on the pavement (p. 51). In another there is a hallucinated close-up of several decapitated roosters (p. 132). These images supplement the sexual theme in that the insecurity of the protagonist and the culture he represents are characterized by a pervasive fear of emasculation. Horse imagery is also prevalent throughout the novel. Moors on horseback are shown ravishing Spanish virgins, temples, and the countryside. Mindful of Jung's careful delineation of the symbolic sexual value of the horse,

---

[5] Carl G. Jung, *Psychology of the Unconscious*, trans. Beatrice M. Hinkle (New York: Moffat, Yard and Co., 1916), p. 480.

[6] *Ibid.*, p. 481.

we find, once again, the themes of sexuality and a repressed incest wish conveyed by another motif.[7]

Many insects appear, the spider being most important, since it is a symbolic representation of the yoni.[8] *Araña* first appears at the beginning, in reference to the chandelier hanging over the protagonist's bed (p. 14). In a library scene, some of the insects squashed inside the books are spiders, and they are prominent in a flashback to Alvarito's school days and his traumatic experience, when forced to witness an insect being devoured by a carnivorous plant with "hojas velludas" (p. 107), while the science teacher talks about the similarity between what is taking place and the spider's method of capturing its prey: " . . . cuando la víctima toca la tela, todas sus tentativas de desprenderse agravan inexorablemente su situación . . . y ella no tiene prisa : su mirada es fría . . . lentamente le hunde los guelíceros . . . procurando alargar su agonía, va disolviendo y chupando todas sus partes blandas" (p. 108).

The bull also reinforces the sexual theme (Zeus assumed the form of a bull in order to ravish Europa). The narrator's continuous references to "Tonelete" (Manolete), might be interpreted as an allusion to the prevading sexual fear in Spanish culture best illustrated in the classic symbolic confrontation of

---

[7] *Ibid.*, p. 308. Because of sexual overtones the horse, according to Jung, is traditionally considered a wicked animal with connections to the devil. It is said that witches have intercourse with the devil when he assumes the form of a horse, a belief which has led to the horse becoming a phallic symbol. The horse is also a libido symbol, as is the mother idea. Yet the horse is not, nor does it symbolize, the mother. The two symbols intersect in their significance at some point, however, and their common feature is the libido, especially in the libido where there is repression of incest.

[8] Erich Neumann, in *The Origin and History of Consciousness*, trans. R. F. C. Hull, Bollingen Series XLII (New York: Pantheon Books Inc., 1954), p. 87, sees the spider as a symbol of devouring chasm; it represents the female spreading her net over the unsuspecting male.

man and bull. The protagonist's sexual fears, resulting from deficient and puritanical instruction, are visible in his constant free association with syphilis, used in a recurring pun where the substitution of *sífilis* for *sílfides* takes place. The protagonist obviously suffers from a morbid fear of venereal disease, but there is also the possibility, since he goes to the pharmacist, that he has contracted syphilis.

The Spanish landscape as seen from Tangiers is termed a scar across the sea. The scar may be a *yoni* symbol, for in one important scene, the narrator enters a cave which turns out to be Spain's vagina. Therefore, it can be inferred that to the protagonist Spain represents the castrating Great Mother and at a distance has the appearance of a woman's genitals. The motif of caves and entering them alludes to a repressed incest wish of the protagonist, an important sexual motif in the novel.[9] Because of his rearing, the narrator is extremely insecure, powerless, and alienated. By returning to the womb—and leaving it—security and a new identity will be gained.

The alliance of church and state has had a deleterious effect on contemporary life, producing a perversion of values which in turn have caused a falsification of tradition. Through some Orwellian rewriting of history, the falsifications have become part of Spanish culture. Throughout the novel the author exposes and satirizes those untruths, including the concept of Hispanidad and that of the *caballero cristiano* of Don Juan Manuel. Ramiro de Maeztu in *Defensa de la hispanidad*, urges his readers to regain a love for Spain and to adopt a national ideal; Spain must return to the ideals of the Golden Age: ". . . su mística, su religión, su moral, su derecho. . . ."[10] The narrator of *Don Julián* scoffs at patriotism and considers it an evil: ". . . la patria es la madre de todos los

---

[9] Jung, p. 375.

[10] Ramiro de Maeztu, *Defensa de la hispanidad* (Buenos Aires: Editorial Poblet, 1942), p. 298. García Morente's views on the subject may be relevant as well, and his "Caballero Cristiano" is probably the one Goytisolo ridicules.

vicios: y lo más expeditivo y eficaz para curarse de ella consiste en venderla, en traicionarla . . ." (p. 134). He criticizes and satirizes the ideal of the *caballero cristiano*,[11] the novel's source being the version of Ganivet, who in re-examining tradition, adds the Senecan element. This version is modified by Goytisolo, who introduces humor in order to destroy the myth.[12]

Ganivet's reinterpretation of Spanish culture (*Idearium español*) emphasizes the role of senequismo: "Cuando se examina la constitución ideal de España, el elemento moral y en cierto modo religioso más profundo que en ella se descubre, como sirviéndole de cimiento, es el estoicismo, no el estoicismo brutal y heroico de Catón . . . sino el estocismo natural y humano de Séneca.[13] Ganivet argues that for Seneca, born in Córdoba, stoicism was an inescapable ingredient of his native culture, " . . . lo encontró inventado ya," and that its essence continued permanently to shape Spanish Christian attitudes.[14] Goytisolo destroys the ideal, embodying it in Álvaro Peranzules, a travesty of the concept: a gentleman who is quite heroic, God-fearing, stoic, suffering for Spain (*le duele España*), as well as an admirer of Manolete, and a mystic.

In his process of demythification, Goytisolo ridicules Seneca, suggesting that the stoic philosopher is a *carpeto*, born in Gredos:

> . . . como en el caso de Cristobal Colón y otras grandes figuras históricas, numerosas ciudades se disputan el honroso privilegio de su nacimiento [de Séneca]: pero los recientes estudios . . . prueban sin nigún género de dudas . . . [que fue] en el centro de la Penísula y no en la periferia . . . en la Sierra de Gredos. (pp. 112–13).

---

[11] Goytisolo's definition is on p. 158 of *Don Julián*.

[12] The giving of new interpretations and perspectives to ideas handed down from previous generations is a characteristic of the shaman according to Andreas Lommel in *Shamanism: The Beginning of Art*, trans. Michael Bullock (New York: McGraw-Hill Book Company, 1967), p. 145. This characteristic of the narrator-protagonist will be examined later.

[13] Angel Ganivet, *Idearium español* (Buenos Aires: Espasa-Calpe Argentina, S.A., 1940), p. 7.

[14] Ganivet, p. 8.

In the novel Seneca becomes other characters, sometimes the Ubicuo, at others Peranzules and even Manolete. As a jeering reference to his Andalusian origin, the author shows him as an old gypsy. In the following scene Seneca is shown defecating as he sings "Les Sylphides" of Chopin:

> . . . en la pelambre crespa, canturrea con descuido un aire de danza de "Las Sílfides" de Chopin: de puntillas te aproximarás a él y descubrirás, acuclillado, un filósofo de catadura de gitano viejo, envuelto en immaculada toga y con la frente ceñida de una corona de laurel: . . . es Séneca! . . . absorto ahora, en industria trabajosa y lenta. (p. 153)

The author seems to associate closely Seneca's name and *senequismo* with the dryness of the *carpetovetónico* landscape and the people's soul (p. 153). By ridiculing patriotism and Seneca, Goytisolo once again topples some important idols venerated by Spanish society.

Literature has contributed a number of fabrications and myths now accepted—wrongly, according to Goytisolo—as part of the national culture—for example, the Golden Age concept of honor and the Generation of '98 outlook on Castile and its general perspective on Spanish tradition and history. The Golden Age and the Generation of '98, therefore, become objects of attack through desecration, parody, and perversion of literary texts. Among false cultural values exposed by Goytisolo is the concept of honor. The author attacks the prevalent concept of honor—one of the worst cultural myths—in Spanish literature during the Golden Age which he calls *Cartón Dorado*. To show dramatically his dislike, the narrator squashes several insects between the pages of an anthology at a point where, in a play by Lope (*El castigo sin venganza*), a duke is about to avenge his honor: ". . . alcanzando el primer volumen de la pila y depositando entre sus páginas una hormiga y seis moscas: en el quintaesenciado diálogo de Casandra y el duque: esto disponen las leyes del honor . . . cerrando de golpe, zas!, y aplastándolas" (p. 37). The narrator thus sublimates his anger and silently but visually protests against one of the many flaws he finds in Spanish culture.

In the same library scene, the narrator continues the *auto da fe*, passing from the Golden Age to the view of Castilla by the Generation of '98: ". . . entre los lentos paisajes del Noventa y Ocho: graves, monacales, adustos: por la llanura inacabable donde verdea el trigo . . . centrando tu interés en una araña de dimensiones medias . . . y ajustando apretadamente las páginas" (p. 38). The author feels the need to touch the *intocables* of the Generation of '98. Prior to this novel, Goytisolo had written a collection of essays about the ossification of contemporary Spanish literature and criticism. Most writers, he believes, continue to imitate those of the Generation of '98; since the members of that generation seem to be deified, their writings form the basis of everything written. He finds no negative criticism of them but, rather, a supersaturation of praise:

> El espectáculo sería cómico si no fuese realmente trágico. Hojear las revistas literarias españolas nos permite ver hasta qué punto el culto del Noventa y Ocho ha esterilizado a nuestros ensayistas. . . . Nadie . . . se aventura por terrenos desconocidos; el ensayista español de hoy avanza prudentemente envuelto—sería mejor decir: acorazado—en una tupida malla de citas de algún "intocable."[15]

In *Reivindicación del conde don Julián*, the narrator feels that the works of the Generation (creators of "false" myths) must be the butt of parody and travesty. Don Álvaro, as he is about to die, says: "Cu-Cu-Cu: cuna, culebra . . ." (p. 181). This might be an allusion to Azorín's cuclillo: "Un cuclillo canta lejano: 'Cu-cú'; otro cuclillo canta más cerca: 'Cu-cú.' Estas aves irónicas y terribles, ¿se mofan acaso de mi pequeña

---

[15] Goytisolo, *El furgón de cola*, p. 81.

filosofía?"[16] Unamuno's "me duele España" is ridiculed throughout the novel. Ganivet's views on Seneca and stoicism are mocked (*passim*). Poems of the Machado brothers are used frequently to criticize and satirize the Generation's concern with Castile.[17] But most demeaning of all, their writings on the landscape of Castile are used as a Baedeker or campaign plan for the Moorish invasion of Spain: ". . . gracias a un puñado de hombres ilustres: maestros universalmente queridos, admirados y respetados . . . espulgadores de remotos linajes . . ." (p. 138). ". . . monopolistas y banqueros de la recia prosa de hoy, podrás identificar y recorrer el paisaje de la fatal Península" (p. 140).

The Spanish language, Goytisolo feels, must also be abused and vilified. He considers language to be the only subversive tool left in contemporary society. Thus, by undermining the aged and decadent Spanish language, considered by *carpetos* and *capras* and the Royal Academy their sole priceless possession, the narrator creates a chaotic situation. Such a state will help eliminate that undesirable segment of the society. Because the Spanish language has been monopolized by the *Real Academia Española* it is now moribund, and thus Goytisolo utilizes a vast number of foreign words, neologisms, Americanisms, Anglicisms, Gallicisms, and erratic syntax in direct attack on the Academy and all those institutions of the literary establishment such as the *ABC*, publishers' prizes, and government grants, which help stunt the language. In addition, there are references to the subject throughout the novel:

> . . . inventarás senderos y trochas, en abrupta ruptura con la oficial sintaxis y su escuela de dogmas y entredichos . . . (p. 152)

---

[16] José Martínez Ruiz, "Azorín," "La novia de Cervantes," *Antología— Siglo XX—Prosistas españoles*, ed. María de Maeztu (Madrid: Espasa-Calpe, S.A., 1969), p. 117.

[17] In many instances verses from the Machado poems are used. As indicated in previous chapters, Antonio Machado's poetry appears repeatedly in Goytisolo's writings.

146

. . . desde estrados, iglesias, cátedras, púlpitos, academias, tribunas, los carpetos reivindican con orgullo sus derechos de propiedad sobre el lenguaje/es nuestro, nuestro, dicen/lo creamos nosotros. (p. 192)

Elsewhere the author presents three characters, "el tlaxcalteca," "el porteño," and "el yoruba," who represent Mexico, Argentina, and Cuba respectively. Each speaks Spanish with all the idiosyncrasies of his country so that the reader goes from one dialect to another in roughly forty-two lines, at the end of which the narrator tells Julián (and the reader) to join them (pp. 194–95).[18] One way then, of attacking Spain, of slapping the public into understanding, is to destroy and demean the academic concept of language.[19] Furthermore, it is a means of severing one of the few remaining links with the mother country:

. . . cambiando con ellos las fórmulas habituales de cortesía: en castellano no, en árabe : feliz de olvidar por unos instantes el último lazo que, a tu pesar, te une irreductiblemente a la tribu : idioma mirífico del Poeta, vehículo necesario de la traición, hermosa lengua tuya : instrumento indispensable del renegado y del apóstata, esplendoroso y devastador a la vez : arma aguda (insinuante) que conjura (exorcisa) la africana hueste y magnífica (potencia) su denso apetito de destrucción (p. 70)

Savage alteration of Castilian is still more pronounced in *Juan sin tierra*. Some motifs relevant to each of these themes have been cited. Since there are far too many to examine each separately it should be noted that throughout the novel, and during the invasion in particular, there are constant references to the above themes by way of their motifs. The invading Moors, for instance, use the Generation of '98 writings as a

---

[18] Carlos Fuentes, Julio Cortázar, and Guillermo Cabrera Infante are thanked by Goytisolo in an *Advertencia* (p. 241) at the end of the book.

[19] Goytisolo's views on this subject, which appeared in *Libre*, have been quoted elsewhere in this study, p. 3.

guide for the invasion. The language is taken away from those who consider it their unique possession.

When all the false idols have been profaned and left in shambles, the narrator-protagonist emerges with an identity of his own creation which must be reattained through a daily ritual. The novel ends with an affirmation of the need for change, the need to seek an identity. The narrator realizes that, if there is no possible way to change his condition in the physical world, his situation must be made a means for existing, which will endow him with authenticity: he seizes his existence and proceeds to create his essence.

Since the narrator-protagonist is the central point around which everything else in the novel revolves, a brief examination of Goytisolo's method of characterization is now in order. Some of Tomashevsky's views on characterization are pertinent to the study of the protagonist in *Don Julián*, an example of indirect characterization since the reader learns about him through his thoughts, actions, and conduct. He is also a dynamic character since there is a definite change in his personality by the time the novel ends. The reader never learns the protagonist's name, although clearly (p. 58) he derives in part from Álvaro (*Señas de identidad*). After consideration of the preceding statements, Charles Walcutt's view that "character is a function of action" seems pertinent to this study.[20]

In the novel, the development of character can be divided into two phases: self-examination and execution. Both take place in the mind of the protagonist, and each requires mental activity. The phases are subdivided into stages that lead into each other in a circular pattern. In *Don Julián* the protagonist is continually thinking about Spain, himself, and his situation; this is self-examination. While thinking about his

---

[20] Charles Child Walcutt, *Man's Changing Mask* (Minneapolis: University of Minnesota Press, 1966), p. 17.

148

state, he reaches a conclusion, makes plans, and consummates them; this is execution. Characterization, then, is a combination of thinking and acting, but both activities take place in the mind of the narrator.

The narrator-protagonist of *Don Julián* thinks of himself as stigmatized by an origin he did not choose and would like to repudiate—an action he undertakes with violence. Tearing off the tag absurdly appended to him by virtue of his birthplace, he takes an irrational step: to divert his mind from the continuous suffering caused by constant awareness of the decadent state of his native country, he makes, with aid of *kif*, a Kierkegaardian leap into the void of absurdity. Unlike Kierkegaard, he does not rely on God, but upon himself and so transcends reality. He moves into another realm, beyond reality and history, reincarnating the mythic-historical figure of the perverse Count Julián, and helps invade and destroy Spain once again. Contrary to the conventional novel, the action in *Don Julián* takes place in the mind of the narrator-protagonist so that self-examination and execution can be witnessed only by the reader, not the other characters in the novel. The development of the protagonist takes place in several stages: some lead to his assuming the identity of Julián and Tariq, while others present the invasion and end with the return of the protagonist to his original state. The former are part of "self-examination"; the latter belong to "execution."

The psychological state of the narrator that leads to his assuming the identity of Julián is presented by Goytisolo in three steps. The narrator undergoes a progressive splitting of personality in the first two chapters until Don Julián appears. These stages serve to bring forth the causes which lead the protagonist to feel as he does and also provide insight into the narrator's plans for invasion and destruction. The instant Julián takes over the mind of the protagonist, the "execution" part of the novel begins.

A closer examination of these stages of characterization

is needed. In the first, the reader obtains a commanding perspective of the narrator's situation with the opening statement of the novel, "tierra ingrata . . . jamás volveré a tí" (p. 11). The author wants the reader to be aware of the exiled status of the protagonist. In addition, it is the only time the first-person point of view is used. Thereafter the author uses the second person throughout, which dramatizes the situation highly, forcing the reader to become directly involved in the drama. In the case of other exiles, or even Spaniards within the country, the effect of the direct address will be even more dramatic. A more detailed examination of point of view will be undertaken later.

The second stage begins with the change to the second person. This technique allows Goytisolo to "leave" the novel and prevents confusing interference by the author during the free association episodes when the narrator dwells on his status, his feelings toward his native country, and his desire for its destruction. The following illustrates some of this despairing pessimism: "madrasta inmunda, país de siervos y señores . . ." (p. 15). The desire for annihilation originates in the protagonist's view that, while Spain continues as it is, people will immediately classify him as something he is not. An umbilical cord (which he wants to cut) still ties him to his native land, "unido tú a la otra orilla como el feto al útero sangriento de la madre . . ." (p. 13). He realizes he must devise a process that will allow him to gain his independence from the detested mother: "Inventar, componer, mentir, fabular, repetir la proeza de Scherezada . . ." (p. 13). The author is preparing the reader for what is to take place in the mind of the protagonist later in the novel: "Compensación mental, neurosis caracterizada: arduo y difícil proceso de sublimación . . ." (pp. 13–14). The narrator realizes that in order to continue living, in order to have a reason, a meaning, for life, he must find ways of sublimating his bitterness and hate as well as obtaining a new identity. *Kif* and Count Julián provide him with it: "Acumulando gota a gota tu odio . . . nuevo conde don Julián, fraguando sombrías traiciones . . ." (p. 16).

The third stage begins when the protagonist leaves his apartment (p. 20) and begins his internal and external odyssey, walking the streets of Tangiers. The narrator must condition himself to reach the moment when he can, by hallucination, become Don Julián, a transformation produced by thinking of his traumatic childhood experiences and assimilating the free associations and flashbacks, waiting for the right moment to go to the cafe and begin smoking *kif*. Free associations and flashbacks are sometimes combined to meld past and present, a result comparable to Proust's madeleine soaked in lime-flowers. An example of such combination takes place when the narrator enters a drugstore and receives an injection of penicillin (p. 30). There is a shift from present to past and vice versa, in a kind of cinematic "time montage," whereby inner life (the past) is synchronized with outer life (the present). The pricking of the needle reminds the narrator of a natural science classroom where he, a child, was forced to witness the killing of an insect by an arthropod (in another instance an insect is devoured by a plant). This traumatic scene, with its obvious criticism of the Spanish educational system, illustrates one of the many reasons for the protagonist's hatred of the ossified social structure of his native country. Many other flashbacks and free associations underscore reasons for his hate and his search for reinstatement. While he cannot alter his past, he is free to alter its significance by an act of choice; so he chooses to use symbols as a way to change the course of events. The three steps enumerated above (first-person point of view, second-person point of view, and street roaming) explain the protagonist's state of mind and lead to the metamorphosis late in the second chapter, the onset of "execution."

In the last part of the second chapter, Julián begins to

take possession of the narrator—the first of two stages that reveal the "execution." The selection of Count Julián as the principal surrogate figure for the narrator is extremely important to the themes and symbolism. Because of Julián a metamorphosis takes place in the Peninsula; by opening the doors to Islam he introduces an entirely different culture, an action bringing upon him the curse of most medieval writers. As the epigraph from the *Crónica general* indicates, Julián was (and perhaps still is) considered the most despicable and evil figure in the history of Spain. He consummated the Marquis de Sade's crime of *effet perpétuel* (referred to in an epigraph to the novel): Julián is brought from Hades to repeat his betrayal of Spain. The narrator feels that Spain's pervasive evils desecrated his childhood and forced him to flee the country as an adult, a state of corruption parallel to that which existed in Rodrigo's court prior to the invasion of the Moors. Ramón Menéndez Pidal indicates that the reign of the Visigoths "mostraba grandes grietas de ruina" in the seventh century and that Rodrigo came to power after a civil war.[21] Rodrigo, tradition holds, ravished Julián's daughter, Cava. The protagonist must avenge himself just as Julián avenged the ravishing of his maiden daughter. The narrator, in order to sublimate his violent desires for revenge, ritualizes Julián's act of *effet perpétuel*. Thus, the mythic-historical event becomes a ceremony, a religious performance. This activity, though only taking place in the mind of the protagonist, can be considered as the second phase of characterization, or execution.

The reasons for the metamorphosis of the protagonist and for his activities when he assumes the role of Julián merit further clarification. His behavior (execution) can be consid-

---

[21] Ramón Menéndez Pidal, "Introducción" to *Floresta de leyendas heróicas españolas*, Clásicos Castellanos (Madrid: Ediciones de "La Lectura," 1925), I, 99.

ered as the reaction resulting from his self-examination. The narrator realizes that attaining vengeance is a great task requiring a heroic figure; the protagonist also sees that the activities in which he is to engage must have a metaphysical level in order to endow them with moral or ritualistic value. Hence his choice of the historico-mythical figure of Julián. This myth, which will be examined as such later, thus becomes the most important thematic cornerstone of the novel.

Reivindicación del conde don Julián is, as a whole, an example of delayed exposition. The reader becomes acquainted with what took place, with what is happening, and with the eventual outcome through hints and the assimilation of seemingly incidental remarks. The novel is narrated throughout from the second-person singular viewpoint, except on the first page where the first person is used. Within the framework of the second-person point of view are constant "flashbacks," a result usually of free associations. There are also instances of stream-of-consciousness narrative and typographical experimentation. The use of the "tú" form probably has a dual purpose: first, it involves the reader directly; and, second, it shows what could be called an interior dialogue in which the state of mind of the narrator-protagonist is bared to the reader. Because of the use of the second-person point of view, the narrative becomes discourse; it ceases to be a printed medium and is transposed to the oral plane. Hence, it is *parole*[22] the reader encounters throughout *Don Julián*. The following diagram illustrates the involvement between the author, the narrator-protagonist, and the reader:

Author ♦ narrator ♦♦ protagonist ♦♦ reader.

---

[22] Saussure's views on the dichotomy of language, with which Goytisolo appears to agree, were referred to in the preceding chapter, p. 129. Goytisolo's belief in the importance of the individual's speech over society's normative usage is observed throughout *Don Julián*.

An example of flashingback as a result of free association is observed in the injection of penicillin scene in the pharmacy when the protagonist recollects having seen an insect being devoured (pp. 30–31). The following excerpt illustrates the stream-of-consciousness technique that appears frequently:

> . . . buenosdiascaballero, mamalapobrecomosiempre, sentinta-añosyaylasaludylosdisgustos : cacareos de gallina, llanto de niño, sífilis de xopén! : tus manos se han aferrado tenazmente a su cuello y el fondo musical ahoga el gemido agrio : globo que se deshincha, serrín que escurre, aplastado abdomen que expulsa liquida masa abdominal : . . . (p. 236)

Typographical experimentation also appears throughout the novel, but doubtlessly the most important narrative technique is the second-person singular viewpoint which causes the reader to become directly involved in the narration and thus an accomplice in the act of *effet perpétuel*.

There is temporal and spatial unity in the novel: it takes place within twenty-four hours, and the protagonist remains in the city of Tangiers. Reality, however, is broken consistently so that conventional time and space are no longer accurate tools to determine where and when the narration occurs. The reader as a result must conclude that what he is witnessing takes place in a mythical dimension where myth, history, literature—everything known to man—have undergone a metamorphosis to serve its creator's purpose, that of the nar-rator-protagonist. The protagonist re-creates the past, the present, and the future to avenge himself, and what takes place within his mind is timeless, whereas the world outside has moved less than a day during his entire odyssey. By the same token, space knows no bounds while he is engaging in a voyage through time and myth, but in the external world he is confined to a small section of the city of Tangiers.

Thus, the novel takes place on two planes: the real—out-side the protagonist's mind—in which he exists from day to day, sleeping in his apartment and walking the streets of

Tangiers; and the imaginary—literary-historico-mythical time and place wherein the narrator submerges himself, after smoking *kif*, to find an identity and change his past, the level to which he must go to obtain purification. These two levels are interwoven to such an extent that frequently it is difficult to separate them. As a result, time and place are suspended and dislocated; past, present, and future, the real and the imaginary, fiction and history are fused while the protagonist engages in his daily communion with Spanish culture.

The most important bound motif of the novel, and the only one to be examined here, is the mythification of Julián.[23] This historico-mythical figure serves as the basis for the story of Goytisolo's novel. In the examination of characterization, the reader saw the protagonist's awareness of his need to give a metaphysical dimension to his activities in order to endow them with ritualistic value. The choice of Julián (as well as Tariq) to serve as his alter ego is logical, since great actions, whether good or evil, require great people. Keeping this view in mind, consideration of the general nature of myth is in order before continuing with the examination of this bound motif as it relates to the protagonist and his characterization.

Bronislaw Malinowski explains that myth is an important aspect of religion: "It is a story which is told in order to establish a belief, to serve as a precedent in ceremony or ritual or to rank as a pattern of moral or religious conduct."[24] Moreover, it is a repetitive restatement of the past in the present, whose elements function as a means to reach the supernatural. A basic characteristic mentioned by Malinowski is re-enactment of an authentic past event. In *Don Julián*, the narrator

---

[23]The importance of using a well-known historical figure with somewhat of a mystic-mythical aura will be shown shortly.
[24] Bronislaw Malinowski, *Sex, Culture and Myth* (New York: Harcourt, Brace and World, Inc., 1962), pp. 249–61.

re-enacts Julián's revenge just as a priest goes through the ritual presumably performed by Christ in the Last Supper. In both instances the ceremony brings the original act back to the present and somehow causes that particular moment from the past to be relived. Such an accomplishment is sufficient to give the narrator an identity and a meaning for his life.

As an elaboration of the concept of myth and its relation to the novel, William Y. Tindall's definition merits examination: "Myth is a dreamlike narrative in which the individual's central concerns are united with society, time and the universe. Both expression and sanction, it organizes experience, uniting fact with imagination, the conscious with the unconscious, the present with the past."[25] In *Don Julián* the narrator's main concern is his identity and his relationship to his native country, the universe, and the present, past, and future. Goytisolo utilizes Julián (as well as Tariq, another surrogate figure) to re-create a mythic-historical situation. The narrator with the aid of *kif*, memory, and hate becomes a shaman whose body is used to reincarnate the souls of Julián and Tariq and of every Spaniard, whether exiled or inside the country, and resuscitate his youth. Once this metempsychosis takes place, Spain is destroyed and a new Spain will rise from the ashes. The central concerns of Goytisolo are thus conceived from, and united with, society, time, and the universe: ". . . hacer almoneda de todo: historia, creencias, lenguaje : infancia, paisajes, familia: rehusar la identidad, comenzar a cero : Sísifo y, juntamente, Fénix que renace de sus propias cenizas: una dosis de hierba más fuerte que ordinaria basta. . . . Tariq está junto a ti" (p. 135).

As a result of his alienation, then, the narrator seeks an identity through ritualistic revenge—a crime of *effet perpétuel*. His use of the imagination to mold reality presents a striking

---

[25] William York Tindall, *James Joyce* (New York: Charles Scribner's Sons, 1950), p. 102.

parallel with de Sade, whom he quotes in an epigraph to the novel. Comparing Lawrence Durrell's *Alexandrian Quartet* with the Marquis de Sade's works, Joseph H. McMahon makes observations applicable to Goytisolo's novel:

> The thread common to both is the effort made by each man to use the imagination as the mediator between individual consciousness and whatever it is we are trying to pinpoint when we speak of reality . . . it gets at a fundamental potential schizophrenia in the individual: his perplexity at the tension between the call of intersubjective reality and the smaller but usually more persuasive forces which urge him to revolt in order to maintain awareness of his own existence. In Durrell, as well as in de Sade, these forces—and the visions accompanying them—are intimately linked with the operations of the imagination. For Sade, the link is sturdy enough to support uncritical use of the image-making faculty . . . what he offers is the example of an imagination obsessively applied to reality because reality is there in its singular unpleasantness and the imagination is determined to force it through the imagination's sieve.[26]

Camus says in *L'Homme révolté* that "Sade est l'homme de lettres parfait. Il a bati une fiction pour se donner l'illusion d'être."[27] Simone de Beauvoir writes: "Literature enables Sade to unleash his dreams and then to capture them."[28] These views also apply to Goytisolo's novel. Through his imagination and *kif*, the narrator's dreams become a reality and give him an identity, a purpose, authenticity.

To recapitulate, the reader finds that what the narrator has accomplished through his daily ritual is to create his own essence or authenticity. He understands what he represents in the eyes of others and in his own, and decides to change that perspective by bringing Julián to life so that he may destroy

---

[26] Joseph H. McMahon, "Where Does Real Life Begin?" *Yale French Studies*, 35 (1965), 97.

[27] Albert Camus, *L'Homme révolté* (Paris: Librarie Gallimard, 1951), p. 66.

[28] As cited by George May in "Fiction Reader, Novel Writer," *Yale French Studies*, 35 (1967), 7.

Spain. This action becomes the narrator's reality, his everyday essence, with the result that he becomes autonomous and whole, ". . . hablando de mismidad, en-sí, paraen-sí" (p. 55), because he creates his own necessity and his own world of internal coherence and order. His invasion is like the song of the saxophone that Roquentin speaks about in *La nausée*:

> Elle n'existe pas. C'en est même agaçant; si je me levais, se j'arrachais ce disque du plateau qui le supporte et si je le cassais en deux, je ne l'atteindrais pas, elle. Elle est au delà—toujours au delà de quelque chose, d'une voix, d'une note de violin. A travers des épaisseurs et des épaisseurs d'existence, elle se dévoile, mince et ferme et, quand on veut la saisir, on ne rencontre que des existants, on bure sur des existants dépourvus de sens. Elle est derrière eux: je ne l'entends même pas, j'entends des sons, des vibrations de l'air que la dévoilent. Elle n'existe pas, puisqu'elle n'a rien de trop: c'est tout le reste qui est trop par rapport à elle. Elle *est*.
>
> Et moi aussi j'ai voulu *être*. Je n'ai même voulu que cela; voilà le fin mot de ma vie: au fond de toutes ces tentatives qui semblaient sans liens, je retrouve le même désir: chasser l'existence hors de moi, vider les instants de leur graisse, les tordre, les assécher, me purifier, me durcir, pour rendre enfin le son net et précis d'une note de saxophone.[29]

By setting himself a goal and living for it, the narrator can, to some degree, be considered authentic. Man, according to Sartre, does not attain authenticity by following a set of rules: authenticity is a way of life. Man must live devoid of dogma; he must lose himself outside of himself. In addition, an important part of the authentic life is the pursuit of transcendent goals.[30] Instead of flight, existentialists advise affirmation of life and reconciliation with the individual self. The protagonist of the novel seems to follow these views when, closing his eyes to sleep at the end of the novel, knowing that the invasion and destruction have been consummated

---

[29] Jean Paul Sartre, *La nausée* (Paris: Librairie Gallimard, 1938), p. 218.
[30] Norman N. Green, *Jean Paul Sartre, The Existentialist Ethic* (Ann Arbor: University of Michigan Press, 1960), *passim*.

and that Julián is gone, he says: ". . . lo sabes, lo sabes: mañana será otro día, la invasión recomenzará" (p. 240). Thus, the circle has been closed, but the following day that circle, the ritual, must begin once again.

The two most important dynamic motifs, the catalysts that trigger the events of the novel, are the use of *kif* and the flashbacks to traumatic events. The latter maintain the protagonist on a hypersensitive and bitter level which the *kif* unleashes in the form of destruction. After examination of these two motifs, characterization will be considered once more, because the novel is basically the portrayal of an individual. An important characteristic of the protagonist is his ability, like that of Proteus, to change into different personalities. *Kif* and flashbacks help. So, Alvarito, the protagonist as a child, appears frequently, in addition to Julián, Tariq, and familiar figures from Greek mythology. Such powers and others still to be examined give the impression that the narrator is endowed with some sort of shamanic gift. Eliade lists five important elements present in every shaman: technique of ecstasy, mastery over fire, magical flight, healing, and control over spirits.[31]

The technique of ecstasy is pertinent to the dynamic motif since *kif* is one of the ways of conjuring literary-mythic-historical figures to help him achieve his revenge. In addition, *kif* is part of the protagonist's ritual day after day, since he seems to look upon it as a communion of sorts: "Entre espirales de humo aromatizado, saboreando la abrazadora comunión de un vaso de hierbabuena: hachich aliado sutil de tu pasión destructiva" (p. 126). The second element, mastery over fire, is present in the narrator since Prometheus is one of his alter egos. The purpose of his daily ritual is to "bring light" to all his compatriots. A more detailed study of Prometheus

---

[31] Mircea Eliade, *Shamanism*, trans. William R. Trask, Bollingen Series LXVI (New York: Pantheon Books, 1964), p. 5.

will be undertaken shortly. The shamanic trait of magical flight is evoked whenever the narrator is in a trance, invading and destroying Spain. A specific allusion to flight is noticed in "Tu vuelo acariciante ciñe el lenguaje opaco. . . . el niño vuelve del colegio . . . la escena se repite, vieja como el mundo" (p. 126). The element of healing presents itself when the protagonist is able to bring Mrs. Potiphar back to life after she is bitten by a snake. He can turn Alvarito into different shapes, such as a bird or insect, or have him die a horrendous death only to bring him back to life: "Alvarito-pájaro salta de rama en rama. . . . Alvarito-insecto vuela feliz" (p. 211). The shamanic power to control spirits is possessed by the narrator of *Don Julián* who descends to Hades and assumes the souls of Julián and Tariq in order to carry out his revenge.

Additional motifs are used to remind the reader of the narrator's further shamanic powers. For instance, there are many references to excrement, urine, and masks, the first two recalling Jung's statements that primitive people regard anything discharged from the body as creative or as having some sort of magical power.[32] Excrement is alluded to throughout the novel, but urine seems to have a ritual value. In several scenes people are urinated upon, leading the reader to associate that act with a perverted form of baptism. In most cases either the protagonist or an alter ego (a Moor) performs the act: ". . . vertiendo recia, caudalosamente el rubio desdén fluido . . . eh, que estoy aquí!" (pp. 59–60) ". . . el palpa la inferior hilera de botones . . . el rubio desdén fluido . . . brota un gemido . . . eh, que estoy aquí!" (pp. 98–99)

Another indication that the narrator has supernatural powers is the mask. Eliade says that the mask announces "the incarnation of a mythical personage (ancestor, mythical, animal, god),"[33] and the protagonist assumes the personality of

---

[32] Jung, *Man and his Symbols*, p. 299.
[33] Eliade, *Shamanism*, pp. 167–68.

several historico-mythical figures. The mask has further uses, according to Eliade; primitive people used it as either a disguise or defense against enemies and evil spirits.[34] Just before the invasion, either Tariq or Julián speaks to his hordes of removing the heavy masks that burden them: ". . . nada os resistirá la máscara nos pesa : el papel que representamos es falso : una imperiosa necesidad de aire agita nuestros pulmones : la sangre circula rápida . . . el cuerpo aguarda . . . virilidad retenida . . . mi felonía se prolongará ocho siglos" (p. 137).[35]

Throughout *Don Julián* there are allusions to Greek mythology, whose purpose appears to be a symbolic re-enactment of the particular event with some idiosyncratic attributes added by the narrator-protagonist, as in the figure of Don Julián. Before examining these mythological allusions, a few observations about myth and its relation to symbol are in order. Cassirer, in *Language and Myth*, relates the mythological symbol to productive force: "Art, language, myth . . . appear as symbols; not in the sense of mere figures which refer to some given reality by means of suggestion and allegorical renderings, but in the sense of forces each of which produces and posits a world of its own."[36] William York Tindall in *Forces*

---

[34] *Ibid.*, p. 166.

[35] The reader should note in this passage the use of the first- and second-person plural viewpoints as well as the first-person singular. There are several exceptions of this type throughout the text. Here Julián or Tariq is addressing his troops; hence the second-person singular cannot be maintained. Thus, these viewpoints essentially fall within the category of dialogue. It is also pertinent to note what Andreas Lommel says in *Shamanism*, p. 147: "Shamanizing consists essentially in rendering the mythological images of the group tradition lively and productively, in employing them to strengthen the collective soul by depicting them and making them conscious. Thus, the shaman's activity is to an important extent an artistic one: miming, acting, singing, dancing and painting." He emphasizes that without artistic creation there is no shaman and that the shamanizing is always done in a trancelike state, which most of the time is artificially induced.

[36] Ernest Cassirer, *Language and Myth*, trans. Susanne Langer (New York: Harper and Brothers, 1946), p. VIII.

in Modern British Literature further elaborates on symbolism and its relation to myth: ". . . Myth seems to hold clues to a reality that philosophers, psychologists, historians, and theologians approach but never master through discursive reason. In short, if we take symbol according to its roots as putting together or according to usage as showing forth, myth is symbol."[37] Mythological evocations in Goytisolo's novel may also be thought of as archetypes following Northrop Frye's definition: "A recurrent image . . . a symbol which connects one poem with another and thereby helps to unify and integrate our literary experience."[38]

By studying Goytisolo's use and variation of symbols or archetypes, as understood in the sense just mentioned, the reader will be able to understand the devices used in his symbolic invasion of Spain. All the literary, mythic, and historical references in *Don Julián*—the significance of which is suggestive rather than revealing—serve as a means of achieving many-leveled meanings and perspectives, irony and satire, pain and pleasure. Classical myths relevant to the protagonist and which may be considered dynamic are those of Proteus, Prometheus, Orpheus, Aeneas, Theseus (with allusions to the Labyrinth and the Minotaur), the story of Sisyphus, and that of the lotus-eaters. The one appearing most frequently is that of Proteus, whose peculiar power was to change his shape at will. The narrator himself is endowed with the power to have historical and literary figures interchange personalities with one another, presenting, at times, a grotesque tableau.

---

[37] William York Tindall, *Forces in Modern British Literature* (New York: Vintage Books, 1956), p. 312.

[38] Northrop Frye, *Anatomy of Criticism* (Princeton: University Press, 1957), p. 99. In addition, the Jungian interpretation of archetypes will also be pertinent. To Jung, archetypes are structural elements of the collective unconscious and serve to give a pictorial form of the instincts. These images have their closest counterpart in mythological types.

The narrator's personality is in a state of constant flux, changing either at will or unconsciously to blend with the surrounding environment and carry out his plans. At the beginning he is faceless and without an identity—a voice emanating from the pages. But as the novel progresses, his past, his present, and his make-believe future begin to appear. After becoming Orpheus, he descends to Tartarus:

> . . . todo por el módico precio de tres dirhames . . . al servicial Plutón que se expresa en francés . . . estás en el umbral del Misterio, en la boca de la infernal Caverna . . . que conduce al reino de las Sombras, del Sueño y de la Noche, ínclito Eneas súbitamente abandonado por la Sibila. (p. 84)

There he releases Julián and Tariq whose souls he brings back to earth to proceed with the invasion.

The Protean change of personality is observed as well in a male character to whom the reader has access only through the eyes of the narrator. Known variously as el Ubicuo, Figurón, Moscardón, Tonelete, and by other names, this person's identity changes from that of a historical figure to a contemporary dictator, popular hero, or typical cafe bore—to a literary entity. The different personalities are interchangeable and the reader can determine that they are the same only by noticing a few common characteristics. Goytisolo himself comments on the protean element in an interview in *Le Monde*:

> Les personnages surgissent, disparaissent, se métamorphosent selon les besoins rhétoriques de la narration. Ce sont des personnages sans consistance psychologique, des personnages protéiformes: Tonelete devient successivement el Ubicuo, Figurón, Sénèque, le chevalier chrétien, Moscardo, Unamuno, etc.[39]

This fusion, a series of grotesque images, identifies Seneca with Tonelete (Manolete); Ubicuo with Franco; Figurón with Unamuno: ". . . tras la mesa de un rectoral despacho cubierta

---

[39] Claude Couffon, "*Don Julián* ou la destruction des mythes," *Le Monde*, 11 September 1970, p. VI.

de papeles y libros y un austero crucifijo Kierkegaardiano . . ." (p. 116). Álvaro Peranzules (famous Count of León, uncle of the Infantes de Carrión) is a combination of the Spanish Christian gentleman and Moscardón (a typical Spanish exile, habitué of street cafes). Seneca becomes not only a source of the Spanish spirit, but also a despised dictator and a popular hero: "rasgos faciales de finura aguileña, disposición capilar de matador de toros, patillas peinadas a lo flamenco / Séneca?/sí, Séneca" (p. 110). He is also an embodiment of the old gentry and a boring "cafebug":

> Figurón te tiende una tarjeta rectangular con la inscripción DON ÁLVARO PERANZULES ABOGADO y se empareja contigo . . . don Álvaro se expresa en un castellano purísimo y, acentuando la digital presión sobre el brazo, te arrastra a un típico café madrileño . . . local muy castizo adonde suelo ir por las tardes: tertulia de carpetos auténticos que avanzan por la vida con rumbo fijo. (pp. 79–80)

By such bizarre amalgamations, Goytisolo ridicules and "destroys" long-held ideas about Seneca while, at the same time, attacking Franco's regime and the people who support it. He demythifies Seneca, presenting him as a common man, exposing the absurdity of the Spanish perspective of him: ". . . lees a menudo Séneca?/no, dices/tienes que hacerlo : hay que desterrar las actitudes cómodas e intranscendentes : someter la realidad a los imperativos absolutos del espíritu : a un orden jerárquico, vertical" (p. 81).

Another example of the use of the Proteus myth is the fusion of Isabel I with Santa Teresa and a nightclub stripper. Isabel's description is highly idealized to present a violent contrast with what is about to happen: "Isabel la Católica es de mediana estatura, bien compuesta en su persona y en la proporción de sus miembros muy blanca y rubia, los ojos entre verdes y azules, el mirar gracioso y honesto: es generosa,

164

expansiva, justiciera, alegre" (p. 162).[40] Shortly thereafter she becomes a nun in a mystical trance. The nun, however, upon hearing the music of the Rolling Stones, metamorphoses into a stripper in a highly erotic state who is flagellated by the narrator. Thus, Isabel and Santa Teresa, the Christian woman and the Church, become a hypererotic female involved in a sexual happening.

Through the use of the Proteus myth, the Cid, the Spanish hero par excellence, becomes the most hated individual in the history of Spain—Julián. This metamorphosis takes place as the narrator quotes a poem by Manuel Machado in which the name of Julián is substituted for that of the Cid: ". . . por la terrible estepa castellana, al descanso, con cientos de los suyos, polvo, sudor y hierro Ulyán cabalga" (p. 192).

In a further Protean application the donkey Platero is knifed by Pascual, a juxtaposition of the violence of Cela's *La Familia de Pascual Duarte* with the innocence and beauty of Juan Ramón Jiménez' *Platero y yo*. Such a tableau produces a grotesque, electrifying effect enhanced by the fact that the narrator foretells the reader's own behavior. When the juxtaposed scene takes place, the reader is not only the witness of the execution, but the executioner as well:

> . . . el animal es pequeño, suave y camina resollando como si viniera de muy lejos: con una mano le darás de comer mientras que, con la otra, empuñas el afilado cuchillo y se lo hundes con lentitud en la garganta: la sangre brotará morada y espesa: sus ojos de azabache implorarán como dos escarabajos de cristal

---

[40] The description of Isabel I has been taken from an elementary school textbook by Pedro Alvarado, entitled *Los españoles de ayer, Isabel la Católica*, p. 3. (This is the only information available in a photocopy of a page of that text received from Boston University.) The destructive irony of the author needs no elaboration.

negro . . . la viejita tratará de interponerse y correrá la misma suerte. (p. 147)[41]

Another important use of the Proteus myth combines the narrator's childhood (perhaps Goytisolo's), with a mysterious figure named Caperucito (an obvious travesty of the Red Riding Hood tale) and Alvarito (who perhaps now represents the collective childhood of the Spanish people):

> . . . la madre de Alvarito, y no hay para menos, lo quiere con locura . . . que todo el mundo da en llamarle Caperucito Rojo, hasta el extremo de haber caído en olvido su verdadero nombre . . . (p. 206); . . . tu odio irreductible hacia el pasado y el niño espurio/que lo representa/exige los fastos de la muerte ritual y su ceremonial/mágico. (p. 213)

The myth of Orpheus also represents an important theme in the novel. He is not only the musician who entices people into listening to his songs, but is capable of transcending life and death (Orpheus was so determined to rescue Eurydice from Hades that he descended to the underworld and was allowed to return with her on certain conditions). Luis del Corral writes about the application of Orpheus in contemporary literature:

> Orfeo ha vencido, además de las barreras entre la vida y la muerte, todas las otras barreras existentes entre los objetos, todas las fronteras divisorias de las cosas, y ha abierto para el hombre el "espacio interior del mundo." . . . dentro del "espacio interior del

---

[41] Cf. Cela's text: "Fue cosa de un momento. Me eché sobre ella y la clavé; la clavé lo menos veinte veces. . . . Tenía la piel dura: mucho más dura que la de Zacarías. . . . Cuando de allí salí saqué el brazo dolido; la sangre me llegaba hasta el codo. . . . El animalito no dijo ni pío; se limitaba a respirar más hondo y más de prisa, como cuando la echaban al macho." Camilo José Cela, *La familia de Pascual Duarte* (New York: Las Américas Publishing Company, 1965), p. 61. In Jiménez' text the description of Platero is as follows: "Platero es pequeño, peludo, suave; tan blando por fuera, que se diría todo de algodón, que no lleva huesos. Sólo los espejos de azabache de sus ojos son duros cual dos escarabajos de cristal negro." Juan Ramón Jiménez, "Platero," in *Literatura del siglo XX*, ed. by Da Cal and Ucelay (New York: Holt, Rinehart and Winston, 1968), p. 229.

mundo" no existe verdadera discriminación de número, figura o tiempo. Muy en especial, ha quedado anulada la conciencia angustiosa del tiempo.[42]

Goytisolo's narrator has Orphean powers. The reader falls under his spell and follows him to Hades (a bathhouse) from where he brings back to life Julián and Tariq who can advance his plans of destruction: ". . . abarcando las tersas superficies pulidas, eludiendo la mórbida carnosidad innecesaria: sin Radamanto, sin Tisífone, si . Cerbero: hechas las abluciones rituales, cumplida la ofrenda. . . . Tariq, Tariq! : agnición de la humana fraternidad! : sólita epifanía del verbo!" (p. 85).

In another scene, where tourists prepare to enter a cave which becomes the vagina of Spain, Orpheus is observed descending once again:

. . . los turistas bajan del autocar . . . (p. 167); . . . estás en el umbral del Misterio, en la boca de la infernal Caverna . . . Orfeo sin lira tras las huellas de Eurídice . . . nuevo Teseo, inspirado Alcides te internarás en la oblicua garganta abierta en la excavación pelviana rastreando el caliginoso lecho del Aqueronte y la vasta y muerta extensión de la laguna Estigia a través de los tortuosos cuellos del útero y los esponjosos sacos vaginales. (pp. 168–69)[43]

This time he introduces the hordes of Arabs who ravish Spain. Goytisolo here shows the prostitution of Spain to contemporary economic goals and, at the same time, the narrator's desire to return to the womb.[44]

This desire can also be linked with the narrator's pursuit of a new identity which can be attained by being reborn.

---

[42] Luis Diez del Corral, *La función del mito clásico en la literatura contemporánea* (Madrid: Editorial Gredos, 1957), p. 161.

[43] Several references to Charon, or Archeron, the ferryman of the Styx, serve to reinforce the descent of Orpheus to Tartarus. There are also references to *obolo* (p. 169), the small coin that Charon receives for his services (in some cultures coins are placed in the eyes of the dead to pay Charon, although the reason may also be to keep the corpse's eyes shut).

[44] Jung, *Psychology of the Unconscious*, p. 375, says that the descent into the earth symbolizes entering the mother's womb.

According to Jung this is a form of the incest wish, although the person's

> . . . desire does not aim at cohabitation, but at the special thought of becoming a child again, of turning back to the parent's protection, of coming into the mother once more in order to be born again. But incest stands in the path to this goal, that is to say, the necessity in some way of again gaining entrance into the mother's womb. One of the simplest ways would be to impregnate the mother, and to reproduce one's self identically. But here the incest prohibition interferes. . . . A very simple method of avoidance is to transform the mother into another being.[45]

Jung adds that the desire to overcome the incest taboo forces the individual to engage in inventive fantasies as well as mythical ones, allowing the libido, taking an active part, to flow. By penetrating and ravishing Spain, the narrator has attained a new identity and, at the same time, shown the deterioration of Spain which, wide open to the world of tourism, is commercialized and prostituted.

In addition to those of Proteus and Orpheus, the myth of Prometheus occupies an important position in the novel, illustrating the narrator's alienation from society and his obsession to expose the servitude to which his countrymen have been relegated by a totalitarian government. The relevant elements of the Promethean story include ability to foresee the future, artistic qualities, and eternal punishment. An analogous situation can be observed in the novel. The narrator foresees the future and relates it in a poetic manner. He is also punished, but, in his case, he is both Prometheus and eagle: he embarks on a daily, symbolic destruction of Spain, the destruction of which is consummated by the end of the day. Yet during the night the same evils the narrator sets out to denounce and destroy are reinstated, and the narrator must begin the invasion anew the following morning: ". . . mañana será otro día,

---

[45] *Ibid.*, p. 251.

la invasión recomenzará" (p. 240). The narrator is Prometheus because he brings the light to his countrymen, but he is the eagle as well since he must "tear out" all the evils of the Spanish society he sees: ". . . encadenado a una roca del Caucaso, un águila dibuja/en lo alto porfiados y agoreros círculos/acecha largamente/y de improviso/cala vertiginosa sobre él/y le devora el hígado" (p. 210).

It may be pertinent to recall also the haruspical symbolism in psychic life that the liver had for the ancient Greeks by an examination of several further allusions to the liver and Prometheus:

> . . . espiándote con sus ojos móviles, escurridizos, durante la exposición del sombrío cuadro: revestido de peto, careta, guante y manopla, presto a manejar el sable . . . unas pastillas paeso, pa el hígado . . . (p. 23). . . . el hígado, como de costumbre: o una trastada juguetona del riñón: la crisis pasó y, gracias a Dios: pero la procesión va por dentro: un cálculo sí, una piedrecilla . . . (p. 24); . . . el sable hundido hasta la empuñadura: en tanto que tú te escabulles por la tangente . . . espiándote con sus ojos móviles, escurridizos, durante la minuciosa exposicion del sombrío cuadro : el hígado, sí señor . . . (p. 25); . . . perseguido de una horda de mendigos que corren detrás de ti, te tiran de la manga, te rodean, amenazan, suplican, intentan cortarte el paso : el hígado, sí señor. (p. 74)[46]

The beggar above has somehow taken the form of an eagle, his eyes moving about, pecking on the narrator's liver. He tries unsuccessfully to avoid this daily encounter—he is marked by his position as a shaman with supernatural powers. In the eyes of the beggar, these powers in contemporary society have been reduced to the position of affluent foreigner and from the standpoint of the narrator to the position of "seer."

The purpose of the myth of Sisyphus in *Don Julián* parallels that of Prometheus. While Prometheus is tortured daily by

---

[46] According to Neumann, *The Origin and History of Consciousness*, p. 26, in haruspicy the liver (and kidneys) is examined because it is considered a divinatory center.

an eagle, Sisyphus is tormented every day by his having to push a large rock. Both myths stress the protagonist's involvement in a daily ritual. As evening falls and the invasion is consummated, the narrator brings his "rock" (daily invasion) to the summit, only to see it roll down, reaching the bottom as day breaks; he wakes up and sees the scar (Spain) across the sea. By accepting this daily ritual the narrator attains authenticity and gives himself a meaning for life in addition to a new identity.[47]

The allusions to the phoenix in the novel (when not referring to Lope de Vega), reinforce the motif of recurrence provided by the myths of Prometheus and Sisyphus. Just as the phoenix burns utterly and springs anew from the ashes, so every morning does Spain, and the narrator is the catalyst, prime mover of this ritual.

Allusions to Theseus, the Cretan Labyrinth, and the Minotaur are important to the general theme: the decadence of Spain. The totalitarian government has forced many Spaniards into exile, among them the narrator: ". . . adiós, Madrastra inmunda, país de siervos y señores : adiós tricornios de charol, y tú, pueblo que los soportas : tal vez el mar del Estrecho me libre de tus guardianes : de sus ojos que todo lo ven, de sus malsines que todo lo saben" (pp. 15–16). So, the reader learns of the narrator's state of anxiety. Being in an alien culture, with only his memory—most recollections, unfortunately, unpleasant—he must develop new goals, new standards, a new reality, find a myth to bring him out of the labyrinth and defend him from the Minotaur. Tangiers is a large labyrinth in which the protagonist finds himself: "Por los recovecos del urbano laberinto . . ." (p. 89). But the labyrinth is also within; he carries it wherever he goes: "El laberinto está

---

[47] Cf. Camus' views on Sisyphus. Albert Camus, *The Myth of Sisyphus* in *Existentialism from Dostoevsky to Sartre*, ed. Walter Kaufman (New York: Meridian Books, 1965), p. 312.

en tí" (p. 52). He is both Minotaur and victim, "minotauro voraz, mártir comestible: juntamente verdugo y víctima" (p. 52). For Jung, the Minotaur is the symbol of decadent Crete and in most cultures the Labyrinth "has the meaning of an entangling and confusing representation of the world of matriarchal consciousness."[48] If this idea is applied to the novel, the allusions to the Minotaur and the Labyrinth may indicate the author's concern for a decadent Spain and his unconscious desire to overcome the matriarchal power he feels Spain has over him. The narrator thus reaches the conclusion that only his country's destruction can bestow freedom on him.

The narrator's use of *kif* can be considered, to some degree, a parallel to the story of the lotus-eaters. In the novel the narrator refers to the patrons of a cafe where *kif* is smoked as "los asiduos del loto" (p. 41). But in contrast to the lotus-eaters of ancient Greece, the narrator does not forget his national origin. He does obtain supernatural powers which aid him in transcending reality and destroying Spain. The use of narcotics to achieve trances is a constituent element of shamanism.

The preceding are by no means the only mythological allusions in the novel. The classical myths studied thus far are dynamic motifs relevant to the protagonist's character. Many others function as free motifs, far too many to be dealt with in this chapter, but a few have been selected for brief examination. An inherent characteristic of free motifs is their use in digressions. In Don Julián, digressions are usually triggered by free associations, at times induced by *kif* or *hierba*. Situations and characters from Greek and Roman mythology appear on almost every page, an occurrence which may be due to the protagonist's desire to divest himself of his Christian back-

---

[48] Carl G. Jung and Joseph L. Henderson, *Man and his Symbols* (New York: Doubleday and Co., 1964), p. 125.

ground. The betrayal motif permeates the novel since the act of the protagonist is one of high treason and he himself recognizes it as such: "Nuevo conde don Julián, fraguando sombrías traiciones" (p. 16).

The executioner-victim motif obtains in the relationship between the narrator-protagonist and his motherland. He is both victim and executioner, accusing Spain of having victimized him and, at the same time, hoping for and planning her destruction, "juntamente verdugo y víctima" (p. 52). Another example is Alvarito, the protagonist as a child, who is frequently tortured, "fondo sonoro: aullido de Alvarito" (p. 210). This free motif is underscored by the sentence, which can be considered a leitmotif, "CON LOS NIÑOS EL LATIGO ES NECESARIO," which reappears frequently in capital letters, set off from the rest of the test. The executioner-victim motif is closely linked here with sadomasochism. The leitmotif which accentuates it is the following sentence, which, taken out of context, lacks the impact it has when seen as part of the entire novel: "DONNEZ VOUS VOTRE SANG SAUVEZ UNE VIE" (printed in capital letters, it is set off from the rest of the text). Sadism appears in the rooster imagery and in the killing of Platero, and also when the narrator-protagonist watches a group of young boys kill a cat (p. 18). Sadomasochism is patent in the relations between Alvarito and the Moor, since the former appears to enjoy his suffering as much as the latter relishes inflicting it. The motif of homosexuality (Alvarito and the Moor) recalls Jerónimo and Álvaro in *Señas de identidad*. The narrator-protagonist also appears to be attracted to a young boy who wants to be his guide, an offer which he accepts even though he lives in the city.

The novel abounds with allusions to films. The most important one is James Bond's adventure, *Thunderball*, an amphibious invasion of the United States. After the protagonist enters the theater, four pages describe what is taking place in the film (pp. 75–78). The name of the film, JAMES BOND,

OPERACIÓN TRUENO, is the leitmotif which reappears throughout the novel. It should be noted that the invader of the Península is called "hijo del Trueno" (p. 142), perhaps a reminder of the film invasion. These three leitmotifs—executioner-victim, sadomasochism, Bond—are combined by using two words of the first two examined and one word from the film. They appear one word at a time, on the left side of the page:

DONNEZ
SANG
BOND
NIÑOS
LATIGO (p. 74)

Through the combination occurs an amalgamation of a number of themes and motifs—in essence, Goytisolo has literarily and symbolically interwoven them.

María Móntez, John Hall, and their films are mentioned, movies set in a medium similar to the one in which the narrator-protagonist finds himself. The protagonist, however, does not have the benefit of technicolor: "...no embellecido por el fausto del hollywoodiano tecnicolor : el de las películas de María Móntez y John Hall con sus cromáticos mercados de los tiempos de Aladino y Ali Baba" (p. 43). Peter O'Toole and his adventures in *Lawrence of Arabia* also figure (p. 46), and it is interesting to note that in *Juan sin tierra* T. E. Lawrence's exploits form a very important motif. Hitchcock's film, *The Birds*, which also deals with an invasion, is cited, the birds "volando en bandas, como en el film de Hitchcock sobre la aterrorizada ciudad : ..." There is also an allusion to a Bergman film, perhaps *The Seventh Seal*, a poignant illustration of a procession during Holy Week: "... los encapuchados que ven avanzar titubeando, como en la inolvidable película de Bergman, pertenecen, ladies and gentlemen, a todas las categorias de la sociedad: . . . (p. 183). Each film utilized adds background atmosphere and aids in the description of the surroundings where the protagonist either finds himself or believes himself to be.

Another free motif comprises constant reference to musical compositions, dancers, and composers from Chopin to Gershwin and The Rolling Stones. An interesting use of this musical motif, an example of laying bare, appears at the end of the novel after the invasion has been completed. An orchestra's performance comes to a close:

> . . . clarinetes y saxos, violines y oboes, atabales y bajos, mandolinas, rebeles : la improvisada orquesta colectará a su paso la quieta aprobación de los espectros que rondan el paseo : en sordina, de forma casi inaudible, insinúa el tema descendente del Adagio cual si quisiera adormecer, acunar : a la altura del hotel El Djénina, los músicos enmudecen sucesivamente y, como en "Los Adioses" de Haydn al príncipe de Esterhazy, apagarán las candelillas verdes, guardarán las partituras, enfundarán los instrumentos antes de abandonar de modo definitivo la nocturna, fantasmal procesión : en tres ocasiones, por la abrupta cuesta de Grotius, el motivo principal vibrará aún con una distribución cada vez más reducida y débil hasta que el movimiento, y con él toda la sinfonía, se extinguirá suavemente en un melancólico solo de flauta. (pp. 238–39)

In the above excerpt, particular attention should be given the statement about theme and motifs, which may allude to Goytisolo's intentions in the construction of his work. If that is so, the passage quoted would be an example of laying bare with Goytisolo showing the reader the blueprints, as it were, of his creation. Elsewhere in the novel the musical motif is combined with the sexual one, and the two become the leitmotif, "erección musical" (pp. 77,165). The famous Russian dancers, Pawlowa and Nijinsky, are mentioned when the narrator equates the "grace" suddenly appearing in an invalid's gait shortly after he receives alms, with that of the dancers:

> . . . cuando to tiende la mano y le das unas monedas tu gesto te parece en seguida sacrílego : limosna a un rey? : el pordiosero se

aleja ascilando como una peonza y su pie contraído tal pezuña de chivo cobra de pronto, al andar, la gracia alada de una Pawlowa o un Nijinsky. . . . (p. 44)

Literary allusions form another important free motif, not to be mistaken for a theme already examined in which the protagonist desecrates literary texts, nor to be considered as part of the technique of literary borrowing, to be examined shortly. Essentially, this motif consists of dropping names, alluding to works, or mentioning them without direct quotes. In one example the narrator speaks of the "proeza de Sherezada" (p. 13). He also mentions the nineteenth-century Russian romantic poet Lermontov, "romántica, lermontoviana-mente. . ." (p. 15). When he talks about the city of Pompeii, he cites Bulwer, (p. 19). Proust and Heidegger are mentioned (p. 138), as is *La gloria de don Ramiro* (p. 176).

An important free motif recurring throughout the novel involves myriad references to organs of the body and organic systems: the digestive system, liver, vagina, penis, and heart. The digestive system is mentioned first: " . . . atrapado, preso, capsulado, digerido, expulsado : el consabido ciclo cital por los pasillos y túneles del aparato diges-tive-reproductor. . ." (p. 13). The liver, the vagina, and the penis and how they relate to different themes and motifs, having already been discussed, need no further elaboration. The heart appears in a scene in which the narrator describes a statue of the child Jesus with "el corazón atravesado de alfileres" (p. 180).

Allusions to the five senses form another free motif in which sight is very important, since the narrator-protagonist roams the streets of Tangiers observing everything about him and is frequently affected, directly or indirectly by it. The sense of smell also predominates: " . . .avivando, el muy cegato, el proceso natural de descomposición : olores densos, emana-ciones agrias que voluntariamente aspiras con fervor catecúmeno, como en una severa y exigente iniciación órfica"

175

(p. 43). The sense of touch is particularly noticed in the library scene when the insects are squashed between the pages of several books. At least three aspects of hearing can be identified: it is naturally present whenever someone speaks to the protagonist, a characteristic of dialogue in most novels. Also, quite normally, the reader has access to extraneous sounds to which the narrator-protagonist is exposed but cannot control. Such an example is observed when, while in his room, he hears someone playing a musical instrument: "Abierta la ventana, la melodía irrumpe" (p. 16). Third, and most originally, the entire novel strives to be an oral rendition rather than formal written prose, making hearing the most prevalent of all the senses. The fifth, taste, is evoked whenever the narrator drinks tea and smokes *kif*.

Several types of fetishism make up another free motif: feet, urine, feces, and vagina. The last three have already been discussed; the first is noticed in the following scene in which the narrator describes a woman's toes and the color of her toenails, equating them with cherries, suggesting an erotic fixation on female feet: " . . .sobre las macizas colmnas sostenidas por zapatones con suela de corcho y abiertos por delante : autorizando así la clamorosa manifestación de los dedos : irregulares, palmipartidos, autónomos : con diez toques de laca rojiza, como otras tantas cerezas rubicundas, apetitosas : . . ." (p. 48).

The final motif is the Quixotic behavior of the narrator-protagonist—he is *literally* fighting windmills. He goes through his odyssey "a tientas y a ciegas" (p. 83), ironically enough for one who is trying to divest himself of his culture.[49]

---

[49] Goytisolo's intentions are observed in the prologue to *Blanco White*, where he writes about his perspective of Spain and his Quixotic fight against her: ". . . la lucha despiadada contra el mito, contra todas las adherencias histórico-culturales que envuelven un nombre, lo lastran, lo petrifican, lo falsean. España, el nombre de 'España,' cubre difícilmente la proteica realidad peninsular. Es un mito también, un nombre que ha envejecido y contra el que el escritor parte en guerra: guerra fantasmal, desproporcionada, como la que

Three arcane figures serve as "bridges" between major themes between motifs, or between themes and motifs. They are James Bond, Potiphar's wife, and Álvaro-Caperucito: father, mother, and son. By means of this triad, a highly elaborated thematic unity is attained. James Bond, the only noticeable father-image in the novel, represents strongly sexual masculinity and a heroism echoing *el caballero cristiano*, in a twentieth-century setting. His normal, caricatural superman image is retained, with references to Bond's adventures in *Thunderball*, where he thwarts an underwater invasion of the United States, revealing one of his thematic relationships to the novel. Bond is thus the only character in *Don Julián* capable of stopping the invasion of Spain, the only one who can rescue Caperucito from the wolf. But he, according to the narrator, will not intervene: "Estamos seguros que morirá/entre atroces dolores/si Bond no lo remedia/pero Bond no intervendrá" (p. 213). Bond therefore introduces either the image of the absent father unable to help or deliberate refusal—rejection by the father. He also serves to bridge the themes of invasion and sex.

Potiphar's wife (often called Putifar), a Protean figure, is more important for sexual connotations than for her contribution to the discussion of myth. Like her biblical counterpart, she represents aggressive and vindictive sexuality. In some of her other protean figures she is a surrogate mother-figure, dissolute Spain, the Virgin Mary, the Church, and the perverting, encroaching U.S. economy with its materialistic culture. In another incarnation she appears as an American tourist: " . . . agrupada ahora alrededor del guía como medroso rebaño al Tiempo que acribillan la explanada con sus máquinas fotográficas . . . una imponente hija de la Revolución Ameri-

---

opuso el caballero don Quijote a los formidables molinos de viento. Dicha empresa debe adoptar la forma de una liberación del lenguaje de los grillos discursivos a que durante siglos ha estado sujeto" (p. 98).

cana" (pp. 46–47). Later she appears in a flashback as a flower vendor who debased Alvarito:

> . . . la vendedora de flores . . . tocada con un fez rojo . . . la boca embadurnada de rouge : el escote inmenso, enunciativo, escabroso . . . (p. 99); . . . zapatones con suela de corcho . . . Putifar, Putifar! . . . sabes dónde está la gruta?/no!/acá!/ agarrándole de la cabeza . . . levantándose la falda . . . a penetrar en el virgiliano antro. (p. 100)

Putifar is killed by a serpent and her corpse is defiled by gnomes from the Zoco Grande as they strip her of her jewelry, a scene which parallels what happens to Mary during the sack of the temple:

> . . . bruscamente abre su boca dilatable . . . y hunde los dientes huecos . . . en la mejilla bultada y carnosa . . . Mrs. Putifar tocada con el fez rojo . . . hace esfuerzos desesperados por mantener el equilibrio . . . cuando se derrumba . . . sugiere un melancólico templo en ruinas (p. 67). . . . los gnomos orientales . . . se precipitan . . . y le despojan de sus joyas y adornos : con irreverencia . . . levantan la falda y se arriman a orinar a la gruta. (p. 68)

Later she has recuperated from her death: "Repuesta de su muerte y profanación, la hija de la Revolución Americana emerge con el papel de fumar, el fez rojo" (p. 69). Her holding the serpent seems to be an allusion to the Virgin and Child.[50] This being the case, "Mrs. Putifar" bridges several motifs and themes: the sexual, the incest wish, the tragic results of inadequate sexual instruction given to adolescents in Spain, atavistic remnants in the Catholic Church, the criticism of contemporary economic policies, and the attack against the *carpetos* and *capras*, since she is a member of a similar social stratum in the U.S. which exerts influence in Spain.

---

[50] Neumann, p. 49. According to Neumann: "The fully human end-figure, the human Madonna with the human child, has her fore-runner in the figure of the human mother with her companion snake in the form of a child or a phallus as well as in figures of the human child with the big snake." Mother and child originally had the heads of snakes, Neumann says, but in the course of time both became humanized.

Alvarito-Caperucito is the most complex of the three recondite figures because of the great number of themes and motifs he bridges and the many related concepts and allusions he incorporates. Alvarito-Caperucito represents the adolescence of every Spaniard—the narrator's in particular, blighted by the deleterious influence of Catholic education. The Church has continued bolstering the sexual fears that gave rise to Rodrigo's legend in which a serpent emasculates the last Visigothic king for his sins against the flesh. The Caperucito story elaborates on the impact this sexual phobia has on youth. The girl of "Red Riding Hood" is metamorphosed into a boy, and the author substitutes for the wolf a Moor and his magic serpent, a valid substitution since Jung says that in some variations of the tale a serpent takes the place of the wolf.[51] When Caperucito goes to visit his grandmother, the usual questioning about her appearance takes place. Caperucito is then sodomized by the Moor and his neck is severed (p. 210). Decapitation constitutes a symbolic representation of the emasculation motif.[52] Alvarito-Caperucito undergoes ritual deaths, all suggesting the emasculation motif: he is devoured by hungry dogs (p. 210); he perishes in the Cretan Labyrinth (p. 210); an eagle rips his liver (p. 210); having assumed the form of a bird, Alvarito is strangled by a serpent (p. 211); as an insect, he is swallowed by a carnivorous plant (p. 211). Goytisolo reiterates his wrath against institutionalized malforming of the perspective on sex, so that the individual, plagued by fears, is unable to engage in normal private and public social relations with his peers.

---

[51] Jung, *Psychology of the Unconscious*, p. 524. In a footnote he elaborates by saying that the "Deluge" is of one nature with the serpent and that in the Woluspa the flood is the result of the Midgard serpent rising. The Midgard serpent, interestingly enough, is also called "the all-prevading Wolf." This fact leads to substitution, in the fairy stories of Red Riding Hood, of a wolf for a serpent or fish. (The importance of this fairy tale to the themes of the novel will be examined later.)

[52] Neumann, p. 159. Neumann says: "It is correct to interpret beheading . . . as castration. . . ."

To illustrate the narrator's psychotic seizures, Goytisolo shows him submerged and overcome by violence. The narrator, aware of his situation and its causes, seeks retribution, a revenge which, at the same time, will have a therapeutic value. Regarding his present state as a consequence of the ravishing of his youth by Spanish culture, he concludes that in order to attain peace with himself, a meaning for his life, he must revalidate himself. Alvarito-Caperucito's ritual deaths are some of the means by which he goes about reaching this goal. Alvarito also represents the narrator's youth, and the Moor, Alvarito's beheader, is an alter ego of the protagonist. Thus, there is a mystic fusion of victim and executioner: "Tú eres el laberinto: minotauro voraz, mártir comestible: juntamente verdugo y víctima" (p. 52). Alvarito-Caperucito links the various motifs and themes of vengeance, sexual perversions, legend, incest wishes, social and religious protest, the need for a father (a possible allusion to the many children who lost their fathers in the Spanish Civil War), and the attack against language and literature, illustrated by the travesty of the Red Riding Hood tale.

Moreover, Alvarito-Caperucito is a sacrificial lamb that purifies Spain, avenges the narrator's past, and provides him and the reader with catharsis. Spain's destruction brings a new identity to the narrator, erasing the past: " . . . tu odio irreductible hacia el pasado y el niño espurio/que lo representa/exige los fastos de la muerte ritual y su ceremonial/mágico" (p. 213). The ritual shedding the child's blood washes away Spain's sins, reconstructs the past of the narrator, and brings the protagonist a new life. Alvarito-Caperucito's death might be associated with ancient fertility rites in which the sacrificial victim's flesh and blood were sprinkled in the fields. In *Don Julián*, the protagonist is the high priest in the oblation. The various themes, motifs, and bridges appear to be linked together somewhat as in a musical composition in sonata form. Each theme has its own motifs; there are free motifs and leitmotifs with ideas of their own or ones reflecting some theme, and the bridges link everything together in a unified whole.[53]

Other techniques utilized by Goytisolo in his construction of *Reivindicación del conde don Julián* are laying bare, literary borrowing, the staircase device, retardation, and defamiliarization. Some of these have been treated earlier, but the first example of laying bare appears at the beginning of the novel when the narrator alludes to Scheherazade's behavior. The reader is also informed of the author's purpose when the narrator speaks of rejecting official syntax: " . . . inventarás senderos y trochas, en abrupta ruptura con lo oficial sintaxis y su secuela de dogmas y entredichos : hereje, cismático, renegado, apóstata : violando edictos y normas, probando el sabroso fruto prohibido" (p. 152).

Literary borrowing may remind the reader of a famous poet's dictum that mediocre poets imitate, great ones steal. Goytisolo steals from many writers to compose a literary collage. For example, one of Iriarte's verses appears to be quoted although his name does not figure in the *Advertencia* (p. 241), "panal de rica miel" (p. 20). Allusion to Larra occurs in the following: " . . . como observó Fígaro, según la mayor o menor cantidad de moléculas que los integran : sólidos, líquidos y gaseosos : abajo, el sólido de los sólidos" (p. 21). Some verses from Fray Luis de Leon's poem "La profecía del Tajo," are quoted (p. 45), and opening words of the *Quijote* appear, somewhat changed, throughout the novel: "Del país cuyo nombre no quieres acordarte" (p. 72). Darío's "Marcha Triunfal" is quoted as the narrator watches *Thunderball*: "¡Ya viene el cortejo! ¡Ya viene el cortejo!" (p. 76). Furthermore many works

---

[53] A detailed study will be needed, however, to establish how much truth there is to this hypothesis. Manuel Durán also mentions the musical form of the novel in "Vindicación de Juan Goytisolo: *Reivindicación del conde Don Julián," Insula*, No. 290 (enero 1971), 4.

of writers of the Golden Age and the Generation of '98 are desecrated. At the end of the novel, Goytisolo lists most of the sources for his collage.

The staircase-like device to be considered next is in itself a form of retardation—a device examined shortly. The story of "Caperucito Rojo," appears for the first time on p. 13 and thereafter is intercalated throughout the novel. It merges with the main story at the moment Spain is invaded by the Moors and Alvarito-Caperucito is ravished and killed by one of them. Other instances are the constant apparitions of Álvaro Peranzules, the young guide, and the beggar who is always talking about his liver. These narrative parallel the novel's main stream and, in some instances, as Caperucito does, merge with it. The device of retardation has many forms, of which the preceding is one. Repetition is another, and in *Don Julián* it prevails throughout. In its more developed form, entire episodes may be reiterated, as is the case of the bedroom scene. In a less complex version, sentences (leitmotifs are examples) reappear throughout the novel. The simplest aspect is the use of two or more synonymous expressions following each other without any need to clarify further what is being described: "Cuando la ruina sea completa y la bancarrota absoluta" (p. 199), and again: "El celeste chivo desmaya, palidece y se vuelve indolente, abúlico : menguado ya" (p. 12).

Reivindicación del conde don Julián may be an exponent of artistic motivation. It has introduced nonliterary material in a new and original interpretation; the ordinary has become unfamiliar, and the old and habitual new and unusual. Through defamiliarization many aspects of Spanish culture are desecrated and ridiculed: long-held beliefs are questioned and sacred cows massacred. Goytisolo also tries to show that realism is not inherent in Spanish literature through his hallucinated invasion and destruction of Spain. In his prologue to *Obra inglesa de D. José María Blanco White* he says that

> Los novelistas latinoamericanos pueden reivindicar, pues, el nombre de Blanco White en su loable propósito de ensanchar las

bases del "realismo" al uso e incluir en él visiones y sueños, pesadillas . . . y mitos. Algunas de sus obras son la demostración práctica de que ese "realismo" mutilador no es inherente ni mucho menos a la literatura de expresión castellana. En el mundo industrial de hoy—el de los Estados y burocracias soviéticos o capitalistas—el poder subversivo de la imaginación resulta más necesario que nunca. (p. 64)

He goes on to explain Blanco White's defense of the *inverosímil*:

. . . en su defensa de lo inverosímil, nos percatamos de que no cae, como la mayoría de sus coetáneos, en la trampa de la ilusión realista: así, en lugar de condenar la inverosimilitud de la predicción de las hechiceras en *Macbeth*, la juzga en función de sus efectos sobre el desenvolvimiento posterior de la acción. La introducción de lo inverosímil, dice, rompe con la monotonía de los acontecimientos humanos y da variedad y color a las situaciones. Los errores en que incurren algunos autores fantásticos no se deben a que expongan sucesos o actos inverosímiles, sino a que "los efectos y expresiones no corresponden a los caracteres ni a la situación." (p. 65)

Interestingly enough, these views parallel Tomashevsky's concept of realistic motivation as applied to literary fantasies (Lemon, p. 83), raising the question whether *Don Julián* may not be an exponent of realistic rather than artistic motivation. There seem to be aspects of both types in Goytisolo's novel.

In conclusion, the contrast between the study of character by nineteenth-century novelists and that by Goytisolo may be established by citing Sharon Spencer who says that

. . . psychology and especially the discoveries of Freud, has shown us how very little of the truth about human beings lies on the surface that novelists learned how to depict so brilliantly during the nineteenth century, and how very misleading that surface can really be. To portray character with depth and truth, the novelist must abandon the surface and find some way of penetrating the inner reality of his subject.[54]

---

[54] Sharon Spencer, *Space, Time and Structure in the Modern Novel* (New York: New York University Press, 1971), p. XVI.

Goytisolo has managed to accomplish it in *Don Julián* and his desire to change Spain has been one of his motivating forces.

Chapter VI

Juan Sin Tierra

Goytisolo's latest work, *Juan sin tierra*,[1] like the two previous ones, deals with Álvaro's search for an identity and his eventual self-discovery. The possibility exists that this may be the last of the series, for which reason it is termed *The Mendiola Trilogy*. This work is not only written under Formalist influence, but also speaks about the Formalists' theories. The title refers to "Jean sans Terre" or John Lackland of England (1167–1216), the astute but unpopular ruler forced by his rebellious subjects to accept the Magna Carta. Goytisolo suggests parallels between the narrator of the novel, himself, and the English ruler, "herederos de Juan sin Tierra" (p. 89). The literal "sin tierra" is applicable to all three, and Don Julián's tradi-

---

[1] Juan Goytisolo, *Juan sin tierra* (Barcelona: Editorial Seix Barral, S.A., 1975). Hereafter all references will be given in parentheses in the text. Since Goytisolo uses periods erratically, they will be inserted in this study to maintain uniformity of style. Additionally, virgules will be used to indicate the variations in line-length of the prose whenever the typographical style varies from normal margin-to-margin. It is pertinent to know that the distribution and sale of this work was prohibited within Spain at the time this study was written. Juan Goytisolo was kind enough to ask Seix Barral to send a copy to the writer of this study.

tional role as a criminal and traitor has a parallel in John, probably a murderer and possibly the most despised large figure in English history. Hence, the motif of destruction, of a crime of *effet perpétuel*, is present in this work also.

As in previous novels, epigraphs refer to important themes developed in the book. The first one, "La cara se alejó del culo," from a work by Octavio Paz, is a broad concept embracing the sexual phobia experienced by most Spaniards—expounded upon at length in *Don Julián*. The other two epigraphs refer to the wanderings which Álvaro will undertake through Africa, the Arab world in particular, several times assuming the T. E. Lawrence identity, and ultimately changing his medium of expression from Spanish to Arabic.

Because of its radical difference not only to novels in general but to Goytisolo's previous works, *Juan sin tierra* could be classified as an entirely new genre in the vein of *Finnegans Wake*. Samuel Beckett's comment on Joyce's *magnum opus* is pertinent: "It [the novel] is not to be read—or rather it is not only to be read. It is also to be looked at and listened to. His writing is not *about* something; *it is that something itself.*"[2] Goytisolo's work has elements of a travelogue, a book of memoirs, and even a diary "to see clearly," as Roquentin said in *La nausée*.[3] The intentions of the author appear to be to embark the reader upon a voyage of self-discovery in which fact and fiction, the present, the past, and the future are intermingled. Frequent use of the second-person singular point of view contributes, as in *Don Julián*, to amalgamation of the protagonist and the reader. Unlike *Don Julián*, however, the author (who shows himself in the act of writing) indicates

---

[2] Samuel Beckett, "Dante . . . Bruno . . . Vico . . . Joyce," in *Our Examination Round His Factification for Incamination of Work in Progress* (London: Faber and Faber, 1921, 1961), p. 14. The italics are Beckett's.

[3] "Tenir un journal pour y voir clair," from Jean-Paul Sartre, *La nausée* (61st ed.; Gallimard, 1950), p. 11.

that he is the narrator-protagonist and fuses himself with protagonist and reader.

This chapter will examine the *caro-culo* and destruction themes, narrating motifs, the divisions of the work, time and place, a few recurring motifs, literary borrowing, and laying bare.

The *caro-culo* theme, suggested throughout the work by leitmotifs, seems at first a fetishist obsession with feces, although a broader interpretation to be examined shortly may also be valid. In the first chapter there is what could be called a *tratado escatológico*. The Spanish term *escatología* refers to both eschatology and scatology, a fact which permits Goytisolo to shift from the white owners of the *ingenio* using a water closet for the first time to a treatise on the theory that the saints, Mary, Jesus, and others detached from the material world do not defecate as do other mortals, since defecation is a sign of evil, of damnation. Alvarito therefore does not want to defecate:

> . . . su aguda conciencia de la naturaleza corrupta del cuerpo humano, con su fuerte inclinación al desahogo animal y sus secreciones impuras, le privaba del sueño : mentalmente, contraponía la melancólica realidad de la expulsión visceral con el bello ideal de esos santos y bienaventurados del Paraíso, cuyos residuos, nos dice San Bernardo, se transforman en un líquido refinado y suave, parecido al bálsamo de benjui y la esencia de almizcle : el acto cotidiano de defecar en su primoroso orinal de porcelana esmaltada, obra de un artífice de nombradía, lo llenaba de angustia y de desconsuelo. (pp. 219–20)

The broader interpetation takes into account ramifications of the Octavio Paz epigraph and also the drawing of large buttocks, which cannot be mistaken for mountains, on the cover of the book. Goytisolo seems to be saying that mankind, in its mistaken concept of virtue and purity, has forgotten its natural origin and suppresses anything that might bring it into focus. Paz, in *Conjunciones y disyunciones*, says that the face wants to forget that it once was very close to the anus and

187

genital organs: "El sexo y todas sus imágenes . . . nos recuerdan que hubo un tiempo en que la cara estuvo cerca del suelo y de los órganos genitales."[4] According to Paz "el sexo es subversivo no sólo por ser espontáneo y anárquico sino por ser igualitario: carece de nombre y de clase" (p. 28). Furthermore, the separation of these two parts, which made man human, has condemned mankind "al trabajo, a la historia y a la construcción de sepulcros. También nos condena a inventar metáforas para suprimirla" (p. 28). He goes on to say that Norman O. Brown has shown that "la 'visión excremental' constituye la esencia simbólica y, por tanto, jamás explícita, de la civilización moderna" (p. 29). Many symbols and images associated with the relationship between the face and sexual organs have through time and history become either very abstract or forgotten, "a medida que aumentaba la sublimación de los instintos" (p. 29). Hence, eventually "la cara se alejó del culo" (p. 29). A leitmotif of this theme is the continuous reference to an "ojo nefando."

The most important narrating motif is the continuation from *Don Julián* of the second-person singular viewpoint. Although used less exclusively, it appears throughout *Juan sin tierra* and serves again to give the reader a sense of engagement and a better perspective of the narrator-protagonist-author since the writing is a confession of sorts in which even the most obscure passages are a symbolic reflection of the narrator-protagonist-author's unconscious. Stream-of-consciousness, dialogue, first-person singular viewpoint (at times arising from dialogue), third-person singular, first- and second-person plural points of view, pastiche, and parody are employed, to name only the most prominent narrating motifs.[5]

---

[4] Octavio Paz, *Conjunciones y disyunciones* (México: Editorial Joaquín Mortiz, 1969), p. 28. Hereafter pages cited will be given in the text.

[5] Pastiche and parody also appear in *Señas* and *Don Julián*, but their purpose in those two novels was not of a narrative nature, as is the case in *Juan sin tierra*.

Since the second-person singular viewpoint pre-dominates, as in *Don Julián* where it was studied at length, only the other narrative motifs will be examined here. These illustrate the variety of perspectives Goytisolo wants to induce his reader to experience. A typical instance of stream-of-consciousness is observed in the following excerpt where the narrator recalls an experience in the Paris subway:

> . . . no en el sutil laberinto de pasillos y túneles ideado quizá por un topo enfermizo en su insomne delirio praguense (crujido lastimoso de los portillos de cierre automático, NICOLAS FINES BOUTEILLES demencialmente multiplicado en los escalones, planos indicadores de la red de autobuses, consignas de seguridad que nadie lee, reclamos de DU BON, DU BON, DUBONNET entrevistos a la súbita y rauda iluminación de los vagones, solicitaciones tentadoras de una próspera sociedad de consumo. (p. 94)

An example of dialogue, reminiscent of Hemingway's style, is this exchange: "Y ahora?, te dice/apostaté, le dices" (p. 154). The first person-singular viewpoint, popular in picaresque novels and in keeping with Goytisolo's parodic intent, is illustrated in this segment: "Mi nombre es Vosk : mi patria, una de las ciudades más claras e ilustres de Sansueña" (p. 263). The third-person singular is used when the narrator describes an event taking place in Spain: "Al *parecer* el infante don Sancho en la rota cabal de Zalaca, convocó el rey a sus sabios" (p. 185). The use of "old" Spanish in the above gives the text a certain aura of verisimilitude which could well deceive some readers. The first- and second-person plural are used, as in *Señas*, to bring into focus a chorus, occasionally the Spanish establishment. In the following example, where both viewpoints are mixed, body lice are addressing humans: "Nostros, muy a pesar vuestro, vivimos y nos regalamos en el interior de vuestros hogares" (p. 172). These two viewpoints appear separately as well, although their purpose is different; for instance, the first-person plural in the excerpt that follows seems to be the voice of the Spanish regime: "Yes, OUR COUNTRY IS DIFFERENT/ esta expresión, popular hoy en el orbe entero gracias a la próvida y eficiente labor de nuestros consulados y agencias turísticas" (p. 189). The second-person plural, on the other hand, is the voice of a priest exhorting black slaves to resign themselves stoically to their fate: "No maldigáis por consiguiente las penalidades que os toca vivir" (p. 195).

Goytisolo himself comments directly (in an obvious example of laying bare, to be examined later), unlike his approach in *Señas* and *Don Julián*, on the important devices of first- and second-person singular viewpoints; he indicates how these are subjected to his whims:

YO/TÚ

pronombres apersonales, moldes substantivos vacíos! : vuestra escueta realidad es el acto del habla mediante el que os apropiáis del lenguaje y lo sometéis al dominio engañoso de vuestra subjetividad reductible : odres huecos, hembras disponibles, os ofrecéis promiscuamente al uso común, al goce social, colectivo : indicativos nucleares, herméticos, transferís, no obstante, vuestra unicidad cuando de un mero trazo de pluma os hago asumir el dictado de mis voces proteicas, cambiantes : la sintonía general que emitís propicia el escamoteo sutil fuera de la comunicación ordinaria : quién se expresa en yo/tú? : Ebeh, Foucauld, Anselm Turmeda, Cavafis, Lawrence de Arabia? (pp. 158–59)

In an interview conducted by Julio Ortega, Goytisolo contends that there is no such thing as unity of protagonist or character and that the reader should experience *Juan sin tierra* as if in a dream. Because

. . . Los pronombres personales del discurso narrativo no expresan una voz individual, sino todas las voces o ninguna. Como señaló Benveniste, los yo, tú, nosotros, no se refieren a una realidad objectiva, como la mayoría e los signos nominales, sino a una realidad de discurso, a un mero proceso de enunciación. Ni el tú intrepelado ni el yo interpelador poseen una identidad precisa y concreta, y el lector no sabe a ciencia cierta quién es el sujeto emisor y quién el receptor. . . .[6]

Nevertheless, the narrator, the person who always talks about

[6] Julio Ortega, "Entrevista con Juan Goytisolo," *Juan Goytisolo*, ed. by Julián Ríos (Madrid: Editorial Fundamentos, 1975), p. 127. Hereafter pages cited will be given in the text.

the act of writing, is the same. Hence there is unity of character here. If Goytisolo is referring to the individual(s) this narrator creates, then he is correct in saying that such unity does not exist.

Pastiches appear in the form of literary texts either in their original form or modified to suit the purpose of the narrative; they may be in the form of words, sentences, paragraphs, subchapter headings (epigrams), to name only a few, written in foreign languages. An example of a modified literary quotation is obseved in Goytisolo's rendition of Manuel Machado's verse from "Felipe IV" (it also appeared in *Señas* and *Don Julián*), "Siempre de negro hasta los pies vestido," which is transformed in *Juan sin tierra* to "'blanco de la cabeza a los pies" (p. 98) and refers to Lawrence.

Juan sin ierra is divided into seven chapters each of which is further subdivided. The manner in which these subdivisions occur, however, varies from one chapter to another. For instance, whereas the first chapter's subdivisions are separated from one another by blank spaces, Chapter Two utilizes Arabic numerals. Chapter Three's divisions each begin with an epigram that has a connection with its content. The fourth also has epigrams, but they are in Latin. Chapter Five's subdivisions use Roman numerals. The sixth chapter returns to the initial use of blank spaces, and the last chapter uses three asterisks arranged triangularly which may be intended as the conventional symbol used in printing to call attention to important passages. Furthermore, in geometry, points in a triangular position mean "therefore" and always come last.

Examples of the relationship between the epigrams and subdivisions are best found in the fourth chapter where the Latin sentences (sometimes quotations from the classics or ancient proverbs) are either a direct or indirect succinct statement of a point to be elaborated upon. The first epigram could be translated as "We sing a little about greater things."[7] In this

---

[7] PAULO MAJORA CANAMUS, p. 179.

section the narrator recalls Spain and his relation to his country—the inquisition, Spain's Civil War, and the absurdity of it all. The last portion of the section, however, changes in tone, and the narrator speaks of the imminent danger from the outside which threatens to corrupt contemporary Spain, an idea in keeping with the motif of paradox Goytisolo maintains throughout.

The next subsection bears an epigram quoted from Virgil's *Aeneid* (Book II, line 11). Asked to tell about the Trojan War, Virgil begins his narration by saying (loosely translated) "My mind shudders to have recalled." ("ANIMUS MEMINISSE HORRET"). Examination of the contents reveals the caustic nature of the epigram, which heads an account in "old" Spanish of the deleterious influence of baths on the noblemen, who would engage in homosexual encounters and thereby lose their "temple bélico" (p. 185).

Another section begins with "FINIS CORONAT OPUS," an ancient proverb translated as "The end crowns the work," but which according to H. T. Riley, could also mean "The end sanctifies the means."[8] In this section, the priest Vosk tells the slaves they must accept their miserable condition in life as a means to gain eternal salvation:

> . . . por eso os aplicamos los tormentos del agua y cordeles, del sueño, la garrucha, el ladrillo y os hemos conducido al auto de fe con cadenas, grillos, mordaza : para que el demonio no os instigara a recaer en sus perversas doctrinas ni incurrir en la execrable promiscuidad de los más brutos animales : . . . . (p. 195)

Another bears the epigram "SALUS POPULI SUPREMA LEX EST," translated by Riley as "The well-being of the people is the first great law." He indicates that it derives from the Laws of the Twelve Tables at Rome, and that Aristotle has a similar maxim. After examining the contents of this section,

---

[8] *Dictionary of Latin Quotations,* ed. by H. T. Riley (London: Henry G. Bohn, 1856), p. 126.

the irony of the epigram is again evident. The fragment presents the voice of the *status quo* rationalizing the totalitarian government of Spain as a means to purge all evil from the country:

> los resultados de nuestra enérgica, eficaz terapéutica son archipatentes : los gobiernos responsables del mundo entero nos envidian ese órgano depurador magistral que, adaptado a los problemas y exigencias de cada época, mantiene siglo tras siglo nuestra salud moral gracias a la radical eliminación de los presuntos portadores de gérmenes y el establecimiento en nuestras fronteras de un hermético, infranqueable cordón sanitario. (p. 199)

Another epigram, "MONSTRUM HORRENDUM, INFORME, INGENS," taken from Virgil in the *Aeneid*, describes Polyphemus after his one eye had been put out by Ulysses and may be translated as "A horrible monster (portent?), misshapen, huge." The contents of the section deal with the deviant few in Spain who worship "a los reptiles y otros animales lascivos" (p. 205), particularly the devil who sometimes takes the form of the "híspido simio," the latter reference being to King-Kong, obviously a symbol of the libido.

The section that begins with the epigram "HOC VOLO, SIC JUBEO, SIT PRO RATIONE VOLUNTAS," presents the recurring theme of how the saints, the royal family, and those sympathetic to the regime do not defecate the same type of wastes as other humans. Their feces, a voice claims, exhale "armonía y fraganca" (p. 209). The epigram, from Juvenal, may be translated as "So I will it, so I command it, let my pleasure stand for my reason." Significantly, the person speaking throughout the section could be Spain's ruler.

The last section to be examined bears the epigram "AD AUGUSTA PER ANGUSTA," a parody of Virgil's telling the Romans that they must endure, prevail, in order to reach the stars. "To great things through adversity" is a loose translation of the epigram, seemingly an expression of hope that the narrator is sending to his erroneously inhibited (that is, constipated), mother country, "la de un país (el suyo) secularmente estreñido" (p. 226). He gives us a solution to all her troubles a return to defecating in "la zanja publica" (p. 228), in other words, a reduction of the distance between "la cara y el culo."

It appears, then, that the smooth transitional unity of *Don Julián*, particularly, where themes and motifs are linked to each other and one section or chapter leads to another, is not present in this work for the reason that its construction is closer to poetry. Goytisolo himself said in an interview that "la construcción de *Juan sin tierra* se acerca mucho a la de la poesía" (*Juan Goytisolo*. p. 127). While a novel such as *Don Julián* is based on a logical and temporal order, poetry depends on a spatial order through a combination of repetitions and symmetrical expositions on the printed page. Hence each chapter could be considered a strophe within which several ideas are developed and sometimes repeated. The last strophe (Chapter VII) brings all the motifs together and delivers the decisive and unexpected final blow. Additionally, the distribution of chapters follows a geometric pattern so that from the musical composition of *Don Julián*, Goytisolo goes to a geometric construction in which there is a linguistic base. This point is explained by Goytisolo in the same interview in the following manner:

> . . . Las agrupaciones textuales distribuidas en los diferentes capítulos del libro obedecen a una única fuerza centrípeta, distinta de las unidades de la perspectiva clásica: al núcleo organizador de la propia escritura, a la fuente de producción textual. Ello no quiere decir que haya un lenguaje único en todo el libro ni mucho menos. El centro lingüístico a que me refiero debe crear la unidad de la novela en la medida en que no se sitúa en ninguno de los estratos lingüísticos sino en el punto en donde convergen sus diferentes intersecciones. Todo esto puede parecer bastante abstracto, pues, como ves, estoy pasando de la música a la geometría. (p. 127)

The time and space of the work are unconventional and non-Euclidean; in fact Einstein's fourth dimension is suggested. The book is being written in a small room, during the summer of 1973 (p. 119), but the reader can neither ascertain how long it takes the author to complete it nor make conventional conjectures about the story time. In the following excerpt the author speaks about the act of writing and the place in which he finds himself:

> . . . sin otro auxilio que el papel y la pluma, a una nueva, imprevisible incursión por la cuarta dimensión einsteiniana : enclaustrado, como siempre, en la minúscula habitación : sin abandonar el ámbito de tu propia escritura : centrando tu interés en la trayectoria ejemplar del país que ha dejado de ser el tuyo y no significa hoy para ti más que esto. (p. 179)

On the other hand, if the author's continual allusions to himself are disregarded, then time and place in the book expand over several centuries as well as many continents. Most of the first chapter takes place on a Cuban sugar plantation, at the end of the nineteenth century; in Chapter Three the author travels through the Middle East; in other instances he is simultaneously in Madrid, Paris, and New York: "Y frente a los escaparates de Galerías Preciados, la Samaritaine, Macys [sic] o Blomingdale's [sic]" (p. 69). Consequently, unity of time and place could be limited to one night in a single room, the time and place of the narrator-protagonist-author's composition of the work. On the other hand, what takes place in the book has no limits, and Goytisolo has indicated that there is no unity of time, place, or character.[9]

The Protean motif pervasive in *Don Julián* is more so in this work. A number of figures and voices originate in a small room and change continually,[10] assuming mysterious, artistic, literary, and historical figures, to name but a few. In these metamorphoses some have a unifying thread such as the name Vosk, given to a priest, a colonel, and a disenchanted profes-

---

[9] *Juan Goytisolo*, p. 127.
[10] These voices are in keeping with the presentation of the work not only as prose but also as oral literature.

sor and critic dressed as a woman.[11] Moreover, the name Vosk suggests the possibility of a reference to the painter, Hieronymus Bosch, to whom the narrator alludes here:

> . . . junto a tí, un caballero flamenco, cuyo apellido bordado en rojo sobre el bolsillo izquierdo de la chaqueta establece una mentida, casi insultante relación fonética con aquel remoto, visionario paisano que magistralmente pintara al diablo expeliendo a las almas protervas por la pupila de su ojo nefando. (p. 308)

The passage above refers to Bosch's "Hell," the right panel of "The Garden of Worldly Delights." There is also a direct relation to the "cara-culo" theme, the "ojo nefando," being a leitmotif thereof.

Some of the literary figures, or their voices, appearing through Protean changes are Lawrence of Arabia, Ibn Turmeda, and Père de Foucauld whose writings are alluded to frequently. Lawrence, for instance, appears in the subsection of Chapter III, bearing the epigram "El Octavo Pilar de la Sabiduría." The oft-used paradox motif is used to confuse the reader, to make things strange or, as the narrator says, "enseñarle a dudar" (p. 146). This motif is best seen in the appearance of contrasting personalities with the same name. Also germane are radical shifts from one line to the next in terms of the political or philosophical perspective expounded:

> . . . coger el libro o volumen que las encierra, recorrer dolorosamente sus páginas y oír su testimonio sobre unos tiempos en los que, como escribiera el liberado Poeta, su sinrazón con génita, ya locura hoy, como admirable paradoja se im-/ponía/pero escuchando todavía/escuchando/hasta esa epifanía gloriosa que todos recordamos, cuando la pertinaz subversión interior, con ayuda extranjera, intentó abolir matrimonio y familia, supeditar lo espiritual a lo material, imponernos comités en lugar de cofradías,

---

[11] The surprising revelation that the beautiful damsel is in reality a man reminds the reader of the discovery in Grande *Sertão: Veredas* by Guimarães Rosa, that Diadorim is a woman, and also of a similar outcome in *Mademoiselle de Maupin* by Gautier.

substituir nuestra querida Giralda con un sucio casquete de astrakán. (p. 182)

The sexual motif also permeates the work, perhaps even more strongly than in *Don Julián* and previous novels. Blacks are portrayed as extremely promiscuous, forever engaging in intercourse in all possible positions, and King-Kong, a libidinous symbol, comes from Africa. But most important, the act of writing itself becomes a form of onanism: ". . . mientras buscas a tientas la secreta, guadianesca ecuación que soterradamente aúna sexualidad y escritura : tu empedernido gesto de empuñar la pluma y dejar escurrir su licor filiforme, prolongando indefinidamente el orgasmo" (p. 255). The homosexual motif is enunciated when the protagonist, wanting to scandalize the tourists, embraces a tattered beggar, covered with suppurating sores (p. 64). Unlike similar scenes in previous works, however, the character's behavior here is an act of defiance, somewhat like Esproceda's poem, "El mendigo," in which the beggar enjoys offending people with his foul-smelling body.[12] Beggars appear almost as frequently in *Don Julián*.

The recurrent motif of smell has several purposes: it offends, as with the beggar; it is a source of pleasure and a form of social criticism. The following is a twist of a well-known proverb substituting *hueles* for *andas*: "Dime como hueles y te diré quien eres" (p. 211).

Racial black and white are juxtaposed, particularly in the first chapter where the author contrasts the living conditions and behavior of the owners of the *ingenio* with that of the black slaves. Father Vosk repeatedly tells the slaves that their color is a sign of evil for which they are being punished and that they

---

[12] The following is an excerpt from Espronceda's "El mendigo": "y me gozo/cuando aspira/mi punzante/mal olor." The reader may speculate whether the parallel of the beggar's Romantic rebellion is unconsciously present in Goytisolo.

must accept their condition. An example of pastiche, and a means of social criticism, is the insertion of a description of the manner in which blacks were transported from Africa to the New World.[13] Black and white racial implications are further developed in a parody of the Annunciation in which Christian and African gods are fused. In Goytisolo's version, God elects "entre todas las negras a la gorda cachonda del disco" (p. 51). The reference to a phonograph record is an allusion to one the narrator has in his room which has a photograph of Celia Cruz on its cover. The Holy Spirit is to appear to her in the form of a dove:

> . . . humilde ahora, recatada, modosa : vacando a sus tareas domésticas en compañía de su esposo purísimo : a la espera sin duda de la insólita visita de la Paloma : disponiendo entre tanto los futuros pañales del niño : del para siempre bendito fruto de su vientre : tú mismo. (p. 52)

The last two words above, involving the reader as well, seem to indicate that the narrator considers himself a sort of grotesque and absurd Messiah. Alvarito, offspring of this union, would redeem the world. Unexpectedly, however, the devil-related African deity Changó appears, kills the dove, and has intercourse with the woman through a Don Juanesque deception:

> . . . viéndole revolcarse y morder y desplegar cruelmente las garras al tiempo que la embobada madre prosigue su esotérico duo con la casi digerida visitadora, embaucada sin duda por el leve rumor de plumas que, fuera ahora, ladinamente agitarás tú : simulando carantoñas, arrullos y mimos, imitando con la uña el roce del pico y con los labios un tenue batimiento de alas : amor mío, alma mía, rey mío, Paloma mía, eres Tú? : y tú : sí, mi negra, sí, soy yo, tu Palomica. (p. 57)

---

[13] In *Juan Goytisolo*, an essay by Severo Sarduy (p. 175), there is mention of two possible works as sources for the descriptions of the "ingenio": *Los ingenios de Cuba* by Eduardo Laplante and *Isla de Cuba pintoresca* by Federico Mialhe.

Hence as the product of a *negra gorda cachonda* and an African devil that has devoured the Holy Ghost, Alvarito's role as redeemer is quite grotesque, in keeping with the general make-up and purpose of the book.

The executioner-victim motif also appears in the section entitled "Tras las huellas del Père de Foucauld," alluding to martyrdom and to mystic flagellation: " . . . a los arrebatos y éxtasis inefables que unen un arpegio común verdugos y víctimas, comisarios y oposicionistas, herejes e inquisidores : imitando hasta en el estilo la abrasadora sed de los místicos, su insaciable y mordiente voracidad" (p. 165). Here Goytisolo is criticizing saintly behavior as being actually a form of eroticism. The narrator's view of the act of writing as a kind of onanism ("Placer solitario de la escritura!" p. 298) is also exhibitionism, because the reader is exposed to the narrator's act. Since exhibitionism, according to the *Psychiatric Dictionary*, is a form of sadism, there is then a sadomasochistic relationship between the narrator and the reader, for the latter becomes a voyeur. This point coult be extended to viewing the narrator as an executioner and the reader as his victim.

The act of "confusing their language," as the narrator indicates, has echoes of the Tower of Babel. The correctness of this observation is made evident by the author's excessive use of foreign languages (beyond that in *Señas* and *Don Julián*) giving this text an even greater appearance of collage. Specific examples of techniques of linguistic confusion employ anagrams and puns. In the following example some proverbs have been modified to absurdity:

> . . . los lugares comunes brotan sin retención de sus labios, y astuta, perfidamente confundirás sus lenguas/en país de riegos el huerto es ley, dice uno/hasta el cuarenta del cayo no te quites el rayo, dice otro/la cerveza es la madre de todos los quicios, dirá un tercero. (p. 107)

Another motif, remarkably reminiscent of Unamuno's *Niebla*, is the ability of the characters to plead with the narrator-protagonist-author:

. . . no soy más que una voz : me ha reducido usted al murmullo de un vago e inidentificable discurso : no voz mía siquiera, sino de usted, de mi amo : va usted a abandonarme así? : no se compadece usted de las lágrimas de mi corazón desgarrado? (p. 307)[14]

The film motif, according to Goytisolo, is also very important to protagonist-reader identification:

. . . en *Juan sin tierra*, las referencias cinematográficas desempeñan, como te dije, un papel muy importante en la medida en que el tú interpelado se confunde sucesivamente con los protagonistas de "King Kong," "Locura de amor" y "Lawrence de Arabia." Y, por cierto, al atravesar el territorio sirio, Lawrence sueña en el personaje del Estilita que Buñuel retrató en "Simón del desierto" (*Juan Goytisolo*, p. 136).

The first time King Kong appears he is in the process of rubbing with one finger the thighs of a woman he holds in his hand. An article in *Esquire* tells how this scene, of which there were photographs, was cut from the final version of the film. King Kong symbolizes the libido phobia experienced by most Spaniards. There is more than one girl in Goytisolo's rendition of that scene:

. . . las raptadas doncellas tiemblan de inconfesable dicha sobre su vasta palma velluda y el antropomorfo las observará con arrobo y rozará delicadamente sus muslos con el extremo de su dardo lingual : buscando el exquisito néctar periódico como esos oseznos golosos, peritos en miel de beja, que introducen el hocico en las colmenas sin reparar en la cólera del insecto ni su mortificante picadura. (p. 75)

King-Kong, also on the cover of *Don Julián*, eventually is metamorphosed into Queen-Kong. "Lawrence of Arabia" with

---

[14] There are also many allusions to "the other": ". . . el olor a incienso de su niñez (del otro, del muerto) insidiosamente envolverá la cola de penitentes a casi cinco lustros de distancia" (p. 289), which alludes also to lost childhood, as in the following: ". . . tu cuitado niñez : tuya? : no, del otro : del infante exquisito (ejecutado luego)" (p. 277). Moreover, the desire to make his reader doubt has also echoes of Unamo. The treatment of Unamuno in this book presents quite a contrast with the savage attack in *Don Julián*. Unamuno's influence on Goytisolo pervades the work.

Peter O'Toole is re-enacted by one of the characters as he travels through Arab territory in Chapter III. The names of Buster Keaton (p. 106) and Terence Stamp (p. 107) also appear. As in *Don Julián*, the films reflect a mood or atmosphere the narrator wishes to introduce.

Another motif comprises instances of literary parody. An apparent report on why the knights of Don Sancho were weak and unable to fight, written in "old" Spanish, states that the baths were at fault because the gentlemen were prone to engage in homosexual behavior:

> . . . al perecer el infante don Sancho en la rota cabal de Zalaca, convocó, el rey a sus sabios y obispos con fin de averiguar por qué había decaído el temple bélico de sus caballeros, y respondieronle ellos que porque entraban mucho a menudo a los bannos e se davan mucho a los bycios a los apetytos defrrenados del cuerpo enon es farto enxiemplo notorio e palpable el/que quisyere consyderar en este desonesto, vill. (p. 185)

Goytisolo here criticizes the fear of sex in Spanish society, passing to parody of a different sort when the narrator hears a poem in echo-form that begins

VERSOS ESPERANZADOS DEL DAÑO
Y EL REMEDIO

¿Qué arma esgrimen con saña?
Guadaña.
¿Quién deja exhaustas tus venas?
Las penas.
¿Y quién prueba tu prudencia?
Paciencia.
De este modo, tal dolencia
tardo remedio te alcanza
pues demoran tu esperanza
penas, guadaña y paciencia (p. 260)

The beautiful damsel singing these lyrics, the narrator later discovers, is a young male professor and critic named Vosk.

The young man tells the narrator of his plight: it appears that he has been a very successful critic of conventional novels who, upon the appearance of new novelists following formal views, finds himself alone:

> . . . enmudeciendo las plumas de quienes escribían conforme a mis dictados y desatando las de una hueste de autores entregados al cultivo de una escritura formal y abstracta, mera expresión enajenada, a menudo esquizofrénica, de obsesiones y complejos personales que, en lugar de ser reflejo objetivo del mundo, postulan tan sólo el intento de liberación, desesperado y parcial, de una mentalidad enferma : en vano peleé, discutí, insistí, porfié : mis desvelos resultaron inútiles. (p. 266)

Vosk's statement is probably a reference to Goytisolo's own experience; his *Problemas de la novela* attacks writers who were *deshumanizados* as well as those who deviated from conventional portrayal of reality (he has since repudiated that work).

Further literary parody involves Vosk and the narrator's finding a manuscript by a conventional novelist who committed suicide, and even a sonnet against Formalism (p. 268), in which the poet asks Literature to escape from Formalism and return to him. [15]

Another formal aspect noticed in *Juan sin tierra* is literary borrowing, although the device is not present to the same extent as in *Don Julián*. Its purpose is not so much to desecrate literary texts (a frequent occurrence in the earlier work), as to present new experiences for the reading public and, as the narrator-protagonist says, "enseñarle a dudar" (p. 146). Literary borrowing also occurs when the narrator-protagonist becomes acquainted (in a pastoral setting) with a damsel who is really a male professor and critic who considers George Lukács an evangelist; he seems incongruously to be a character from a

---

[15] Other motifs in the work include references to U.S. culture (p. 69), snakes (p. 80), spiders (p. 70), masks (p. 81), Putifar (p. 135), syphilis (p. 64), use of *kif* (p. 137), and mythological figures (*passim*).

realistic novel. These two individuals find and begin reading the manuscript of a realistic work, whose author committed suicide as a result of the attacks on him by avant-garde writers. Thus, there is parody of the pastoral novel as well as of social realism *á la* Lukács:

Capítulo XVII

Donde Se Describe El Puerto De Toledo Con Otros Pormenores Necesarios A La Comprensión De Esta Veridica Historia (p. 273)

Goytisolo cites parallels to a scene in *Don Quijote*, where there is a polemical exchange about reality between a priest and an innkeeper, and in an answer to a question posed by Julio Ortega in the interview quoted earlier, Goytisolo elaborates on his belief that writers do not and cannot live in a vacuum; they are, and should be, influenced by one another. He uses *Don Quijote* as an example of literary borrowing (although he does not use the term):

> . . . La lectura de *Don Quijote* nos introduce en una auténtica galería de espejos literarios, en una complejísima relación de signos que corresponden a realidades literarias y extraliterarias extremadamente diversas. Pues como vio muy bien Américo Castro (uno de los rarísimos españoles capaces de una lectura activa de los clásicos) la novela cervantina no responde tan sólo a las exageraciones y extravagancias del género caballeresco: enlaza, en realidad, con la totalidad del *corpus* literario de la época (novela pastoril, novela italianizante, relato morisco, comedia lopesca, etc.) (*Juan Goytisolo*, p. 122).

Furthermore, Goytisolo continues to say, even though Cervantes did not influence authors of his own country, he managed to affect many writers elsewhere:

> La lectura creativa de la tradición literaria a que nos convida Cervantes no despertó ningún eco en su propio país—la meseta peninsular resultó una vez más un amazacotado ladrillo en el que la semilla de la libre invención quijotesca no pudo arraigar—pero sí lo

halló, en cambio, en Francia e Inglaterra, permitiendo la creación de obras tan dispares como *Le neveu de Rameau, Jacques le Fataliste, Tristram Shandy, Pickwick Papers* o *Bouvard et Pecuchet*, novelas cuyo único común denominador es su deuda manifiesta con Cervantes (p. 123).

As an example of literary borrowing, as well as a mixture of different types in the same text, Goytisolo cites the polemical exchange concerning reality, between the priest and the inn-keeper mentioned previously equating this scene with a hypothetical film in which John Wayne, as a hero of the Far West, encounters Dillinger and Frankenstein: " . . . una película en la que un héroe típico del Far-West (John Wayne) tropezara, digamos, con Dillinger o Al Capone (James Cagney) y fueran a ver juntos un film de Frankenstein protagonizado por Boris Karloff" (p. 123). Goytisolo's borrowing from Cervantes seems to parallel the purpose of Cervantes as well: to destroy reality, or the appearance of reality, for which many writers strive, and endow the reader with a totally new, and perhaps even rewarding, experience. Literary borrowing is more specific in references to and use of aspects of T. E. Lawrence's *The Seven Pillars of Wisdom* and the film "Lawrence of Arabia." The narrator-protagonist appears to be establishing a parallel between Lawrence and his fascination with the Arab world and his own decision to abandon Spain for the Moslem culture.[16]

The most important formal aspect of *Juan sin tierra* is laying bare. Throughout the novel the narrator-protagonist-author is concerned with the act of writing while engaging in it. It is as if the blank page becomes a mirror where the narra-

---

[16] Additionally, there are the three epigraphs at the beginning of the novel from Octavio Paz, T. E. Lawrence, and Jacques Berque, and an epigraph to Chapter VII from *La Celestina*. Within the text, some modified verses from Darío's "Sonatina" appear: ". . . pavos reales, parlanchina Sansueña dice cosas bonales" (pp. 316–17), only a few of the many examples of literary borrowing in *Juan sin tierra*.

tor-protagonist-author reproduces himself so that there may be symbiosis of the creator and the created. "Drawing Hands" by M. C. Escher may give a graphic illustration of Goytisolo's probable intentions. Moreover, the act of writing is not only creative, but also procreative since it can become a sexual engagement between the blank page and the pen, where the ink becomes semen (p. 255). The process of writing becomes a challenge to both reader and writer as the novel develops, and a combat between the two ensues. By means of this struggle the author hopes to have enlightened the reader by teaching him to doubt á la Unamuno:

> . . . seguirás el ejemplo del alarife anónimo y extraviarás al futuro lector en los meandros y trampas de tu escritura : alzarás bloques de piedras sonoras, las substraerás crecer y agruparse, atraerse, excluirse, dóciles a los campos magnéticos y afinidades secretas que imantan la búsqueda aleatoria del zahorí : . . . captar al intruso ingenuo, seducirlo, embaucarlo, envolverle en las mallas de una elusiva construcción verbal, aturdirle del todo, forzarle a volver sobre sus pasos y, menos seguro ya de su discurso y la certeza de sus orientaciones, soltarle otra vez al mundo, enseñarle a dudar. (pp. 145–46)

The process of laying bare offers, after the narrator-protagonist has traveled through Arab territory and has had many adventures, a recapitulation of his activities:

> . . . has recorrido de un extremo a otro el ámbito del Islam desde Istanbul a Fez, del país nubio al Sáhara, mudando camaleónicamente de piel gracias al oficioso, complacente llavín de unos pronombres apersonales prevenidos para el uso común de tus voces proteicas, cambiantes has gozado del vasto, enjundioso trasero de la ilustre Queen-Kong
> emulado la hazaña del Estilita en lo alto de la buñuelesca columna
> combatido contra el ejército turco en la desolación de la estepa jordana
> ascendido el valle del Nilo de Alejuandría a Luxor cruzado el desierto en campañía de Ebeh
> sufrido cristiano maritirio en Tamanrasset
> azotado al Père de Foucault en el tumulario alminar de Ghardaia (pp. 174–75)

This very much resembles the conclusion of an essay wherein the points established are summarized.

There is also a scene in which the narrator-protagonist-author takes part in a panel discussion and the audience asks questions about his work. The questions are the sort of negative criticism that Goytisolo and those contemporary novelists who follow a Formalist bent usually encounter. A few examples follow:

UN SOCIÓLOGO CON GAFAS
si no me equivoco, la acción de una gran parte de su novela parece situarse en el Sáhara : díganos, por favor, qué significa para usted el desierto?

UN ALUMNO DE LA ESCUELA DE PERIODISMO
yo no hallo en su obra ningún trasfondo humano o social, el dramatismo de la lucha por la existencia : o es que, en su opinión, la vida de los beduinos en un medio duro y hostil no plantea problemas?
(murmullos de aprobación)

UNA JOVEN DE PECHOS ABULTADOS
sus personajes son nulos, vacíos, huecos, inexistentes : ni yo no nadie puede creer en ellos : tendría usted la bondad de explicarnos de dónde los ha sacado?

UN MOZO AÚN IMBERBE, PERO MUY INSOLENTE
algunos opinan que escribe usted sus paparruchas cuando está grifado y, a juzgar por lo que he leído, pienso que tienen razón!
(risas) (p. 283)

The questions directed at the novel are perhaps an indication of the type of reaction Goytisolo expects. Furthermore, Vosk foresees future criticism, as he enumerates nine flaws in the book:

(a) abuso de extranjerismos
(b) falta de rigor lingüístico
(c) registro dudoso de la realidad
(d) incapacidad de transmitir fría y objetivamente los hechos
(e) Acumulación insubstancial de obsesiones personales, enfermizas y mórbidas
(f) empleo consciente de mitos substitutivos

(g) renuncia a toda pretensión de verdad
(h) estilo cada día más incorrecto
(i) incesante erosión del idioma (pp. 287–88)

As the novel continues, the narrator-protagonist-author is committed to a mental institution because of his deviant writings and a Doktor Vosk examines him. A bit later, Goytisolo describes the purpose of writing and the process the writer must follow to achieve it, indicating that theatricality must be eliminated in the novel and that it must be transformed into discourse. The latter concept, observed in *Don Julián* is more apparent in *Juan sin tierra*. He rejects the character of flesh and blood, stating that the dramatic progression of the narration should be replaced by an ensemble of textual cluster, moved by a centripetal force emanating from the author's pen. There should not be a logical, temporal progression, but rather a combination of elements on the rectangular space of the writing page in an emulation of painting and poetry, with perhaps a return to the typographical experimentation of the twenties:

> eliminar del corpus de la obra novelesca los últimos vestigios de teatralidad : transformarla en discurso sin peripecia alguna : dinamitar la inveterada noción del personaje de jueso y carne : substituyendo la progression dramática del relato con un conjunto de agrupaciones textuales movidas por fuerza centrípeta única : núcleo organizador de la propia escritura, plumafuente genésica del proceso textual : improvisando la arquitectura del objeto literario no en un tejido de relaciones de orden lógico-temporal sino en un ars combinatoria de elementos (oposiciones, alternancias, juegos simétricos) sobre el blanco rectangular de la página : emulando con la pintura y la poesía en un plano meramente espacial : indiferente a las amenazas expresas o tácitas del comisario-gendarme-aduanero disfrazado de crítico : sordo a los cantos de sirena de un instrumental e interesado contenidísmo y a los criterios mezquinos de utilidad (p. 311)

The motivation appears to be twofold: first, because of the many reasons indicated by Goytisolo himself and second, perhaps more important, as an act of revenge. Goytisolo's creation is in itself a form of destruction, not only of the language, but of many long-established literary precepts, in addition to the sexual mores of Spain. In his role as gadfly, the narrator-protagonist-author is an all-destructive entity who does away with time, space, culture, myths, the protagonist of conventional novels, the conventional novel, reality, and finally, the Spanish language. The narrator-protagonist-author actually will discard his native language:

> si en lo futuro escribes, será en otra lengua : no en la que has repudiado y de la que hoy te despides tras haberla revuelto, trastornado, infringido : empresa de sedición interior que compensa el presente que muy a pesar tuyo le ofreces : agregando tu artefacto a su monumento, pero destilando al mismo tiempo el agente (cáustico, corrosivo, mordaz) que la corrompe y desgasta : . . . con la conciencia neta de que el mal está hecho : progenitura infame, su (tu) subversión (idealógica, narrativa, semántica), proseguirá independientemente su labor de zapa por los siglos de los siglos. (pp. 319–20)

He then proceeds to renounce Spanish: he writes it phonetically, with a Cuban speech pattern at first, then disregards the rules of "doña Hakademia" (the real Academia Española), and finally shifts to Arabic, first in Roman characters and at the end in Arabic script:

*

*   *

> . . . de ty mim-mo i la posyvilidá dep-presal-lo lyberándote de tu hantiryor ympot-tura i, grasias ha la prat-tyca dun lenguage cueppo, dun belbo beldadelamente echo canne, de tebdá kif uáhed l-arbi al idu sghera ua min baád al idu Kbira bex temxi l-xamá ua tqrá al surat eli tjab
>> qul ya ayuha al-kafirún
>> la a budu ma ta budún
>> ua-la antrum abiduna ma a bud
>> ua-la ana abidum ma abattúm
>> ua-la antum abiduna ma a bud
>> la-kum dinu-kum ua-li-ya din (pp. 320-21)

What he set out to accomplish in *Don Julián*, a crime of *effet perpétuel*, is consummated in *Juan sin tierra*. Baroja's cyclop would have summarized his intentions by saying, ironically perhaps: "Destruir es cambiar. No, algo más. Destruir es crear."

Conclusion

Spanish novels from 1940 to the early sixties, with few exceptions, were a continuation of the type of novels published in Spain in the nineteenth century and the first four decades of the twentieth. In contrast, during the same quarter century, Latin Americans produced a respectable number of experimental novels, comparable with those of James Joyce and William Faulkner—to whom they probably owe their inspiration. Since 1966 the Spanish novel, too, seems to be seeking new directions. In that year *Señas de identidad* by Juan Goytisolo was published, and the author, who admits to a degree of influence from some Latin American writers, can be considered foremost among novelists such as Benet and Leyva whose works are helping the Spanish new novel regain recognition in world literature. More important than the Spanish American influence on Goytisolo is that of the Russian Formalists who departed from the traditional dichotomy of form versus content, seeing the work of art as the sum of the devices utilized in it.

The examination of Juan Goytisolo's novels with a Formalist perspective has shown their progressively more complex construction. It is evident, indeed, that Goytisolo's increasing familiarity with Formalist views contributed to noticeable changes in his creativity. This awareness is one of the reasons for the fundamental difference between the early novels, which in most instances are conventional and even immature, and the highly sophisticated and complex *Mendiola Trilogy*, which begins with *Señas de identidad*. The complexity of the trilogy depends particularly on the measured use of those devices identified by the Formalists as retardation, defamiliarization, literary borrowing, and laying bare. Goytisolo evinces more perception and, thus, better control over place and time, being more aware also of the intricacies of story and plot and the importance of point of view.

This study has shown the need for reconsideration of the divisions of Goytisolo's works. Instead of Martínez Cachero's three-part scheme, it is felt that the proper division is into two. The first is an early, conventional phase in which the author's novels follow the forms utilized by most novelists in the nineteeth century and first decades of the twentieth; the second period is a mature one in which constant experimentation is undertaken. Within the early phase, however, there could be two subdividions in which Martínez Cachero's first two demarcations may be used (*Juegos de manor* and *Duelo en el Paraíso* in the first and the trilogy *El mañana efímero* in the second). Martínez Cachero's third period (*Para vivir aquí, Campos de Níjar, La isla, Fin de fiesta* and *La chanca*) is seen in this study as a transitional stage, or hiatus, which leads to Goytisolo's experimental phase.

Despite a fundamental contrast in construction between these two periods, there is a common thread uniting them, via a number of motifs appearing throughout these works. These motifs do not necessarily serve the same purpose in every novel since they are interchangeable: they may be dynamic in one, bound in another, and dynamic and free in a third. The motifs in question are homosexuality, betrayal, masks, escap-

211

ism, executioner-victim, loss of innocence, social criticism, the sex phobia in Spanish culture, and U. S. materialistic influences. Another uniting link is the author's concern with time and space, first observed in *Duelo en el Paraíso*. A brief summary of each novel's Formalist aspects, together with a discussion of flaws in construction, will establish, *a vuelo de pluma*, the progressively complex construction of the books.

The first novel, *Juegos de manos*, is conventional and somewhat primitive, developed with what are later deemed the worn-out methods of the novelists of the last century. It is basically a psychological study of a group of angry young men. The characters, however, by nineteeth-century as well as Formalist standards are not well developed; they remain static and their behavior at the end of the novel is unmotivated and forced. The point of view utilized varies from section to section and lacks the smooth transition necessary to develop the type of character study the author is trying to portray. There seems to be no awareness of the importance of time and space so evident in later novels. Some motifs seen in the other works appear here for the first time: escapism appears as a bound motif, executioner-victim and betrayal are dynamic, while homosexuality and Protean changes (masks) are free. The story and plot can be summarized, a situation contrary to that of more recent novels.

Duelo en el Paraíso, on the other hand, shows some early experimentation. The author, perhaps influenced by Faulkner, experiments with time and space. Unfortunately, lack of control leads to chaos, the novel's major flaw. Point of view is complex and there is a great deal of experimentation, but progressions from one viewpoint to another lack smoothness. Social criticism appears as a bound motif; escapism, executioner-victim, betrayal, loss of innocence are dynamic; homosexuality, Protean changes (masks) and a mother-figure appear as free. This novel foretells the type of works Goytisolo will write in his mature period.

With the trilogy *El mañana efímero* Goytisolo both regresses and progresses. *El circo* is probably his weakest novel, even though there are aspects which will be better developed in later works. In *El circo*, increasing awareness of time and place is noticeable, with the beginning of use of epigraphs as a means of giving a succinct perspective of the story. The point of view, unfortunately, is chaotic and there is seldom sufficient motivation for the continuous shifting of viewpoint. The motifs of escapism and betrayal are found in this novel as bound, dynamic, and free. Social criticism, homosexuality, United States' influence, and executioner-victim appear as important free motifs. The novel's major flaw is the contrived and unfinished characterization of Utah; he is not a character from a conventional novel and is a failure as an experimental one.

Fiestas, in contrast, is a superior work. With a better perspective of the genre, Goytisolo uses motifs as building blocks; time and space are handled skillfully and viewpoint flows more smoothly. As in *El circo*, the epigraph has a direct relationship to the story and, consequently, is an important part of it. Some motifs appear under different guises: loss of innocence, betrayal, and executioner-victim are bound; betrayal is dynamic; and social criticism, escapism, and homosexuality are free. *Fiestas* may be considered the best novel of Goytisolo's conventional period.

With *La resaca*, the third of the trilogy, political preoccupation is more evident than in any of the others. The novel at times becomes a political pamphlet rather than fiction, yet there is indeed a concern with construction which overcomes its documentary aspect. As in the other two of the trilogy, an epigraph gives perspective to its content. Its epilogue calls for a better Spain. As in previous novels, the shifting viewpoint from character to character and from one family to another gives a collage effect. As in *Fiestas*, there are instances of suspension of time, offering a simultaneous perspective of things occurring at the same moment. Additionally, the story time is provided throughout, providing awareness of the progression of time within which the events in the narration are developing. Social criticism, loss of innocence, betrayal, escapism, and executioner-victim are present as bound motifs. The last three are also dynamic because they influence the development of events. Among the free motifs are social criticism, homosexuality, loss of innocence, and some criticism of the United States. Here Goytisolo seems to view prose fiction as an instrument for the ethical and social improvement of mankind, and not until *The Mendiola Trilogy* will his political views be relegated to a less pervasive level.

In Chapter III a transitional period is examined comprising *La isla* and two travelogues, *Campos de Níjar* and *La chanca*. A definite connection is seen between awareness of the precarious social conditions of the murcianos in *Fiestas* and, particularly, *La resaca* and the novelist's subsequent travels throughout Southern Spain which are recorded in his travelogues. His interest in this region gives rise to an admiration for Arab culture. In Chapter Three, it was noted that a few motifs from the travelogues appear in *The Mendiola Trilogy*: use of cannibis, the language, the Arab Culture, and criticism of Spain's past sins. Consequently, the importance of this period is not be underestimated; Goytisolo's later works were germinating during these years.

The value to Spanish literature of Goytisolo's latest three novels is considerable and his influence will be felt for years to come. With *The Mendiola Trilogy* Goytisolo embarks on a multifarious odyssey: whereas the purpose of his earlier novels was fundamentally one of social criticism, in his last three novels protest is not as important as literature itself, the Spanish language, the sexual taboos of Western civilization, and the identity of man. With *Señas de indentidad* Goytisolo begins his experimental phase, the most noticeable aspect being the variation of narrating viewpoints. Although varied and shifting, they are kept under control by their smooth gliding into each other. Balanced use of themes and motifs develops the plot.

The story is succinctly given in the epigraphs, as in previous novels, and time and place are handled skillfully (as in *Fiestas*) so as to keep the reader aware of the flow of time and the shifting of place.

Because of the complexity of its plot, *Señas de identidad* has a myriad of free motifs: homosexuality, the overpowering mother-figure, sex phobia, social criticism, loss of innocence, executioner-victim, betrayal, and escapism. Two motifs are used to a greater extent than in earlier novels—a linguistic one which involves a great deal of experimentation and frequent allusions to Arab culture. The techniques of laying bare, de-familiarization, and retardation found throughout *Señas* constitute the first definite instance of the Formalists' influence upon Goytisolo.

Reivindicación del conde don Julián, the second of the tri-logy, is a totally new approach to fiction-writing in Peninsular literature. As in previous novels, the epigraphs give a hint to the reader as to what is about to happen. The plot of this novel is extremely complex because of a combination of several themes and motifs. Some of the motifs observed throughout this study are developed into themes in *Don Julián*. For in-stance, the sexual phobia, the deleterious influence of the United States, social criticism, and the language are fully de-veloped themes with their own motifs. Additionally, the mo-tifs of betrayal, homosexuality, masks (Protean changes), es-capism, executioner-victim, and loss of innocence appear in different guises throughout the work. Unlike his earlier nov-els, *Julián* possesses a unity of character, time, and place, setting this work apart from previous ones as well as from *Juan sin tierra*. The only developed character is the protagonist, since all the other figures enter and exit very quickly. The novel takes place in Tangiers and occurs within twenty-four hours; there is unity of action insofar as most of what happens transpires in the mind of the protagonist (Goytisolo thus seems to abide here by the old unities).

Of particular interest, too, is the utilization of laying

bare, literary borrowing, retardation, and defamiliarization. The first of these four appears at the beginning of the novel when the narrator alludes to Scheherazade, and thereafter it recurs throughout. Literary borrowing is perhaps the most important device, endowing the work with a collage texture, as well as being a means to criticize and praise Peninsular and Spanish-American writers. Through retardation Goytisolo manages to suspend time, return to the past, and remind the reader of what has happened and what is about to take place. Defamiliarization is in some instances used in conjunction with literary borrowing, as in the example of Platero and Pascual Duarte.

Many critics, and even Goytisolo himself, have commented on the musical construction of *Don Julián*, in addition to its collage aspect. With *Juan sin tierra*, on the other hand, Goytisolo enters the realm of poetry—of oral poetry in prose. The work is basically a new genre, a work of the future which, as with Joyce's *Finnegans Wake*, will not be readily accepted nor understood by most readers. The book seems at first total chaos, but careful reading reveals an orderly disorder. There is no unity of time, place, character, viewpoint, story or plot, and only in the chapters and subdivisions is there evidence of a particular pattern. The work is actually an oral prose poem which happens to be transcribed (some aspects of the technique are present in *Señas*). Each chapter and its subdivisions may be considered as strophes which have themes and motifs of their own. Certain themes and motifs, however, run throughout the work giving it unity. The use of epigraphs, in particular, facilitates a general perspective of two major themes. The motifs of homosexuality, language, Protean changes, escapism, executioner-victim, social criticism, and sex phobia are continually encountered.

Two important Formalistic aspects are literary borrowing and laying bare. The use of literary texts may be as frequent as in *Don Julián* and the purpose, with a few exceptions, is the same: to criticize as well as praise. Laying bare, on the other hand, is perhaps the most important device used since the author frequently engages the reader in a dialogue where he expounds on his views of literature and the purpose of what he is writing, somewhat as Sterne does in *Tristram Shandy*. (Significantly, Goytisolo translated Victor Shklovsky's essay on *Tristram Shandy*.) The narrator's voice, nevertheless, takes on Protean changes so that the reader is confronted with the sound of many voices, at times expressing conflicting views.

In essence, *Juan sin tierra* is a destructive tool. As Goytisolo commented in *Libre*, the themes of homosexuality, sexuality, and others which in the past were considered of great social impact have no longer any shock value. Language and only language is the new subversive vehicle to obtain that desired effect. Hence the intention of the narrator-protagonist-author is that of annihilating, through an original and sadistic use and abuse of the language, all those aspects he considers deleterious not only to Spain, but to Western culture in general. Language per se, a creative medium and the primary one of which the work is composed, becomes paradoxically the most destructive tool available. Moreover, through the process of destruction the book has created a new perspective, a new manner of examining mankind in general and Spanish culture in particular.

In this study Juan Goytisolo's novels have been examined from a Formalist perspective that shows his progression from a conventional to a Formalist influence. Each has been studied from a similar angle, and a comparative view shows that Goytisolo's works have become progressively more complex and better written. This study has also demonstrated how important Juan Goytisolo is to contemporary Spanish literature. It is hoped that this investigation may contribute in some way to placing the Spanish author in perspective as the foremost writer of the new Spanish novel.

Bibliography

Works by Juan Goytisolo

Goytisolo, Juan. *Campos de Níjar: Relatos*. Barcelona: Editorial Seix Barral, S.A. 1960.
———. *El circo*. Barcelona: Ediciones Destino, 1957.
———. *La chanca*. Paris: Librería española, 1962.
———. *Duelo en el Paraíso*. Barcelona: Ediciones Destino, 1955.
———. *Fiestas*. Barcelona: Ediciones Destino, 1958.
———. *El furgón de cola*. Paris: Ruedo Ibérico, 1967.
———. *La isla*. Barcelona: Editorial Seix Barral, 1961.
———. *Juan sin tierra*. Barcelona: Editorial Seix Barral, S.A., 1975.
———. *Juegos de manos*. Barcelona: Ediciones Destino, 1954.
———. "La novela española contemporánea." *Libre*, No. 2 (diciembre, enero, febrero, 1971–72), 33–40.
Obra inglesa de D. José María Blanco White. Edition and Introduction by Juan Goytisolo. 2nd Ed. Barcelona: Editorial Seix Barral, S.A., 1974.
———. *Problemas de la novela*. Barcelona: Ediciones Destino, 1959.
———. *Reivindicación del conde don Julián*. México: Editorial Joaquín Mortiz, 1970.
———. *La resaca*. París: Librería Española, 1961.
———. *Señas de identidad*. 2nd Ed. México: Editorial Joaquín Mortiz, S.A., 1966.

Works Cited

Beckett, Samuel, "Dante . . . Bruno . . . Vico . . . Joyce" in *Our Exagmination Round His Factification for Incamination of Work in Progress*. London: Faber and Faber, 1921, 1961.

Brantley, Jon D. *The Fiction of John Dos Passos.* The Hague: Mouton and Co., 1968.

Buckley, Ramón. *Problemas formales en la novela española contemporánea.* Barcelona: Ediciones Península, 1968.

Camus, Albert. *L'Etranger.* Paris: Librairie Gallimard, 1951.

————. *The Myth of Sisyphus* in *Existentialism from Dostoevsky to Sartre.* Edited by Walter Kaufman. New York: Meridian Books, 1965.

Cano, José Luis. "Tres novelas." *Insula,* No. 36 (marzo, 1958), 6–7.

Cassirer, Ernst. *Language and Myth.* Translated by Susanne Langer. New York: Harper and Brothers, 1946.

Cela, Camilo Jose. *La familia de Pascual Duarte.* New York: Las Americas Publishing Company, 1965.

Cirre, J. F. "Novela e ideología en Juan Goytisolo." *Insula,* No. 230 (enero, 1966), 1, 12.

Couffon, Claude. "*Don Julián* ou la destruction des mythes." *Le Monde.* September 11, 1970.

Cox, Randolph Calvin. "Aspects of Alienation in the Novel of Juan Goytisolo." Unpublished Ph.D. dissertation, University of Wisconsin, 1972.

Diez del Corral, Luis. *La función del mito clásico en la literatura contemporánea.* Madrid: Editorial Gredos, 1957.

Durán, Manuel. "Vindicación de Juan Goytisolo: *Reivindicación del conde don Julián.*" *Insula,* No. 290 (enero, 1971), 1, 4.

Eliade, Mircea. *Shamanism.* Translated by William R. Trask. Bollingen Series LXVI. New York: Pantheon Books. 1964.

Erlich, Victor. *Russian Formalism, History-Doctrine.* :'S-Gravenhage: Mouton and Co., 1955.

Frye, Northrop. *Anatomy of Criticism.* Princeton: Princeton University Press, 1957.

Fuentes, Carlos. *La nueva novela hispanoamericana.* Mexico: Editorial Joaquín Mortiz, S.A., 1969.

Ganivet, Angel. *Idearium español.* Buenos Aires: Espasa-Calpe, S.A., 1940.

García Berrio, Antonio. *Significado actual del formalismo Ruso.* Barcelona: Editorial Planeta, 1973.

Gil Casado, Pablo. *La novela social española.* Barcelona: Editorial Seix Barral, 1968.

Gimferrer, Pere. "El nuevo Juan Goytisolo." *Revista de Occidente,* No. 137 (agosto, 1974), 15–25.

Greene, Norman N. *Jean Paul Sartre, The Existentialist Ethic.* Ann Arbor: University of Michigan Press, 1960.

Hutman, Norma Louise. *Machado: A Dialogue with Time.* Albuquerque: University of New Mexico Press, 1969.

Iglesias, Ignacio. "Juan Goytisolo: *Fiestas* y *La resaca.*" *Cuadernos del Congreso por la Libertad y la Cultura.* No. 36 (mayo-junio, 1959), 114–15.

Jimenez, Juan Ramón. "Platero" in *Literatura del Siglo XX.* Edited by Da Cal and Ucelay. New York: Holt, Rinehart and Winston, 1968.

Juan Goytisolo. Edited by Julián Ríos. Madrid: Editorial Fundamentos, 1975.

Jung, Carl G. and Joseph L. Henderson. *Man and his Symbols.* New York: Doubleday and Co., 1964.

Jung, Carl G. *Psychology and the Unconscious.* Translated by Beatrice M. Hinkle. New York: Muffat, Yard and Co., 1916.

Lommel, Andreas. *Shamanism: The Beginning of Art*. Translated by Michael Bullock. New York: McGraw-Hill Book Co., 1967.

Maeztu, Ramiro de. *Defensa de la hispanidad*. Buenos Aires: Editorial Poblet, 1942.

Malinowski, Bronislaw. *Sex, Culture and Myth*. New York: Harcourt, Brace and World, Inc., 1962.

Martínez Cachero, José María. "El novelista Juan Goytisolo." *Papeles de Son Armadáns*, 95 (febrero 1964), 125–60.

Martínez Ruiz, José ["Azorín,"] "La novia de Cervantes" in *Antología—Siglo XX—Prosistas españoles*. Edited by María de Maeztu. Madrid: Espasa-Calpe, S.A., 1968.

May, George. "Fiction Reader, Novel Writer." *Yale French Studies*, 35 (1967), 5–11.

McMahon, Joseph H. "Where Does Real Life Begin?" *Yale French Studies*, 35 (1967), 96–113.

McVan, Alice Jane. *Antonio Machado*. New York: Hispanic Society of America, 1959.

Meerts, Christian. *Technique et Vision dans "Señas de identidad" de J. Goytisolo*. Analecta Romanica Heft 31. Frankfurt: Vitto-Rio Klostermann, 1972.

Menéndez Pidal, Ramón. Introduction to *Floresta de leyendas heróicas españolas*. Vol. I. Madrid: Ediciones de "La Lectura," 1925.

Neumann, Erich. *The Origin and History of Consciousness*. Translated by R. F. C. Hull. Bollingen Series XLII. New York: Pantheon Books Inc., 1954.

Nora, Eugenio de. *La novela española contemporánea*. Vol. III. 2nd ed. Madrid: Editorial Gredos, 1970.

Olmos García, Francisco. "La novela y los novelistas españoles de hoy. Una encuesta." *Cuadernos Americanos*, CXXIX (julio-agosto, 1963), 211–37.

Paz, Octavio. *Conjunciones y disyunciones*. México: Editorial Joaquín Mortiz, 1969.

Rodríguez Monegal, Emir. "El arte de narrar." *Marcha*, No. 10 (julio, 1959), 22–25.

Russian Formalism. Edited by Stephen Bann and John E. Bowlt. New York: Harper and Row, 1973.

Russian Formalist Criticism, Four Essays. Translated and with an introduction by Lee T. Lemon and Marion J. Reis. Lincoln: University of Nebraska Press, 1965.

Sartre, Jean Paul. *La nausée*. 61st Ed. Paris: Librairie Gallimard, 1938.

Sbarbi, José María. *Gran diccionario de refranes de la lengua española*. Buenos Aires: Librería "El Ateneo," 1943.

Scholes, Robert. "Formalism and Structuralism." *Novel*, II, No. 2 (Winter, 1973), 134–51.

Sobejano, Gonzalo. *Novela española de nuestro tiempo*. Madrid: Editorial Prensa Española, 1970.

Spencer, Sharon. *Space, Time and Structure in the Modern Novel*. New York: New York University Press, 1971.

Tindall, William York. *Forces in Modern British Literature*. New York: Vintage Books, 1956.

———. *James Joyce*. New York: Charles Scribner's Sons, 1950.

Walcutt, Charles Child. *Man's Changing Mask*. Minneapolis: University of Minnesota Press, 1966.

Wellek, René and Austin Warren. *Theory of Literature*. New York: Harcourt, Brace and Company, 1949.

Zamora Vicente, Alfonso. *Camilo José Cela*. Madrid: Editorial Gredos, 1962.

Other Works Consulted

Amoros, Andrés. *Introducción a la novela contemporánea*. Salamanca: Ediciones Anaya, 1966.

A Prague School Reader on Esthetics, Literary Structure, and Style. Selected and translated from Czech by Paul L. Garvin. Washington: Georgetown University Press, 1964.

Baquero Goyanes, Mariano. *Estructuras de la novela actual*. Barcelona: Editorial Planeta, 1970.

Barthes, Roland. *Critique et vérité*. Paris: Editions du Seuil, 1966.

Daiches, David. *Critical Approaches to Literature*. New York: W. W. Norton and Company, 1956.

L'Enseignement de la littérature. Sous la direction de Serge Doubrovsky et de Tzvetan Todorov. Paris: Librairie Plon, 1971.

Handy, William J. *Modern Fiction: A Formalist Approach*. Carbondale: Southern Illinois University Press, 1971.

Langer, Susanne K. *Feeling and Form*. New York: Charles Scribner's Sons, 1953.

The Novel and its Changing Form. Essays, selected and edited with an introduction by R. G. Collins. Winnipeg: University of Manitoba Press, 1972.

Pomorska, Krystyna. *Russian Formalist Theory and its Poetic Ambiance*. The Hague: Mouton and Company, 1968.

Reading in Russian Poetics: Formalist and Structuralist Views. Edited by Ladistav Matejka and Krystyna Pomorska. Cambridge: MIT Press, 1971.

Sans Villanueva, Santos. *Tendencias de la novela española actual (1950–1970)*. Madrid: Cuadernos para el Diálogo, 1972.

Schwartz, Kessel. "Juan Goytisolo, Cultural Constraints and the Historical Vindication of Count Julián." *Hispania*, 54, No. 4 (December 1971), 960–66.

Structuralism. Edited with an Introduction by Jacques Ehram. New York: Anchor Books, 1970.

Todorov, Tzvetan. *Literatura y significación*. Translated by Gonzalo Suárez Gómez. Barcelona: Editorial Planeta, 1971.

Tovar, Antonio. *Novela española e hispanoamericana*. Madrid: Ediciones Alfaguara, 1972.

Varela Jácome, Benito. *Renovación de la novela en el siglo XX*. Barcelona: Ediciones Destino, 1966.

Wellek, René. *Concepts of Criticism*. Edited and Introduced by Stephen G. Nichols. New Haven: Yale University Press, 1969.

———. *Discrimination: Further Concepts of Criticism*. New Haven: Yale University Press, 1970.

Most Recent Works about Goytisolo

Levine, Linda Gould. *Juan Goytisolo: La destrucción creadora*. México: Editorial Joaquín Mortiz, 1976.

Levine, Susan F. " 'Cuerpo' y 'No-cuerpo'—una conjunción entre Juan Goytisolo y Octavio Paz." *Journal of Spanish Studies: Twentieth Century*, V, No. 2 (Fall 1977), 123–135.

Pérez, Genaro J. "Form in Juan Goytisolo's *Juan sin tierra*." *Journal of Spanish Studies: Twentieth Century*, V, No. 2 (Fall 1977), 137–160.

Pérez, Genaro J. "Goytisolo's *Juan sin tierra*." *Hispania*, 60, No. 4 (December 1977), 1024.

Romero, Héctor R. "*Juan sin tierra*: Análisis de un texto literario." *Anales de la novela de posguerra*, I, 1976, 35–107.

Index

226

227

studia humanitatis

PUBLISHED VOLUMES

Laclos. Critical Approaches to Les Liaisons dangereuses. Ed. Lloyd R. Free. xii–300 pp. US $17.00.

JULIA CONAWAY BONDANELLA, *Petrarch's Visions and their Renaissance Analogues.* xii–120 pp. US $7.00.

VINCENZO TRIPODI, *Studi su Foscolo e Stern.* xii–216 pp. US $13.00.

GENARO J. PÉREZ, *Formalist Elements in the Novels of Juan Goytisolo.* xii–216 pp. US $12.50.

SARA MARIA ADLER, *Calvino: The Writer as a Fablemaker.* x–164 pp. US $11.50.

LOPE DE VEGA, *El amor enamorado*, critical edition of John B. Wooldridge, Jr. xvi–236 pp. US $13.00.

NANCY DERSOFI, *Arcadia and the Stage: A Study of the Theater of Angelo Beolco* (called *Ruzante*). xii–180 pp. US $12.00

JOHN A. FREY, *The Aesthetics of the* ROUGON-MACQUART. xvi–356 pp. US $20.00.

CHESTER W. OBUCHOWSKI, *Mars on Trial: War as Seen by French Writers of the Twentieth Century.* xiv–320 pp. US $20.00.

FORTHCOMING PUBLICATIONS

El cancionero del Bachiller Jhoan López, edición crítica de Rosalind Gabin.

Studies in Honor of Gerald E. Wade, edited by Sylvia Bowman, Bruno M. Damiani, Janet W. Diaz, E. Michael Gerli, Everett Hesse, John E. Keller, Luis Leal and Russell Sebold.

HELMUT HATZFELD, *Essais sur la littérature flamboyante.*

MARIO ASTE, *La narrativa di Luigi Pirandello: Dalle novelle al romanzo Uno, Nessuno, e Centomila.*

JOSEPH BARBARINO, *The Latin Intervocalic Stops: A Quantitative and Comparative Study.*

NANCY D'ANTUONO, *Boccaccio's novelle in Lope's theatre.*

ANTONIO PLANELLS, *Cortázar: Metafísica y erotismo.*

Novelistas femeninas de la postguerra española, ed. Janet W. Díaz.

MECHTHILD CRANSTON, *Orion Resurgent: René Char, Poet of Presence.*

La Discontenta and La Pythia, edition with introduction and notes by Nicholas A. De Mara.

PERO LÓPEZ DE AYALA, *Crónica del Rey Don Pedro I,* edición crítica de Heanon and Constance Wilkins.

ALBERT H. LE MAY, *The Experimental Verse Theater of Valle-Inclán.*

JEREMY T. MEDINA, *Spanish Realism: Theory and Practice of a Concept in the Nineteenth Century.*

ROBERT H. MILLER, ed. *Sir John Harington: A Supplie or Addicion to the Catalogue of Bishops to the Yeare 1608.*

MARÍA ELISA CIAVARELLI, *La fuerza de la sangre en la literatura del Siglo de Oro.*

MARY LEE BRETZ, *La evolución novelística de Pío Baroja.*

DENNIS M. KRATZ, *Mocking Epic.*